3 –
9J

THE WORLD OF SEAN O'CASEY

The World of Sean O'Casey

edited by

SEAN McCANN

Drawings by John Cullen Murphy

A FOUR SQUARE BOOK

CONTENTS

ACKNOWLEDGEMENTS

The Editor wishes to acknowledge the help given to him by many people, including relatives and friends of Sean O'Casey who put at his disposal letters, documents and manuscripts of a very personal nature.

The following quotations from Sean O'Casey's *Collected Plays* appear by kind permission of Messrs. Macmillan & Co.: 'Shadow of a Gunman' (Vol. I), 'Juno and the Paycock' (Vol. I), 'The Plough and the Stars' (Vol. I), 'The Silver Tassie' (Vol. II), 'Within the Gates' (Vol. II), 'Purple Dust' (Vol. III) and 'The Drums of Father Ned' (Vol. III).

Grateful acknowledgement is also made to Messrs. Macmillan & Co. and to Mr. M. B. Yeats for permission to reproduce the quotation from 'Under Ben Bulben', from *Collected Poems of W. B. Yeats*, which appears on pp. 155–6.

The Editor is indebted to the *Massachusetts Review* and to *Irish Renaissance* published by the Dolman Press, Dublin, for permission to reprint David Krause's article.

INTRODUCTION

By Sean McCann

EVERYONE knows the story of Sean O'Casey . . . he overcame extreme poverty, inadequate education, partial blindness and the tag of 'labourer' to become one of the world's greatest playwrights.

It is the perfect legend. A story anyone can retell. A story that has been retold so often that it has been accepted as a fact. But how true is it? Does the legend stand up to close scrutiny and investigation? This book looks behind and beyond the legend. The individual writers have probed deeper into the story of O'Casey, and have backed up their theories with telling facts – facts that have been dug out of a Dublin that, we had been told, held no secrets of O'Casey's life. Yet the city that reared many a brace of great writers yielded a rich harvest of new facts that go a long way towards clarifying the real story of the Irish beginnings of Sean O'Casey. Gaps, that have glared through many books about the man and through his own telling of the story of his early life, are filled from this rich store-house of previously untapped facts. Poems and letters are published here for the first time; so is the story of the great love of his life.

This book is not a deep analytical study of O'Casey's literary work. This has been adequately done before by Gabriel Fallon, David Krause, Robert Hogan and Saros Cowasjee. It was the man himself who was always in the forefront during the compilation of this book.

Yet it is impossible to look at the man apart from his work. The plays, articles, poems, autobiographies, letters, form their own part of this story but purely as personal responses. In this part of the book the writers face up to the often asked questions – was O'Casey in exile a man without that vital spark of genius? Were his autobiographies wayward and uneven? Were the letters he wrote the mirror of a grouser, a bitter man?

Sean O'Casey, even before he acknowledged an audience's reaction to his first play in the Abbey dressed in working clothes, had gone his own highly individual way. Facing him from youth

9

onwards was the battle of red and green – Gaelic League and Communism, Nationalism and Trade Unionism. The great divisions of Ireland, religious and political, pulled him asunder – and in the pulling set him on a path that was often stormy, stony and sad. He made his own way along this path, a way eventually paved with success. At first in Dublin. And then London. Initially his parting from Dublin was only temporary but then he made his decision. He would stay away, because in London he found the things he craved – adulation, success, money and love. Dublin eventually reconciled itself to the parting but not to his reasons for it. Dublin was intolerant – and intolerable to him. 'It takes both courage and patience to live in Ireland', he said. He certainly lacked the patience.

He moved on to Devon and lived a happily married life – a long life marred by the death of his son. From Devon he fought a running battle with the Irish in Ireland about plays, the Church, censorship, the Abbey, the Abbey directors and theatres in general. He reacted to every return attack and defence with wild gales of fury or laughter. And the battles lingered on. . . .

He found himself hailed and almost forgotten in his lifetime. Lost in deep Devon where the people never really knew who he was other than 'a nice gentleman'. He was hailed 'indisputedly a genius' greater than Brecht or O'Neill, a man almost in the garb of Shakespeare. He was a man of many faces – more than a mere Jekyll and Hyde. This comes through frequently in the contributions to this book. He was always eager for a fight and yet could be calm and kind when face to face with some of the combatants. He loved words, they tumbled from him fluently and beautifully – even in torrid letters to the newspapers. When it seemed that the world was once going to forget him he kissed his fame to life with his autobiographies and continued to press the breath of life into it until, at the age of eighty-four, he died, like so many other great Irish writers, still in exile – unreconciled.

The image of the man given here is not going to please some people – but then this book is not written to please. It is written so that the real life of Sean O'Casey should be known at last.

PART ONE

THE MAKINGS OF THE MAN

1

THE EARLY BACKGROUND

By Anthony Butler

THE gap that separates us from the day in late March when John Casey – later known as Sean O'Casey – was born is more than one of time or physical change. A new philosophy of society rather than the atomic bomb, a shrinking of the international community rather than space travel, sharply and irrevocably divide us from that age. But even when considered in terms of historical chronology the range covered by the years is remarkable.

Some indication of the texture and distance of his first year may be derived from the fact that in 1880 Parnell was only on the threshold of his great political career and Captain Boycott in Co. Mayo was a living issue. It would be another year before the first electric lights would appear in the streets of Dublin, and landmarks like the O'Connell statue were still unknown to the centre of the city.

Abroad, Cologne Cathedral was completed after six hundred years of leisurely building. A rumour circulated that Professor Graham Bell – inventor of the telephone – had discovered a means of transmitting light by wire. Had it been true, television would have been a possibility before the death of Queen Victoria. In fact he had found a means of transmitting sound by light; an obvious anticipation of radio. General Gordon, awaiting his hour of glory in the Sudan, was writing letters to *The Times* solemnly suggesting that the British Government should buy eleven counties in the West of Ireland for £80 million to establish a Crown Estate. Had the suggestion been adopted it would have resulted in the world's first large-scale experiment in socialism.

On the London stage Ellen Terry and Irving were playing, and Dion Boucicault's 'O'Dowd' showed that the old master of Irish melodrama was still a theatrical force. It was the year when Ned Kelly and his bushrangers were finally wiped out in Australia and it also marked the first discovery of a fresh-water jellyfish.

Another look at the year can be obtained through the advertisements which appeared in Dublin publications and we can note the shy announcement of John Murphy, 14 Thomas Street, that: '. . . he had the honour of supplying with bells about forty Bishops'. At the same time it is more impressive to read of Sainsbury's Steam Clock Factory which offered for £40, a Village Church Striking Clock powerful enough to send the resounding impulses of a 10-cwt bell for a distance of two miles. Pickerings Razor Paste enjoyed enormous popularity, and on St Stephen's Green a Mr George Shields summoned the public to his Turkish, Electric, Medicated and Nitro-Hydrochloric Baths.

These are a flavour of the facts which are recorded of the year 1880 and to them must be added another – that Dublin was one of the unhealthiest cities in the world in that era. The death-rate was higher than in many plague-infested cities of the Orient and although disease is not always class conscious, the poverty and the over-crowded conditions in the city slums did aggravate the position.

This, it can be said, is the characteristic of O'Casey's first year which impresses most of those who write of the man and the playwright. It is against this dark background of squalor and human degradation that his emerging genius is so often cast.

In his six-volume autobiography O'Casey himself is never slow to emphasise this part of his life. In the last chapter of *Inishfallen, Fare Thee Well* he smugly accepts a common description of himself: 'It has been often recorded in the Press, by those who could guess shrewdly, that Sean was a slum dramatist. . . . The terms were suitable and accurate. . . .'

He goes on to say that wherever he went he would wear 'the tattered badge of his tribe' and he proclaims with more than a little vanity: 'But he would sew on that badge, soiled with the diseased sweat of the tenements, a coloured ribbon or two. . . .'

Others have no difficulty in accepting this view, and in Chapter 8 of Robert Hogan's *The Experiments of Sean O'Casey* it is bluntly stated that the playwright was a product of the slums. Jules Koslaw in his biography of O'Casey speaks of his social origin in 'gaunt houses' that are slum tenements crowded with poverty-stricken dwellers. In another study an Indian scholar, Saros Cowasjee – although he is less deceived than many – talks of O'Casey and his mother moving into a tenement house in a slum district after the marriage of a sister.

Sean O'Casey, the Man and his Work by David Krause has

sometimes been misinterpreted and Desmond Ryan, the well-known Irish historian, could say in the *Irish Times* of 2 March, 1964: 'And there are rival homes and even rival cradles despite O'Casey's authoritative word and the detailed confirmation gathered by the documented researches of Dr David Krause. It was a tenement house.'

In his book Krause did not state that O'Casey was born in a tenement, although he does remark that the family lived in one of the poorer sections of the city and goes on to assert that after the death of the father Michael Casey '. . . they were gradually reduced to the poverty and hardship of tenement life'. Later he records that for O'Casey '. . . the squalor of the tenements be-came the crucial experience of his life'.

These are a few samples of the manner in which the early life of the writer is normally described. It may seem impudent and absurd to challenge this clearly defined account, a Quixotic tilt at very substantial windmills; but I cannot accept its validity. In questions of this kind it is essential that scholarship should go where the facts beckon and they did not lead me to the charted and familiar territory. It is necessary, therefore, to take a fresh look at the environment into which the writer was born.

He was born to Michael and Susan Casey on 30 March 1880, the last of a very large family of which only three other brothers and a sister survived. Both his parents were staunch Protestants although all other members of his father's family had been reared as Catholics as they were the products of a mixed marriage. The bitter anti-Catholicism of Sean O'Casey's outlook – and he was anti-Catholic rather than anti-clerical – stemmed in some measure from the prejudice of his own home.

There are many question marks in his life but it is strange that the address at which he was born should still be queried now and then. It is necessary to start with this fact and establish exactly where Sean O'Casey first saw the sharp skies of an Irish spring.

He has added to the confusion and in the last chapter of *Sunset and Evening Star* he speaks of himself as a boy sitting on '. . . the doorstep of a Lower Dorset Street house . . .'. David Krause in his book gives the address as 85 Upper Dorset Street, and since his presentation of hard data is usually good this might be accepted by some. On the other hand Saros Cowasjee gives the address as 85 Lower Dorset Street, and this combined with the playwright's own statement might seem conclusive. The

14

Indian student was supported by a very good friend of the playwright, Mr Ronald Ayling.

In a bitter assault on Cowasjee's work in *The Kilkenny Magazine* he corrects what he alleges are mistakes in the text of *Sean O'Casey: the Man Behind the Plays*. One accuracy he concedes to Cowasjee no matter how else he may be in error: 'In one small detail, however, he is right where Krause is wrong; the playwright was born at 85 Lower – not Upper – Dorset Street.'

At first I was inclined to accept Mr Ayling as definitive as I felt that he must write with absolute certainty when he was setting out to chide another for mistakes of this kind. It did not seem possible to me that so stern a critic should err himself on a point which could be easily vertified. Nonetheless I decided to check carefully and bought a copy of Sean O'Casey's birth certificate.

This gave the place of birth as 85 Upper Dorset Street, and mentioned that Isabella Archer – Mrs Casey's sister – was present at the delivery. His father's occupation was listed as 'clerk'. Realising that the local registrar, Mr John P. Nowlan, of 10 Summerhill, might have made a mistake I decided to check further.

I went to St Mary's Church, Mary Street, and with the invaluable assistance of the Rector, the Rev. Canon George D. Hobson, and Mr V. Oakley I examined the baptismal records of 28 July 1880, and found that the address given for John Casey was still 85 Upper Dorset Street. An additional fact which emerged from this examination was the note in the Register which described his father as a mercantile clerk and this suggested that he was not working for the Irish Church Missions at that time as it has been alleged on one or two occasions.

In order to obtain further evidence I checked street directories and found the occupier of 85 Upper Dorset Street listed as 'M. Casey'. As this information was repeated over several years in annual publications the accuracy of the entry could be relied upon. It can be accepted, beyond further question, that Sean O'Casey was born in 85 Upper Dorset Street on the site of which now stands a branch of the Hibernian Bank.

The next step was to try to establish if this house had been a slum or even a tenement in the popular sense of low-quality housing. Again the evidence was against this.

I was fortunate to receive the courteous and very efficient assistance of the Law Agent's Department of the Hibernian Bank in looking through the leases and conveyances of 85 Upper Dorset Street. Indeed, without their guidance I would not have been able to make sense of the great mass of documents involved.

These clearly established that the house was a very valuable piece of property which could not by any stretch of the imagination be called a slum or tenement. A reference to the Valuation

St Mary's Church, where he was baptised

Office revealed that Mr Michael Casey was the rated occupier of the entire premises, with a valuation of £20 which in itself underlined the worth of the building.

The valuations of the houses in Upper Dorset Street at that time established generally that they were of high quality and most of the people living in them came from a good strata of society. It should also be noted that the Hibernian Bank – or any other bank – did not establish branches in low-class housing or in poor

districts during the 1890s, which further establis[h]
level of the district at that time. I think I am justif[ied]
in asserting that it is nonsense to suggest that O'C[asey was born]
into a slum or a tenement. Indeed it would ha[ve been]
surprising if he had been.

His father was an educated Protestant and an educated
Protestant was to the majority of the Catholic population in those
days what a white man was to the natives of Africa in the early
nineteenth century. He belonged to a powerful and wealthy
Establishment; he was a pillar and guarantee of it and so could
claim a good share of the thick cream of patronage which it
distributed to its loyal members.

It was most unlikely that his income was low or inadequate
and the idea that he gave his labour cheaply to the Irish Church
Missions is disproved to some extent by the fact that he called
himself a mercantile clerk in the baptismal records of St Mary's.
I found, however, substantial evidence of his status at the time
his son was born in an authoritative list of the Nobility, Gentry,
Merchants and Traders of Dublin. He was on this and presumably
belonged to the 'Gentry' since he would not qualify for the other
classifications. It is unlikely that anyone living in a fetid, filthy
slum would be so listed, and it is almost certain that he would
not find a place on it in those class-conscious days if he lived
in what Dr Krause described as a poorer section of the city.

The four children who preceded Sean O'Casey received an
excellent education and his sister Isabella – called after her aunt,
I presume – was a fluent French speaker and had more than an
average knowledge of music. His brother Michael was also well
educated and had a good training in art. These accomplishments
were not the standard intellectual equipment of Dublin slum
dwellers in the 1880s or at any other time.

There is no evading the fact that contrary to the popular
biographical pattern which is generally accepted, Sean O'Casey
was a product of the middle class and it is ironic that he emerged
from the petty bourgeois – a social group detested by his beloved
Communists.

This, I am convinced, was of considerable significance to his
life and the future man. Later he was to fight bitterly, not to rise
from a level of under-privilege and poverty, but to regain a
remembered and superior position in society. It is significant that
he does not appear to have found integration with his environ-

...nt until he retired to the gracious and genteel atmosphere of predominantly Tory Devon. Had he found his spiritual home?

Michael Casey, Senior, suffered a back injury in 1883 or 1884, and the family moved to 9 Innisfallen Parade, which was not too far from Dorset Street. Once more there was no removal to a slum or a tenement and the house, though small, was then and is now in a respectable area. Their neighbours in the mid-1880s included, for instance, John Castel, an insurance agent, and James M'Collough, a law clerk, so that we find support for the idea that the tone of the area was not a low one. In those days a law clerk and an insurance agent would have enjoyed a reasonably good status.

The young O'Casey suffered a good deal of ill-health and his eyes gave him endless trouble. He claimed that his father rejected him because of this and in *I Knock on the Door* he recalls with what seems to be genuine intensity his eagerness to do an errand for him. His optical defects had one advantage, however, as they helped to make him a bookworm later and this is commonly recognised as an Adlerian compensation for poor vision.

He grew to an awareness of life, its responsibilities and its terrors, in the shadow of his dying father and this, combined with physical suffering, appears to have had a profound effect on his psyche. It seems to have focused his needs and emotions on his mother who became the source of love and sympathy. At the same time the aggressive attitude he adopted towards other members of his family was a product of the possessiveness he felt for her. All of these characteristics were transferred in later life to other people and to other situations.

His father died at 9 Innisfallen Parade on 9 September 1886, of bronchitis and a form of dropsy. He was aged forty-eight. The death certificate has one surprising entry for which there is no immediate explanation. His occupation is described as that of 'gardener'. There is a minor mystery here which may never be fully solved.

It is difficult to believe that the family was very poor at this time as several members were earning money and they had the sympathetic assistance of the parish authorities – probably a good deal more than Sean O'Casey ever acknowledged. This was one of the great advantages of being a Protestant in an oppressed Dublin; of belonging to a small, powerful and wealthy Establishment.

18

Protestant charity was well-organised and there were many organisations to distribute it, from the highly endowed Association for the Relief of Distressed Protestants to the Protestant Shoemakers Charitable Society. It is almost impossible, therefore, to believe the tales of terrible poverty in *I Knock on the Door* and there seems little doubt that O'Casey touched the picture with something more than truth.

The family belonged to the parish of St Mary's, the church of which has many historical associations. In it Wesley first preached when he came to Ireland and it has many links with Wolfe Tone and other Irish patriots. In passing it may be mentioned that William Bentham, a long forgotten churchwarden of St Mary's, may well have been the inspiration for the name of a character in 'Juno and the Paycock'.

It was a wealthy parish and controlled a large parochial school at 20 Lower Dominick Street (now St Saviour's Orphanage). This building has magnificent Georgian ceilings and plasterwork and it is not the drab place that O'Casey described. His sister Isabella (she is called Ella in the Autobiographies) was a teacher in St Mary's and there she gave her brother his first lessons. A certificate for proficiency in Holy Scripture which he won in 1887 still survives in patched and vivid splendour. On the opposite side of the road was a National School in 43 Lower Dominick Street, and it was in this that the playwright suffered the experience which he alleged was to deprive him of some formal education.

At that time the Rector and incumbent of St Mary's was the Rev. James Hunter Monahan, D.D., who was also Precentor of Christ Church Cathedral. He was a classical scholar of modest range and edited the 'Hecuba' of Euripides. The schoolmaster of St Mary's National School was a Mr James Logan, and both he and the Rev. Monahan were to appear in the Autobiographies; one as the Rev. T. R. S. Hunter and the other as Mr Slogan. Elsewhere in this book the late Dean Emerson draws attention to the fact that the initials 'T. R. S.' were those of the curate, so that the Rev. T. R. S. Hunter might be intended as a composite picture.

O'Casey always suggested that he received very little formal education and he describes how after a savage beating from Slogan he hit the master on the head with an ebony ruler and ran forever from school. Unfortunately his account is curiously confused and obscure. No dates are given and we can only guess how long he was in attendance. The period was probably longer than he was willing to admit as he mentions at one point that the *Boys of London and New York* and *Deadwood Dick* were part of his literary diet while still fairly young. Now Victorian juvenile publications of this kind made little concession in prose style to their readers and his command of English must have been quite good.

It is reasonably certain that after 1887 or 1888 the Caseys lived in the caretaker's apartments of St Mary's Parochial School, 20 Lower Dominick Street, and Isabella Casey was married from there to Nicholas Beaver in early March, 1889. Isabella's daughter, Mrs P. Murphy, confirmed these facts when I interviewed her, as she had been told them by her mother. We may be sure that Sean was attending school at this time as the family could not, in the circumstances, ignore the Rev. Monahan in matters of this kind. Certainly we may discount the idea that Sean O'Casey was largely self-educated or grew up in relative ignorance.

Mrs P. Murphy provided me with some evidence of the general state of the Casey living style in the early 1890s and she had a number of interesting and revealing photographs. One of these has been used in some editions of *I Knock on the Door*. It shows a plump and well-dressed Mrs Casey holding her namesake, Susan, the baby daughter of Isabella. This is not a woman of the slums, few of whom would have the means or the leisure to sit for a studio photograph.

Another picture of roughly the same period shows Sean O'Casey at the age of eleven or twelve. The elegance of his dress is quite astonishing and his suit is of good material and very well cut. He wears what appears to be a new soft flannel hat with a round crown and turned-up brim with a loose cord looped beneath his chin. There is no sign of poverty in his appearance which is further decorated by a large flower in his buttonhole. Quite clearly he comes from a comfortable home and it would be difficult to believe that he ever had to put cardboard in his shoes. If the Casey family suffered poverty in the years between 1887 and 1895 it must have been of short duration and of little consequence. Again, Mrs Murphy gave me assistance and she emphatically denies that the family suffered as outlined in the Autobiographies.

She states that the Casey family moved to Hawthorn Terrace in the East Wall area of Dublin in the early 1890s and from there to 18 Abercorn Road a few years later. Once again there was no question of a slum or tenement experience. They were to live for over twenty years in the Abercorn Road house and it is a solid, two-storeyed house in excellent condition today. Sixty years ago it must have been a good deal better.

David Krause who interviewed the daughter of the then Rector of St Barnabas, the Rev. Edward Morgan Griffin, is able to establish something of the state of the family in 1904. Her recollection of Mrs Casey as a neat little woman, who wore a pretty bonnet and distributed sweets, is not indicative of grinding poverty and it is far from the sombre picture which Sean was to paint.

At this point we may complete the residential record of the playwright in Ireland. He moved from Abercorn Road in 1920, about a year after the death of his mother, and went to live with a friend at 35 Mountjoy Square. Now this was not a slum area or, in the 'derogatory' sense, a tenement district. On the small square lived doctors, solicitors, a hotel proprietor and a Mr W. F. Cotten, a highly placed executive in the Dublin Gas Company. In fact the house beside No. 35 was privately occupied. People of this kind were unlikely to be found in wretched living conditions. It is amusing to remember that the square provided O'Casey with the setting of a so-called 'slum' play.

The last residence of O'Casey in Ireland was 422 North Circular Road and this, while let in rooms and flats, was quite respectable as we know from Gabriel Fallon's excellent account. There was no breakdown in the pattern of decent living and the front door was always shut. My own family lived on the North Circular Road at this time, not too far distant from 422, and they claim it would be grossly absurd to draw any comparison between the houses there and real tenements.

Soberly examined I think my survey goes far to establish that it is very little short of fantasy to describe Sean O'Casey as a product of the slums. They were no major influence in his life and he never lived in them. By contrast with her affluent past Mrs Casey may have thought that Hawthorn Terrace and Abercorn Road were distasteful and her views may have coloured the illusions of her son, but this did not detract from the relatively good status of the houses concerned. At the same time one can understand how foreign scholars have been misled when inadequate knowledge of Dublin was combined with the wild inaccuracies of O'Casey himself.

We should also take note of the fact that O'Casey does not describe any slum or tenement in his account of the earlier years. Poverty is stressed but there is no mention of anything comparable with 10 Francis Street, described in the 1913 Housing Commission Report as housing 107 people with three closets for all of them.

This Report fascinates all who write on the author although it had nothing to do with where he was born or where he lived for some eighteen years before it was issued. David Krause does use it in one respect to establish the poor conditions in which O'Casey lived. In Chapter 4 of *Pictures in the Hallway* the playwright describes how ashes and dirt were removed from the rear of the house in which he lived. He gives a more vivid account in *The Green Crow* published many years later, and dwells on the removal of garbage and filth from the jakes by men with baskets on their backs. Krause equates this with part of the Housing Commission Report which mentions the state of slum houses, with excrement on the stairs and in the passages.

Unfortunately no relationship can be established between the two. O'Casey is clearly giving a picture of a sanitary and cleansing process which, if it had been widely practised, would have had the effect of reducing the worst features of the real tenements. No doubt it was unpleasant while it lasted but its long-term results must have been of value to the residents in keeping their homes sweet and uncontaminated. I might add that the incident in question appears to have been related to 25 Hawthorn Terrace (valuation £8) which was rated in the sole name of Mrs Casey.

One of the factors which led me to re-interpret the facts of O'Casey's alleged slum background was the environments described and suggested in the first three major plays. 'The Shadow of a Gunman' is plainly set in Mountjoy Square, a place in which he had lived for only five months. He did not reach back into his own earlier life for the simple reason that it could not afford him an experience of tenements. But even 'The Shadow of a Gunman' has overtones of respectability and we should consider the character Adolphus Grigson; a solicitor's clerk who wears a heavy top-coat, a soft trilby hat, carries an umbrella and wears a silk scarf. Could anyone suggest that this is a description of a degraded, downtrodden and typical slum dweller?

We can look in the same way at Minnie Powell, who is said to be charmingly dressed in a brown tailor-made costume, shoes and stocking of a dark brown tint and a silk tam-o'-shanter of a rich blue tint. If these are representative of Dublin's poor and suffering I can only repeat that W. B. Yeats will have to take his place as one of them. This at least can be granted, that the characters in the play would be representative of some individuals who lived in Mountjoy Square flats.

'The Plough and the Stars' is also set in a house with a fair social status. The opening scene demands a picture of 'The Sleeping Venus' and other reproductions of good paintings, as well as a bowl of scarlet dahlias and white chrysanthemums.

We may judge how untypical this setting is when the evidence of John Cooke, Hon. Treasurer of the National Society for the Prevention of Cruelty to Children, to the 1913 Housing Commission is recalled: '. . . the notes of a bird in a cage never sound in the ears of those I visited and not a flower in the window sill brightens the tenement room. One copy of the Red magazine and that for firelight. . . . ' It has been stated to me that the Clitheroes of 'The Plough' were never intended to be typical slum dwellers, but this is the point I am trying to make. Tradesmen like bricklayers and carpenters were not normally found in tenements and a Protestant fruit seller like Bessie Burgess would have been as rare as a white blackbird.

'Juno and the Paycock' too has a comfortable environment in a two-roomed tenancy or flat. In this a family of four resides, which is not overcrowding by any means. We are told also that Mary Boyle is a reader of books: that the family has wealthy relations and we see Mary's boy friend – a teacher – enter with gloves and a walking stick. Joxer is sufficiently cultured to quote Lord Macaulay and is offered eggs and sausages with open-handed generosity by 'Captain' Boyle. Poverty is scarcely suggested in this or the other two dramas, and lack of money is never a serious problem.

It must be faced that O'Casey's pseudo-slums do not fester; they do not smell – they are genteel; they are middle-class concepts of what such places might be. Certainly they are not the slums of the 1913 Housing Commission Report and are never presented as such on the stage.

I am convinced that the basic illusion of the O'Casey saga is factually threadbare, but it would be futile to deny that in later life he did suffer poverty. Illness and unemployment reduced him to a wretched condition around 1913 but this was the common lot of many Dublin workers in those days.

Because of his illness and the indulgence of his mother he seems to have been a little work-shy as a boy and a young man. In his first years in employment he lost jobs because he insisted on wearing on his shoulder a chip like a Field Marshal's epaulette. He deliberately sought dismissal or left. It was safe then to be proud and scornful as he could always cadge a living with his family. There was nothing particularly heroic in his attitude.

The company he calls Hymdim, Leadem & Co. in *Pictures in the Hallway* was in fact Leedom, Hampton & Co. of 50 Henry Street (valuation £210), a firm which dealt in china, delph and hardware. Here he started his working life at the age of approximately fourteen and by the standards of his day he was reasonably well paid. The fact that he was a Protestant helped a great deal and with care he might have enjoyed a good future with the company. By the time he separated himself from it he was on the clerical staff. As usual when he became too closely associated with a group he built up aggressions towards members of it which had to be discharged in one way or another, and this led to his dismissal or resignation – if one can decide exactly what happened.

His description of that employment throws one curious light on his own and his mother's characters. Earlier in Chapter 21 of *I Knock on the Door* he describes how he stole a piece of bacon and an egg when out shopping. She mildly reproved him but her real response was to go and buy a head of cabbage to go with them. While he was at Leedom, Hampton & Co. he commenced pilfering on a large scale and he seems to have taken anything that could be hidden under his coat. When his mother became aware of this habit, her first worry was not the moral wrong involved but the grim possibility that he might be caught. According to her son the solution she proposed was worthy of Fagin in *David Copperfield*. She arranged to put deeper and wider pockets in his coat so that he could steal more with greater ease.

The family – or some members of it – seemed to have this light-fingered streak and O'Casey records that his brother Tom while working for the Great Northern Railways would watch for broken crates and boxes in order to take what he could. If the crate proved difficult he would lever it off the wagons so that the fall might open it a little more. Once again the good Mrs Casey thought her duty lay in assisting her son and she pawned

24

the stolen goods when necessary. Sean would not do this – he was afraid.

Frequently the theft by Sean O'Casey of a copy of Milton from the Dublin Bookshop is mentioned as an indication of his love of literature but we cannot consider it as an isolated incident. All through his youth he seems to have been willing to help himself to other people's property without scruple or shame, and the book was only one more object that could be taken.

Mrs O'Casey, at least, will never qualify as a sweet innocent picture of Mother Machree. Sean in several parts of his Autobiographies tells of her taste in beer which she sometimes satisfied at the expense of the rent she had to pay. The frequency of the references indicate that the indulgence was not an occasional one.

When Sean was nineteen a new Rector came to the parish of St Barnabas and gave the young man an intense and renewed interest in religion. O'Casey relates how he joined the choir and became secretary of the local branch of the Foreign Mission Society. He claimed also that he helped to break the power of an extreme Protestant Orange group in the parish.

Around this time also he became a labourer, although it is hard to understand why he could not obtain a better job. He was a Protestant with some education and congenial employment should have been available. It is possible that his contributions to Leedom, Hampton and Co., as well as Easons, may not have been good references in a small city with a long memory. His toil was not altogether manual in the years that followed and he mentions on one occasion that he performed duties very similar to those of a clerk of works.

His resentment against his working-class situation – and he later described his fellow employees as a 'low lot' – may well have driven him towards Irish nationalism, but whatever the real reason he learned to speak the Gaelic language with all the speed and power of his unusual genius. If we can depend on him, he suggests that his first – and almost his last – physical action in the cause of patriotism took place when he was around twenty years of age. In *Pictures in the Hallway* he pompously heads one chapter 'I strike a Blow for You, Dear Land.' Trapped in a riot arising from a Boer War protest he knocked a soldier from a horse in a moment of terror and fear. With the economy of an artist he includes in his description of the day an account of what he implies is an early sexual experience with a music hall dancer. As usual we are intended to be impressed by his feats in this arena as well and his partner in bliss is described as sighing with ecstatic and fulfilled delight as he departs.

Working for the Gaelic League – an organisation devoted to the restoration of the Irish as the common speech of the people – he was initiated into the semi-secret Irish Republican Brotherhood in the early 1900s. In time he was adding members himself and Ernest Blythe describes in *Trasna Na Boinne* how O'Casey brought him into the revolutionary movement.

He had an active sports life and played hurling regularly although his poor sight was a handicap. In one story which has become almost legendary he is described as striking a bird from the air in mistake for the ball.

In due course his interest in games lessened as he turned to a fresh enthusiasm, music – in the unlikely form of the bagpipes. Helping to found the St Laurence O'Toole Pipe Band he acquired kilt, shawl and feathered Balmoral cap, and it can still raise ironic eyebrows to picture him marching through Maynooth College in this costume. It should be noted that kilts, bagpipes and trips to Maynooth, Bodenstown and other places cost money so that we can conclude he was not altogether poverty-stricken in those days.

It should be mentioned that his first published work – an article on education – appeared in 1907 and shows his remarkable grasp of language. His abilities were being recognised, too, by some of the organisations he joined.

He remained a passionate nationalist until some time in 1913 and the great Dublin strike of that year may have convinced him of the merits of socialism. It is a bewildering exercise in dialectics to read his sharp criticism of the Labour movement in the spring issue of *The Irish Worker* in 1913 and his total reversal of views the following year in the same paper. Few conversions can ever have been so rapid and so complete.

After the big strike Jim Larkin, the Irish Labour leader, formed the Irish Citizen Army and O'Casey became its first secretary. His tenure of office was brief and he resigned because he could not tolerate association with the purely nationalist movement of the Irish Volunteers represented in the Army by Countess Markievicz.

The Insurrection of 1916 took place without the assistance or blessing of Sean O'Casey, but then he was never unwilling in later years to admit his cowardice. His nationalism had a renaissance in 1918 when he wrote a lament for Thomas Ashe, an Irish patriot who died on hunger strike in circumstances of great heroism. The same year, however, saw the publication of his history of the Irish Citizen Army which marked his conversion to pacifism – a prudent creed in an Ireland on the brink of renewed revolt.

From that time forward the playwright-to-be gave little to either nationalism or labour as he prepared to seek a more natural outlet for his magnificent dramatic talents – the Abbey Theatre. Of course, in this period also his great love affair with the mysterious Maire – described elsewhere in this book – was engaging his emotional energies. All that mattered in his early life was being eroded – reduced, in the Yeatsian term, to wall-paper.

Since we must rely on O'Casey for the descriptions of his pilferings inevitably the question is raised of how far we can rely on the Autobiographies. They are a major source of information on his early life and I think I have shown that in some ways they are exaggerated and distorted.

Selection of what one considers to be true must be subjective where there is no independent source of confirmation, but an assessment of O'Casey's psychological make-up does help to distinguish truth from fiction. His obsession with presenting himself as poverty-stricken is one element which must at all times be accepted with a grain of salt and there are others.

In essence the Autobiographies are not deliberately falsified but they are experience reconstructed in tranquillity. A yardstick of their method and validity might be the picture he provides of the death of his mother.

He describes with all the selective skill of a true dramatist how, alone and weary, he tries to comfort her with a few things purchased from his first real literary success – the publication of *The Story of The Irish Citizen Army*. She dies and we are moved by the sad details of the funeral; by his isolation and his grief. He breaks a sprig of fuchsia, another of musk and with a scarlet disc from a geranium he makes a simple wreath. It is touching even if theatrical – it is also balderdash.

O'Casey was not alone at the time and the necessary act of registering the death was effected by his brother Michael who, according to the certificate, was present when his mother died of bronchitis and cardiac failure. This took place on 9 November, 1918, at the age of seventy-seven years.

Apart from his brother, O'Casey had the assistance of his niece Mrs P. Murphy and her husband, as well as at least one other friend, a Mr J. Adams. The stage was a little more crowded than the elegant, sentimental writing of Sean would suggest. No mention of others is allowed to mar the aesthetic simplicity of his story. This is perhaps typical of how O'Casey – consciously or unconsciously – tried to mould reality to his own design.

His treatment of his brother in *Inishfallen Fare Thee Well* is also misleading. He conveys the impression that Michael was in the last stages of alcoholism and depicts him – and there are no other words for it – as a brutalised swine. I have spoken to those who knew Michael and they are unanimous in their agreement that he was a generous, kind and good-humoured man who enjoyed a drink and good company. He did not die until the late 1940s.

The playwright also paints his brother Tom's wife as a sullen, dirty slut, and this picture is also denied by people who knew her. It is significant that both Michael and his sister-in-law were not unqualified admirers of Sean and did not hesitate to tell him unpleasant truths when they felt like it. It is easy to see why they like all his critics were selected for the pillory of the Autobiographies.

Another example of his inaccuracy is the description of Mountjoy Square in Chapter 4 of *Inishfallen Fare Thee Well*. I know from personal experience that it is false. I was a regular visitor to friends in the square in the early 1930s – on the same side that O'Casey lived – and even then the houses were in better condition than he said they were in 1920, although they had deteriorated in the interval.

All this should enable us to realise that it is a caricature of reality he presents from time to time; it is an inner vision, a fantasy rather than a recollection of objects and events as they happened. The Autobiographies will one day provide an interesting study for some psychiatrist who is willing to read O'Casey and contrast the known truth with his statements.

I believe there is enough to show that he had an almost textbook paranoid attitude. There was the persecution complex which so often exploded into aggression even in the first years of his life. In *I Knock on the Door* he speaks of his birth into a world 'that was filled with the needs, ambitions, desires, and ignorances of others, to be shoved aside, pressed back, beaten down by privileges carrying godwarrants of superiority because they dropped down into the world a couple of hours earlier'. Thus he wrote of his brothers and sister, and the theme that they didn't want him runs through the earlier chapters of the book. Flugel pointed out that paranoia often leads to crime, and the pilfering fits into the picture in this way.

The Autobiographies also suggest that he could withdraw into a dream world, yet another symptom of the condition I mention. When people criticised him in later life they had to be fitted into his delusions. George Orwell spoke harshly of him and so this was attributed to the fact that O'Casey refused to write a preface for a book; Dublin critics assaulted him because he refused to join in a conspiracy against Yeats; his brother Michael's strictures must be caused by excessive drinking and his sister-in-law was a worthless individual who need not be heeded. Everything was rationalised and explained.

The stress he lays on poverty is another expression of his persecution complex, and for me the discrepancy between the Mountjoy Square I knew and the one he described is a trivial but sharp measurement of his mental condition. It is typical of the way in which he writes of things as seen through the distorted lens of his tortured mind.

Ireland, too, by its revolt brought him face to face with his cowardice and he was forced to ideological evasion by events. In 'The Plough and the Stars' he implies that the men of 1916 were cowardly; they had to be in order that O'Casey might justify himself to his own uneasy conscience. It was a feeling that was to remain with him all his life and much later Krause was to note that he was 'an uneasy rebel'.

Whatever explanations exist for his departure from Ireland, his refusal to return for anything other than brief periods must be related to psychological factors. Could it be that Dublin and all it stood for was a material contradiction of his fantasies and his paranoid world? To return for too long might threaten his ultimate sanity by forcing him to face reality and truth.

It may be countered that his conduct was in most ways normal and sane, but paranoids are like this if their delusions escape the harsh abrasion of truth. This, I think, can be offered as no more than a possible theory but it is not illogical. It is one of the few explanations which will cover most of the facts. Whether it is right or wrong we must admit that there is a great deal in the character and life of this strange man which still requires clarification and, in the most charitable sense, understanding.

2

THE GIRL HE LEFT BEHIND

By Sean McCann

LIFE, joy, happiness, truth, sincerity, courage, friendship, sympathy '. . . having all these and losing Maire I would have nothing. Losing all, except life and truth, and having Maire all are mine, for she is all to me. Even the truth of my soul and the life of my life.'

So wrote Sean O'Casey in 1919 in a letter that has never before been published. He wrote it to the one girl who has remained a mystery woman in his life. He dedicated a play to her, he devoted a whole chapter of *Inishfallen Fare Thee Well* to her. He wrote a multitude of letters and poems to her. And yet this woman has remained mysteriously in the background of the O'Casey story, known only by the fictitious name of Nora Creena.

She has avoided biographers, research students and film makers and those who visited her or wrote to her about her friendship with O'Casey were given a gracious but firm 'no comment'.

Saros Cowasjee in his study of O'Casey* wrote of his attempt to meet the Nora of the Autobiographies. He wrote to her in 1958 but received this reply: 'After mature consideration and having regard to the lapse of time since my friendship with Sean O'Casey, I have come to the conclusion that I can be of no assistance to you in the matter in which you are so interested.'

Other writers who have approached Maire have met with the same firm but polite refusal. So many had tried and failed that I had little hope of breaking such a barrier when I set about collecting the stories of the people who had known O'Casey. I knew of Maire's existence and her married name and address but I felt it would be a waste of time to even approach her. Until one Saturday when talking to Tony Gallagher, a colleague, a chance remark he made turned my deep pessimism into wild hope.

*Sean O'Casey: The Man Behind the Plays, by Saros Cowasjee (published by Oliver and Boyd, Edinburgh.)

'You know her maiden name, I suppose', he said.

'No, I don't', I told him with only mild interest.

When he told me the name I laughed. It just couldn't be. I had a long-lost cousin of the same name. I had often heard stories of her – but never a mention of a love affair with anyone remotely concerned with the world of literature. It was just a coincidence, I told myself. But the thought stayed with me until I had almost willed the Maire of the O'Casey story into the Maire of my own family line.

Tony Gallagher came up with some more information. She had been a schoolteacher – so had my cousin. A quick foray among known relations brought one who knew Maire well. My father's sister, Brigid McCann, had been a childhood friend of Maire but knew nothing of the O'Casey relationship. I read her details of Nora Creena from the O'Casey autobiography and she felt that this could indeed be the girl with whom she played and went theatregoing in the early 1900's.

A visit to Maire was arranged, and the amazing coincidence became a truth. She confirmed she was the Maire in O'Casey's life – and was my first cousin, once removed.

At first she was very reluctant to talk about the O'Casey episode in her life; 'it was such a long, long time ago'. But slowly she unfolded the story and showed me many of the treasures of her association with Sean. Letters and poems, books and plays dedicated to her – very few of them ever seen outside the immediate family circle.

There were books carefully hidden away with exciting dedications.

Two Plays by Sean O'Casey ('Juno and the Paycock' and 'The Shadow of a Gunman') bearing the inscription 'To the lovely and loveable Maura in whom the author found his first inspiration.' Frequently O'Casey used the English spelling of her name.

The Plough and the Stars: 'To Maire – from Sean O'Casey. Dear Maire: There is none like unto thee in gentle loveliness, in kindness and in truth. Sean.'

Then an edition of Shaw's *St. Joan* which carried the double inscription: 'Inscribed to Sean O'Casey's friend by G. Bernard Shaw.' and 'From Sean O'Casey to Maire in remembrance of her lovely charms and charming loveliness. South Kensington, 1926.'

And, then inside the copy of *Juno and the Paycock* the printed dedication 'To Maura and the Abbey Theatre'.

Letters and poems which had been folded away silently for over thirty-five years were revealed, and with them the first lifting of the curtain that had hidden the truth of this, the great early love story in O'Casey's life – the story of the girl who gave him 'the fullest experience of good companionship' he had had in those early days. This relationship began in 1917 and continued, apart from an extended break at the end, up to 1926.

An old family album brought to light pictures of Maire in her early days as a schoolteacher and confirmed the pictures that O'Casey painted of her in *Inishfallen Fare Thee Well* – a good-looking girl with large hazel eyes, a head of heavy brown hair, beautifully rounded chin, delicate full white throat. A girl always meticulously dressed, wearing the large, big-brimmed hats of the time.

Her picture of him is still vivid. Tall, well-built, dark brown hair and glasses. 'He would crinkle up his eyes when they got tired. His eyesight was so poor that he wouldn't recognise you on the other side of the street – even with strong glasses. He was not particular about his dress – I'd say he was careless . . . but he was never unkempt or dirty.

'He was a very good companion to be out with. He had a fine – if often sarcastic – turn of humour. He was full of talk – interesting talk. And so very proud – a pride that could be a weakness – and often embarrassing. On one occasion we went out on the Glasnevin tram and the conductor knew me. When he came around for the fares he handed Sean the two tickets and wouldn't take the money. It was often the thing in those days for a conductor to show his appreciation of some help or kindness by giving you a "free fare". In this case I had helped one of his children at school. But Sean was not a one to accept something that he considered charity. He got excited and very annoyed with the conductor. The tram was almost in uproar. "Does he not think I can pay my own fare and yours too?" Sean shouted. "Do I look in need of charity?" He was in a very bad mood for the rest of the evening – that was the "sour pride" he often talked about.'

Maire says that Sean always wanted people to think he was a lot worse off than he really was in his early days. His home was never, she says, a slum. 'In this way he was a bit two-faced. He had a thing about poverty. He liked to put on the Irishman's poor mouth.'

She remembers giving him a fountain pen early in their association. 'It was one of the very latest – a Waterman – and

Maire – the girl O'Casey left behind

he used it all the time. But later he wrote that he couldn't afford a pen to write with. I know that wasn't true. It was just part of the image that he wanted to paint of himself.'

They met first at the start of an amateur drama club. He wrote that he often encountered her years before as she hurried to a local school. Maire cannot remember this; certainly they never spoke to each other. When they met – and spoke – he was thirty-seven and she was twenty-two. But it wasn't for a year after that, as they say in Dublin, they 'got great' with each other.

She lived then in a street of small, respectable, two-storey houses with her father, mother and two sisters near Dublin's East Wall dock area. In his autobiography O'Casey gives a detailed picture of the house and leaves the reader with the impression that he is describing Maire's home. 'But he was never in my home,' she says. 'He couldn't have had an idea what it was like inside.' Certainly what he wrote bears no resemblance to her childhood home. When pressed she says that he would have been a very unwelcome visitor. Her family were adamant in their refusal to accept him as her boy-friend. 'We were a very Catholic household. My parents would not tolerate a Protestant for a son-in-law. My mother was particularly strong about this – my father was a little more tractable.'

Her friendship with O'Casey triggered off innumerable family arguments. But then arguments between Maire and her family were almost a part of the household scene. The first ones developed when as a child she took a strong dislike for meat – a dislike her family couldn't understand. But she persisted and is still a vegetarian. However with O'Casey the whole family became involved. Mother, father, sisters became a part of the argument ritual. One of her sisters would express her wish forcefully: 'Why, in the name of God, can't you get another boy-friend – one that won't cause continual trouble.'

But it took more than family objections to keep them apart. Maire and Sean met six days a week; never on Saturdays – that was the day for washing the hair, going to confessions and generally preparing for Sunday. 'Sean used to get annoyed when I wouldn't go out on the Saturdays. "You'd think Saturday wasn't a day of the week", he'd say.'

Belonging, as they both did, to that famous Dublin Gaelic club, O'Toole's, they spent a lot of their spare time taking part in the various plays, concerts, musical evenings and sports events. It was at this drama club that they met for the first time. Maire had been asked to take part in a play but felt she would rather do some work backstage, and backstage she met O'Casey. He eventually asked her out after a meeting of the club. Then for the six days of the week they met they did what most young courting couples in Dublin did. She went and saw him play in the piper's band; she listened to him sing ballads and parodies at concerts; they went to dances together and she discovered that he was happier as a 'wallflower' than as a dancer.

Tram rides to the seaside at Dun Laoghaire and Howth. Trips into the strife-torn and wary city. And country walks. One of their favourite places was in Finglas, in west county Dublin – a lover's lane, known as Stella's Walk, between tall, old trees where Stella and Swift had walked before them. On these outings O'Casey talked about writing and writers. About Keats, Shelley, Milton, Dumas, Thackeray and Shaw. And he would read his own articles, poems and stories to Maire. He was excitable – and always more so when he had a piece accepted for publication. He would read it over and over and discuss it with her. And he would do the same with new pieces that had not, up to then, found a publisher.

With his plays it was the same. He read them to Maire. He asked her advice. He told her how he found his characters. She remembers him telling her how he wanted to get authentic notes on a prostitute for one of his plays. 'Eventually one evening he left off his collar and tie and put on a scarf instead – he said it made him look disreputable – and he went down to Burgh Quay. He hoped to meet the right sort of girl there. He didn't have long to wait before one came up to him. He asked her a lot of questions and when he had got most of his information he put on the poor mouth and pretended he had no money. She took pity on the poor starving writer and took him to a cafe and bought him a cup of coffee.' The information he collected that night became the basis for Rosie Redmond, the most illustrious prostitute on the Irish stage.

O'Casey seldom let a character or incident slip from his memory. Even Maire was to figure later in a play – a play that shows up a jealous streak in the man. For some time a bachelor police inspector who had been drafted to Dublin from her father's home town, visited her home. 'To me he was just an old man at the time and I didn't take much notice of him – except when I heard my mother saying how worried she was that an officer of the law should be visiting our house. She'd say, "If the boys (the I.R.A.) get to hear of this we'll be branded".' But no one did get to hear of it and apart from occasionally mentioning the man to O'Casey she forgot all about him. But O'Casey was not convinced that the visits were as innocent as Maire made out. He believed that the policeman was there courting Maire. Eventually he used this as part of 'Red Roses for Me'. 'O'Casey saw himself as the dead hero Ayamonn, Maire as Sheelagh, the girl who put a bunch of red roses on his coffin as she stood outside the church with a policeman by her side.'

Many other incidents stuck in his mind and were used later on. His walks with her through the leafy, lonely country lanes through 'sun-dappled' meadows, and lush green fields. The kisses they shared and the talk they talked. Once they talked about a poem he had written. It was called *The Call of the Tribe*. Sean was thrilled about this. He felt it was the ballad that was needed to lift the hopes of Ireland, a song that could almost be a national anthem. Later he told her that the people at Liberty Hall thought it was good too and they were going to put it to music. But they didn't, and after they handed it back to him, he tore it into little pieces and dejected and depressed walked home. As far as I know this poem has never been published. This may be because O'Casey made only two copies – the one which he tore up in disgust and the other which he gave to Maire. She kept her copy and showed it to me.

THE CALL OF THE TRIBE

Like vultures from dark clouded skies they come swooping
To feast themselves full on inanimate prey,
The legends of England to Ireland come trooping
To bear the best sons of our mothers away.
The bull brazen throat of Britannia's yelling
That Dishonour's dark chalice is empty and dim,
And Ireland's rich blood the world's slaughter tide swelling
Must colour it redly from bottom to brim.

Refrain: *But the children of Ireland with hearts fixed and true*
Shall ever be faithful dear Eire to you!

The rivers of Fodhla are tirelessly flowing
Through different ways to the Breast of the Sea,
And the thoughts of thy children with energy glowing
Form an ocean of love, dearest Eire, to thee;
The children of Labour with red banners waving
Are the strength and the hope of the tribes of the Gael,
They unite to resist the proscription enslaving
That would break the broad heart of their loved Granualle.

Refrain:

An altar of dark stone our foes are now building
To sacrifice Ireland's dear body and soul,
With promises splendid this altar they're gilding
By yielding a little of all that they stole;
But gravely we laugh at their frantic endeavour –
They never shall reap where they think they have sown –
And the altar they're raising thy form to dissever,
Shall become, dearest Eire, thy radiant throne.

He has written of the dejection and depression caused by the failure of the Transport Union to use this poem. And there were many other moments of depression – and humiliation. Out with Maire he records that whenever they saw her sister and her boyfriend approaching Maire would frantically run the opposite way and he would trot after her. He was angry, humiliated and tense, being treated, he felt, like a small boy. He writes that it happened many times, but Maire remembers only the one occasion. They were walking near Rathfarnham and saw her sister approach. 'We did turn away – she was with her boy friend and it saved mutual embarrassment. But I don't remember it happening more than once.' She remembers that O'Casey's pride was hurt and he was annoyed for days.

To this gentle, wistfully patient girl he wrote endlessly. Each morning, although they had been out only the night before, he would send her a letter by post – although they lived only a short distance apart. 'When I left him at night he would go home, write a letter and then put it in a post box near his home in time for the last collection.' Maire did not keep all these letters and those which she did keep have been deposited at the National Library and are not open for public scrutiny until 1980. Before giving them away she copied some into a small notebook. Most of these were in the form of poems, which again, I believe, have not been published. They were all very personal love poems and just a few of them are reproduced here.

THOUGHTS OF THEE

Through all the hours that life shall go,
Sweet hours or sad, hours swift or slow –
Each passing moment brings to me
Full blooming rose-like thoughts of thee.

The shaded woods where linnets throng
The sweet notes of the thrush's song,
The blackbird piping on a tree,
Are all sweet murmuring thoughts of thee.

The brook that kisses as it flows,
Each flower that on its border grows,
Babbling its love is love to me
A limpid lovely thought of thee.

The dawn, casting night's robes away,
To wanton in the arms of day,
Blushing her own fair charms to see
Is morning's tender thought of thee.

When God, the painter, paints his dream,
And night's great orbs are all agleam,
The lights of ships on Heaven's broad sea
The sky is gemmed with thoughts of thee.

When evening gently soothes to sleep
The weary day, and slumber deep
Enfolds each flower in copse and lea,
The silence breathes sweet thoughts of thee.

The celandine, the sensuous rose,
And every lovely flower that grows,
The scented bloom of hawthorn tree,
Are fragrant incens'd thoughts of thee.

The heather robing hillsides bare,
With glowing purple garments rare,
Broider'd with gorse gold filigree,
Are purple, golden thoughts of thee

Through all the hours that life shall go,
Sweet hours or sad, swift hours or slow,
Each passing moment brings to me,
Full blooming rose-like thoughts of thee.

Some of the overnight letters O'Casey posted contained only a poem. Others were letters or notes, sometimes with an introduction to a poem, sometimes a postscript. When he sent her one called *The summer sun is tightly folding* he added this note: 'Maire – Dear, Gentle, Beloved – I offer this little effort to you,

not because of any merit therein, but as an expression from a heart
pressed full with ardent love for you. Maire, I love you. Sean.'

THE SUMMER SUN IS TIGHTLY FOLDING

The summer sun is tightly folding
Dear nature in a warm embrace
With joy his ardent love beholding
All mirrored in her flushing face;
So, Mary, when I'm fondly gazing
Upon your face so richly fair,
Your tender glance sweet hope is raising,
For me deep love seems pictured there.
The seasons shall forget to come,
The summer skies shall ne'er be blue,
And voiceful birds in Spring be dumb
When my heart shall lose its love for you.

At Eve when nature says goodbye,
Before she seeks her couch of rest
The sun's most ardent glances dye
With glowing hues her tranquil breast:
So, Mary, when you whisper sadly,
With pensive air a faint farewell
My throbbing heart's inclining madly
Love's deepest, tenderest thoughts to tell!
When time the sun's warm heart shall chill,
And tides ne'er fret the surging sea,
When falls each everlasting hill,
My heart shall cease to think of thee!

Night's subtle presence interposes
But still the sun – from lands afar –
The bright beam of his love discloses,
In sheen of moon and shine of star:
So, Mary, love is flowing ever
From this true heart in search of thee –
Not space – but death alone can sever
The bond of love that's life to me!
When rivers – weary of their flow –
No longer seek the calling sea –
When life itself no life shall know –
Then shall this heart be cold to thee.

There was one other poem copied into Maire's notebook before the letters were passed away, one that I feel is relevant here and important in the picture and feeling that O'Casey had for his girl with the deep brown hair.

TO MAIRE

Soft shining pearls from Orient seas,
And wond'rous sapphires, brilliant blue,
Entwin'd in beauty, could not make
A garland rich enough for you.

Nor all the emerald's glorious green,
And rubies rich of crimson hue,
Mix'd with soft opal light, could make
A garland fair enough for you.

But in the wood's deep shaded bower,
Where grow rare violets, deeply blue,
I'd gather all these gems of bloom,
And make a garland, love, for you.

And golden celandines, as well,
The perfum'd may, and speedwell, too;
I'd gather all these gems of bloom,
And make a garland, love, for you.

Could I find flowers in far-off fields,
Fairer than those that ever grew –
I'd gather all these gems of bloom,
And make a garland, love, for you.

Ah, could I climb among the stars,
Gleaming in heaven's deepest blue,
I'd seize the brightest orbs of all,
To make a garland, love, for you.

Star-crowned and garlanded with flowers –
Thine own sweet beauty shining through –
I'd clasp thee panting in my arms,
And kiss the ripe, red lips of you!

These then are just a few of the many, many pages that O'Casey wrote to Maire: in return for them what did she ever write to him? She can't remember writing often. She sent him postcards each year when she left Dublin with her family for holidays, and then some letters, brief ones, at the end, to finish off the affair. These final letters caused her real heartsearching. They brought to an end a courtship that lasted over six years during which 'we were never formally engaged but it was believed that we would marry'.

The affair ended because of religious differences. That she wilted, as O'Casey suggested, under family resentment seems certain. But criticism of the local priest, Maire claims, is most unfair. 'My mother did speak to Father Flood about my relationship with Sean and told him that she considered it wrong for a Catholic girl to be going around with a man of little or no religious persuasion. But the priest did not advise her to stop me seeing Sean, nor did he ever advise me to stop seeing him. He said to my mother, "there's good in the worst of us and bad in the best of us". He told me to try and bring Sean to Benediction if I ever got the chance. He felt this would help to convert him – but I never got the chance.'

O'Casey complained to her that she wouldn't talk about religion. 'Why don't you talk to me about religion', he said, 'don't you know we two could never be unequally yoked?'

'But I couldn't talk to him about it', says Maire. 'You'd need to be a theologian to do that successfully.'

In his letters he acknowledged her religion – and asked for her prayers. 'I hope you did not forget to pray for me last night; remember me always in your prayers, I beseech you, my gentle Maire. May God lift upon you the Light of His countenance now and forever.' This he wrote in May 1919.

Towards the end of the same year he was acknowledging the gulf that yawned between them – a gulf that each refused to cross. 'It is not fate, neither is it the will of God, that separated us, but the tyranny of old-fashioned thought that has come between us two. My love forever and forever shall be yours.'

And yet for another five years they walked out together – knowing well the hopelessness of their situation. O'Casey never asked Maire to give up her religion, only to accept him as he was. This she was not prepared to do. And the religious chasm was never bridged.

O'Casey left Ireland in 1926, but he still wrote to her, although at this time he had received her last letter telling him that it was finally all off – that there wasn't a bridge they could cross together. Never was there a note or a letter or word from her, as he claimed, that he should be a success in six months or the affair would end. Always it was a religious gap. 'It was the only thing between us.' And then from London came the last letter she received from him, telling her that he was coming home for a short visit and asking her to meet him, and saying 'many have I tried to love, but none have I loved'. She didn't meet him then or ever again.

Now serene, contented and happily married, Maire lives in Dublin in a solid, red-brick house. Paintings by a friend, a well-known artist, on the wall, comfort all around her, some personal mementos of times 'long, long ago'. And red roses growing in the front garden.

3

CIVIL WAR AND PEACE

By R. M. Fox

I FIRST met O'Casey in the early twenties during the truce just before the Civil War. This meeting took place in Delia Larkin's flat in Mountjoy Square. Yet, in a way, our acquaintanceship had begun before we met. We were both enthusiastic supporters of Jim Larkin in his turbulent leadership of the Labour struggle in 1913, a struggle in which a third of the city population was directly involved.

Much later Larkin had gone to the States and was imprisoned in Sing Sing Jail. I had written an article calling for his release and this was published in a Scottish journal. I was then a student at Oxford and I sent a copy to Delia Larkin, Jim's sister. I was greatly surprised when this article was printed and placarded in *The Gael*, a Dublin periodical. I was still more surprised to find that it was about three times the original length and contained attacks on individuals and groups who were strangers to me. I asked Delia about this. She said she had shown my article to Sean O'Casey who said he might be able to do something with it. He did. I had no kick on this score for we both had the same purpose, to help in Larkin's release. Incidentally this episode reveals the integrity of Sean O'Casey. He would not use my article as a basis for his own work and put his name to it, which is a far commoner journalistic practice. He left me with whatever credit was due.

I was a stranger to the city and Sean O'Casey quickly made himself my friend and guide. So I learned about Dublin and himself at the same time. He was generous with his time and help. My first impression was of a man in his thirties, of slight build, straight, with quick nervous movements, sensitive features and peering eyes. Very soon I noted his gift for incisive comment.

My time at Oxford was coming to an end and he asked what I would do when I left.

'I am coming to Dublin to write', I answered, with all the confidence of youth.

O'Casey looked at me quizzically.

'I've known dozens of people who left Dublin to write', he said. 'But I've never heard of anyone coming here for that purpose.'

In a few years O'Casey himself was to join the wild geese of Irish literature.

He suggested that we should go to the Fowler Hall in Parnell Square, then the headquarters of the Orange Lodge in Dublin. The city was in an angry, agitated mood, for the civil war was brewing and this dignified Georgian building had been seized by the Republicans to house Belfast refugees driven out of the ship-yards and their homes during the 'pogroms' of that period. A great billowing tricolour, in vivid green, white and orange, hung from the upper windows of this mansion as we stood on the steps.

O'Casey explained that he knew the Commandant, and I

Liberty Hall, as it was in 1916 *just after the shelling by the gun-boat* Helga. *It has been demolished and a skyscraper has taken its place on the banks of the Liffey*

waited expectantly as he knocked. Nothing happened at first. A few men drifted down the street. O'Casey hailed a burly, red-faced countryman.

'How are things shaping in your part of the country?' he asked.

'Terrible', said the man, shaking his head, dolefully. 'All the scallywags and corner-boys have arms and we don't know what is going to happen next!'

'You know the remedy for that, don't you?' responded O'Casey. 'Join the Army and get arms! In a properly constituted state every man should be in the Army!'

While this badinage was going on I heard a clicking movement from the letter box lid behind me. The shutter was lifted and it looked as if a piece of gas pipe was resting on the metal easing. Stooping, I peered through the slit. It was a gun and man's eye, alongside, looked into mine. O'Casey parleyed through the letter box and, presently, with a clanking of chains and undoing of bolts, the door opened wide enough for us to squeeze through. In the hallway was an array of sandbags, with a man lying there holding a rifle. Stepping over the bags we went upstairs to the main room where I talked to some of the refugees, mostly old men, women and children.

There were heaps of improvised bedding curtained off roughly with blankets to provide cubicles. They told me stories of men who had to jump from the ships into Belfast Lough and swim to safety, while red-hot rivets (Orange confetti) fell around them. Round the walls were heavily framed, massive portraits of Queen Victoria, Lord Carson and other Orange worthies, gazing down in glassy-eyed disapproval of the scene. The whole atmosphere and setting was of a Sean O'Casey play though none of these had yet been written.

'If you are writing anything about this', said O'Casey softly, 'the Commandant would like to see it before it is published.'

All my dislike of military censorship welled up.

'How can anything I say about these poor people injure the garrison here?' I demanded.

'That's all very well', drawled O'Casey, in his Dublin tones. 'But they have a store of ammunition in the basement and they are expecting attack at any moment. That's why we found it so hard to get in!'

The refugees, I realised, were in a more perilous position than they knew, for they were the camouflage covering for the ammunition dump.

After saying farewell to the Fowler Hall, O'Casey took me over to the Sinn Fein Court, a crowded room where cases were being argued. Of course this was an illegal assembly under British law, but even Unionist lawyers came to plead, for no one would go to the 'legal' British courts. Later we went to the Four Courts – the principal courts of the city. This impressive domed building had been taken over by the I.R.A. that very day and a

45

crowd of curious lookers-on, shawled women and men with caps and mufflers, were gathered round the gates.

Volunteers were busy, with coils of barbed wire, fixing up defences. Three or four young insurgents were sitting round the dome dangling their feet into space while one stood, silhouetted against the sky, blowing a blast of defiant youth over the city. I noticed business men, wearing bowler hats, clutching their umbrellas and scurrying past. They looked up furtively at the bugler who was playing all the calls he knew. Piles of law books were used to block the windows, huge tomes full of legal precedents. But they had no precedent for this. I did not know that the next time I saw that noble building, the dome would be shattered by the bombardment which marked the beginning of civil war.

We mounted the top deck of a tram and, as it swirled round College Green, a motor car in the street backfired loudly. Suddenly I saw that all my fellow passengers ducked their heads. They knew Dublin and didn't trust bangs. O'Casey smiled his sardonic smile.

I have told of these incidents because, not long afterwards – in 1923 – O'Casey had his first full-length play 'The Shadow of a Gunman' presented at the Abbey. This was an immediate success and re-vitalised the theatre which had been languishing. O'Casey, it was evident, was a dramatist of genius who seized on such Dublin happenings for his material and his atmosphere. All the troubled years since 1913 constituted the seed-bed from which the O'Casey drama grew and flowered.

In 1913 O'Casey gave his full allegiance to the fiery industrial revolt of the Dublin workers. He was enthusiastic about the Irish Citizen Army, the strikers' defence force, formed to protect the marches and meetings against police aggression. He became the secretary of the Citizen Army Council and, in the columns of the *Irish Worker*, he wrote 'Citizen Army Notes' and articles in which he urged a militant – even a military – policy. He said workers should be armed if only with halberds or pikes. Along with Larkin he held recruiting meetings for the Citizen Army. When the Irish Volunteers appeared on the scene, after their organisation was launched at the Rotunda in Dublin, O'Casey expressed bitter hostility to that force. He and other Citizen Army men regarded it as a rival body competing for the allegiance of the Irish workers. They complained that prominent members of the Volunteers were opponents of Labour.

O'Casey could never forgive James Connolly, when 1916 approached, joining forces with the Irish Volunteers and leading the Citizen Army into the 1916 Rising, as allies in the national struggle. He accused Connolly of forsaking the narrow path of Labour's emancipation for the broad highway of National endeavour. In his later writings he invariably wrote in a scornful, bitter and even jeering mood about Connolly.

As long as O'Casey was secretary of the Citizen Army Council he did his best to keep the two forces apart. Captain Jack White and the Countess Markievicz incurred his wrath because each, besides being members of the Citizen Army Council, were associated with the Volunteers. O'Casey moved a resolution calling upon them to choose which group they would belong to, and excluding them from the Citizen Army if they did not withdraw from association with the Volunteers. The Army Council did not like this and Larkin made an appeal to O'Casey to withdraw the resolution and cease his enmity. As a result, O'Casey resigned his secretaryship. This incident illustrates his partisan approach and the bitterness of his feelings. In an appeal to the Irish workers he wrote that they would be fools to fight for anything less than their complete emancipation.

This side of O'Casey's thought should be stressed because many writers have persisted in describing O'Casey as a pacifist. There is no evidence in his writings that he believed in pacifism and, indeed, plenty to show that he did not. It is quite true that in his plays he stressed the suffering that war inevitably brings to the poorest and most helpless of the community. As a man of sensitive mind and spirit, an artist with a great capacity for feeling, he expressed a quivering indignation at injustice, cruelty and oppression. But this does not necessarily make a man a pacifist. The difference between himself and James Connolly was that Connolly believed that all the forces making for national independence should come together for, until a nation asserts its freedom, it cannot choose which path it is going to follow. On the other hand O'Casey believed there should be a definite Labour goal from the beginning, expressed in some such phrase as a Workers' Republic. The Citizen Army travelled the road marked out by Connolly so that O'Casey was left as a critic on the sideline ever since. His plays and prose writings have expressed that criticism.

O'Casey's Irish plays, forged in the heat of the National Revolutionary period, constitute his finest work, though we can see in them the self-consuming bitterness of a man condemned to the

47

role of a spectator after having called long and loud for militant action. This situation was inescapable, for the Irish Revolution did not take the road O'Casey wanted. With his views he could do nothing else but stand aside, and the cry of 'Coward!' that greeted his early plays in the Abbey Theatre riots by a small disgruntled group was foolish and uninformed. If one agrees with Connolly's attitude that the only practical stand was to join in the national struggle, one could question O'Casey's wisdom and urge that his reliance on a tiny separate force could lead only to futility. But, given his point of view, he had to stand aside. And his work as a dramatist proved much more important to the nation – and the world – than anything else he might have done.

In 'The Shadow of a Gunman' he took characters from real life and transmuted them into his drama. Two of the men O'Casey had lived with figure in this early play, while he cast himself for the role of the poet. One man I knew was Captain Seamus McGowan of the Irish Citizen Army who appears in the play as Maguire, the rebel with the bag of bombs, who goes 'catching butterflies at Knocksedan'. Another was Michael Mullen who becomes the eloquent but not very courageous Sammy Shields whose motto is that a live dog is better than a dead lion. McGowan was an explosives expert who made bombs in the basement of Liberty Hall. He carried round with him, in a little tin box, the metal splinter of a bomb that went off accidentally and lodged in his forehead for some years before it worked out. He helped to make a machine gun in Liberty Hall before 1916, though this was never used. He was not killed – as in the play – but lived long after 1916 and was proud of being in Sean O'Casey's drama. Mick Mullen, quite understandably, was not. He resented the character O'Casey portrayed.

May Craig, the well-known Abbey actress who appeared with great effect in several of O'Casey's early plays, once told me how, after she had played in the theatre, one night he brought her down to a little huxter's shop and urged her to study the manner and speech of the woman behind the counter. 'She will be your part in my next play', he said. I mention these facts to show how O'Casey not only used the Dublin he knew so well but also drew many of his characters from life.

It is said that O'Casey's first attempt at a play was written in 1913 during the great strike and presented in Liberty Hall basement to interest the men and hold them together. But I have no record of this. Yet G. W. Russell (A. E.) told me once that

O'Casey had submitted many plays to the Abbey – nine or ten, he said – before 'The Shadow of a Gunman' was accepted. 'We could not take them because they were full of propaganda', said A.E. It was not until O'Casey was able to take a more detached, critical, sardonic, cynical and human view of 'the Troubles' that his moment came and the Abbey Theatre opened its doors. And, after some hesitation, the Irish people opened their hearts.

The life of Sean O'Casey was a blend of tragedy and splendour, for he was an authentic dramatic genius. In his poetry and humour he was a true voice of the Dublin underworld, as he gazed from the tenement doorways, with their broken fanlights and dilapidated stairs. An air of decayed grandeur still lingered about these once stately Georgian mansions, which had come down so low in the world. The people, too, in O'Casey's vision, had that fierce flame of individuality which burned through sorry circumstances and held hope of redemption.

With all his bitterness Sean O'Casey remained a very likeable man. I met his wife when she came to Dublin to see the production of 'The Bishop's Bonfire', the last of his plays to be shown in the city.

She is a woman of discernment and of charm. I asked her, 'Is Sean as bitter as ever?' She looked at me in amazement. 'How can a man with a soft voice like that, be bitter?'

4

THE GREAT OCCASIONS

By Donal Dorcey

A VETERAN of both the First World War and the Irish Civil War
once told me that Flanders was a cake-walk by comparison with
West Cork and Kerry. 1922–23, the year of the Civil War, was
the most shameful year in Irish history. It was a horrible dirty
little war when brother set booby-traps for brother and best
friends hoped for a chance to fire on each other. It was a war of
mass executions and inevitable reprisals. Men died in daylight in
city streets and on mined bridges in deserted countryside. It was a
war which Ireland pretends never took place. But it is a war
which no one in Ireland has ever been able to forget.

To write, and present upon the stage, the sort of plays Sean
O'Casey was writing at that time one had to be a little mad and
very brave. Between April 1923 and February 1926, five O'Casey
plays received their first presentation in the Abbey Theatre.
They were (in chronological order): 'The Shadow of a Gunman',
'Cathleen Listens In', 'Juno and the Paycock', 'Nannie's Night
Out' and 'The Plough and the Stars'. In April 1923 the Civil War
was still raging. By February 1926 it had been reduced to a cold
war, but renewed violence was always threatening. Nothing was
forgiven or forgotten. Members of the Republican party elected
to the Dail (the Irish parliament) declined to take their seats
because their party still did not recognise the Free State Government. The reception of O'Casey's early plays cannot be considered without taking this political background into account.

The intensity of feeling his plays aroused was revealed as
recently as 1960, when shots of O'Casey were deleted from an
American television programme about Ireland because Irish-
Americans protested that he was 'a rather shabby expression' of
his country.

The reactions which the plays evoked from their Abbey
audiences were as varied as the content of the plays themselves.
As the plays ranged from searing tragedy to riotous comedy
within the space, sometimes, of a few lines only, so the audience

reactions ranged from the puzzled silence which greeted 'Cathleen Listens In' to the violent demonstrations which halted a performance of 'The Plough and the Stars' and sparked off a heated public controversy. O'Casey was as puzzled by the audience reactions as were the audiences by his plays. The sense of rejection and insecurity the reactions bred in him was a major cause of his decision to live in England.

However, considering the subjects of the plays and the manner in which O'Casey dealt with them in the light of contemporary events, one must be surprised that the reception was so favourable.

'The Shadow of a Gunman' was first presented on Monday, 12 February, 1923. There had been two famous funerals that morning – in London, Sarah Bernhardt's, in Fermoy, Co. Cork, Liam Lynch's. Liam Lynch was one of the leaders of the I.R.A., and had been killed in a raid on his temporary headquarters by Free State troops. His death led to the truce of two and a half months later.

Otherwise, things were very much as they are today. Shell Ltd was proclaiming a 'new super motor oil'; the Prince of Wales had a sore throat; statements were awaited from France and Germany on their relations with each other; a plan for a tunnel under Mont Blanc had been revived; and the Annual Convention of Secondary Teachers was worried about 'inadequate salary scales'. A shallow depression centred off the south-west coast was moving slowly over the country. One sign of the times: a 'strong young girl for scrubbing and washing' was offered 2s 6d per day in the advertising columns of the *Irish Times*.

The Abbey Theatre was the only place in Dublin where one could hope to see a serious play. There were variety shows in the Royal and the Tivoli, musical comedies in the Queen's and the Olympia, all of these twice nightly. In the Gaiety the Rathgar and Rathmines Musical Society was performing, as usual, 'The Gondoliers'. Even then the *Irish Times* critic thought it a bit old hat, though he expressed himself with old hat courtesy.

The Abbey directors were not very impressed with 'The Shadow of a Gunman' and presented it for three nights only at the end of the season. On the same bill was 'Sovereign Love', a well-established one-act play by T. C. Murray. Perhaps they just wanted to placate the determined nuisance who had already submitted half a dozen plays. But 'The Shadow' proved so popular that it was selected to open the next season in fashionable Horse Show Week. On the first night the theatre was less than half full.

On the second night it was three-quarters full. It was booked out for the third night. O'Casey was paid less than £4 for the play, which he considered less than the Abbey could afford. He may not have known that the theatre had recently been mortgaged to clear a debt of £1,153. An annual subsidy of £850 per annum had just been accepted from the then Minister for Finance, Mr Ernest Blythe. Only six professional players were employed at the time by the theatre; the other actors were part-timers. Years afterwards Yeats told O'Casey that his plays had saved the Abbey from extinction.

The *Irish Independent* reported that the audience cheered and laughed at the first night of 'The Shadow of a Gunman'. The queues will last for the whole run, predicted Jacques, the paper's reviewer. There were few plays to touch it in the Abbey's repertoire, he said, and it was 'in a class by itself in satire'. Of the acting, by F. J. McCormick, M. J. Dolan, Eric Gorman, Gabriel Fallon, P. J. Carolan, May Craig and Christine Hayden, he adjudged that better character studies were never given.

Prior in the *Irish Times* was not so unreservedly enthusiastic. 'The play was well received by a large audience. Mr O'Casey took a call at the end.' He was not satisfied with the play: 'If Mr O'Casey will remove the small element of real tragedy from the end of his play . . . and if he will . . . call it a satire instead of a tragedy, there is no reason why it should not live for a very long time. There is really good work in the play and the dialogue is very well done.'

One cannot expect a newspaper critic on one viewing of a new play by a new playwright to risk his reputation by giving unqualified praise. But once a Dublin audience starts laughing it doesn't like being asked to stop. Audience and critics underestimated the tragic element in 'The Shadow of a Gunman' as they did in the rest of O'Casey's plays. Nevertheless, Dublin had recognised the debut of another promising Abbey dramatist.

How did O'Casey himself feel about it all? In his autobiographical *Inishfallen Fare Thee Well*, he wrote that although the audience reaction did not excite him he felt that he had crossed a border into a new kingdom. In later years he was to revise his opinion of the importance of being an Abbey dramatist.

O'Casey was deeply disappointed with the £4 he was paid for the play, especially as he then had no other source of income but his writing. So he went home and started work on another play. It didn't take him long. Perhaps economic necessity is not a writer's best inspiration. The result of his efforts was probably the least successful of his plays. 'Cathleen Listens In' was presented on 1 October, 1923, less than six months after 'The Shadow of a Gunman'. On the same bill were Shaw's 'The Man Of Destiny' and Lady Gregory's 'The Rising of the Moon'. The people who filled the theatre that night might have been drawn by any one of the playwrights. The play was a ruthlessly witty satire in which the Irish political parties of the day were presented as the suitors of a girl called Cathleen, daughter of a man named Houlihan. The audience, said O'Casey in *Inishfallen Fare Thee Well*, received the play in dead silence, as if too shocked to clap. Was this subjective description accurate? Was it just politeness that made J.H.C., the *Irish Independent* reviewer, write 'the audience was rather amused by the idea, obscured as it was by some irrelevant talk at the outset'?

Prior in the *Irish Times* gave a clue to the audience's attitude. He summed up the play as 'a political skit which, with all its abstruse allusions, is a little difficult to follow'. There was plenty of humour in the dialogue, he thought, and O'Casey obviously knew by instinct 'how to make a play "go"'. But the construction could be improved for 'the comedy tails off, and Mr O'Casey should not be so mystifying. If one were able to read the play before seeing it, no doubt it would become quite comprehensible; but at first sight there seem to be several characters in it whose presence has no particular point.' That indefatigable theatre-goer, Joseph Holloway, the architect who designed the Abbey interior, found the audience not completely silent. In his diary he noted: 'Somehow or other, despite 'Cathleen Listens In' being a good shot, it missed the mark, I think, and fizzled out somewhat. . . . The audience was eager to laugh with him but couldn't; only by fits and starts.'

That the audience was confused was understandable. The message was clear enough: all existing parties were destroying Ireland between them. But what hope was there, then, for Ireland? O'Casey made no suggestions, beyond prescribing a period of rest, which was hardly politically practicable. More than that, the play was so written that not all of it could be flatly paraphrased. Many lines were intended simply to accelerate the dramatic movement and had no meaning outside the play itself. Anyone who sought a double meaning in every line would, therefore, emerge quite bewildered from the theatre, having missed the more obvious allusions from being still distracted by the search for non-existent ones.

Had Dublin failed to recognise a work of genius? No. Allegory does not take naturally to the stage. 'Cathleen Listens In', however witty, has virtually no dramatic impact. And it was hardly a play that political enemies would laugh at together. But there were no angry denunciations, no cries for censorship, no violence. No one who visited the Abbey during the week-long run of 'Cathleen Listens In' could have cared very much for the principles O'Casey satirised. He couldn't hope to get away with it for ever.

O'Casey had no sympathy for the audience in the dilemma in which he'd placed it. Still nervous and unsure of himself, he wanted the sympathy to be all one way. On that first night he slipped away unnoticed from the theatre. But out of anger and disappointment grew a new determination – to let nothing deflect him from his vocation to portray the world, as accurately as possible, as he felt, saw and heard it. There was going to be trouble ahead.

So O'Casey worked on and produced 'Juno and the Paycock'. It was accepted by the Abbey – for once even Yeats was enthusiastic – and presented there on 3 March, 1924. It was the only play on the bill, the first time O'Casey was so honoured. His reputation had obviously survived 'Cathleen Listens In', for the theatre was well filled on the first night. The play was well received by the audience and again O'Casey was called on to speak. The theatre was quickly booked out for the rest of the week. But critical reaction was mixed. The critics had had almost a year since 'The Shadow of a Gunman' to think up smart phrases with which to describe O'Casey. Now the first cries of 'cinematic realism' and 'an outrageous mixture of tragedy and comedy' were heard. However, most of the criticism was favourable.

Jacques in the *Irish Independent* complained that there was too much padding, due to a thirst for 'dialogue with a dig in it'. He termed the production a triumph, one of the Abbey's greatest, and said that O'Casey achieved his effects by colour, contrasts and malapropisms. 'Every character in the piece was excellent if sometimes too verbose'. He concluded: 'This play is a distinct advance and a courageous one. It provides entertainment for the many. Better still, it stimulates thought and exercises the intelligence.'

This judgement was surprising when one remembers that the paper for which Jacques wrote was energetically supporting *Our*

Boys magazine, which spear-headed the campaign called 'The Angelic Warfare for Maintaining the National Virtue of our Country'. This campaign blended a theory of racial supremacy in sex morality with the puritanical attitude to sex held by many of the Catholic clergy. The aim was to shield the young people of Ireland from the dangers of 'bad' books, films and cigarettes. Long bicycle rides into the country were recommended to the young. The propagators of the campaign were unaware that what cannot be done in cinemas or while reading books is very easily and frequently accomplished during long bicycle rides into the country. But the campaign was to score one victory in the introduction of the Censorship of Publications Act, 1929.

To return to the critics. A fine tribute to O'Casey's stature as a dramatist was paid by W. J. Lawrence in his review of 'Juno and the Paycock' for the *Irish Statesman*. O'Casey, he wrote, 'is at once an iconoclast and a neo-Elizabethan. . . . He lures us into the theatre under the pretext of affording us hearty laughter, and he sends us away with tears in our eyes and with the impression of direst tragedy heavy on our hearts. None but a neo-Elizabethan could accomplish this, since the secret of juxtaposing and harmonising the comic with the tragic, and thereby throwing the elements of terror and pathos into greater relief, have been lost to the English-speaking stage for over a couple of centuries.'

To which O'Casey would probably have replied that Lawrence had not seen enough of the Irish melodramas of Dion Boucicault, from which he had learned so much of his technique.

Lady Gregory was delighted with the play. 'This is one of the evenings at the Abbey that makes me glad to have been born', she told Yeats on the first night. O'Casey, who liked and respected her so much, was equally pleased. 'Juno' established him as a celebrity in Dublin and gave him his first taste of the fruits of that little glasshouse. Everybody wanted his autograph. There were invitations from the wealthy and influential to At Homes and dinners in exclusive clubs. But fame and flattery didn't please O'Casey. He had none of the conventional shame of his working-class origins. Now forty-four, he was too old to have his head turned. His own opinion of himself was good enough for him. The more Ireland praised him, the smaller she became in his eyes. Having conquered her he was preparing to leave her.

'Turn your back on it all, Sean, a vic o!', he wrote in *Inishfallen Fare Thee Well*. 'Turn your back on the green and the gold, on the old woman that once had the walk of a queen! What's

Ni Houlihan to you, or you to Ni Houlihan? Nothing now.' O'Casey's thoughts were turning to emigration or, at least, to travel. He had never yet set foot outside Ireland. But he had brought the powerful people of Dublin to his feet and his self-confidence was unassailable. It was a strange confidence considering that his reputation and his slender finances were shaky still and that a refusal then to compromise with the Dublin literary establishment could have ruined him.

For it was 'Juno and the Paycock' which first enabled him to live by writing. Dublin was too small to provide a decent income for a playwright but 'Juno' was presented successfully in London and ran for months. This, more than anything else, was what turned O'Casey's thoughts to leaving.

'O'Casey has caught the ear of the public in no uncertain fashion and the theatre is usually over-crowded to hear his plays', wrote Joseph Holloway in his diary for 6 October, 1924. O'Casey's latest work, a one-act play called 'Nannie's Night Out', was running that week at the Abbey with Shaw's 'Arms and the Man'. Everybody had liked 'Juno and the Paycock'; even the nationalists had attended it and, despite its popularity, Yeats had liked it too. Not so with 'Nannie's Night Out'.

Before it was produced there were objections from the Abbey directors and the original ending had to be changed. In the first version Irish Nannie, a spunker or drinker of methylated spirits, who is enjoying her first night in months out of jail, chases a very shadowy gunman from Mrs Pender's little shop, then collapses from the effort and dies, before the audience and her half-naked son. She expires still swearing that she'll die game. None of the characters shows any sympathy for her except for a ballad-singer, who plays a Greek chorus-like role. He furiously accuses the others of hypocrisy, for they drove Nannie to live in the tenements which killed her and took notice of her only when she was drunk.

Whether it was to the sordid manner of Nannie's death or to the social message of the ballad-singer or to both that the Abbey directors objected we know not. But in the version to which they gave their imprimatur the ballad-singer delivered no such speech and Nannie suffered what to the directors may have seemed a fate worse than death. She was arrested for drunkenness by the police and carried off screaming. This drastic change made the play quite meaningless but O'Casey didn't seem to mind. At least he makes no mention of it in *Inishfallen Fare Thee Well.*

He seems to have been rather ashamed of the play and dismisses it as 'a play no one liked except A.E., otherwise known as George Russell, who thought it O'Casey's best work, an opinion that didn't bother Sean for he knew A.E. knew nothing about the drama and felt a little less.'

This is rather unfair to A.E., the man O'Casey lambasted in the same book as 'Dublin's glittering guy'. A.E. seemed genuinely moved in his own ponderous pretentious fashion by the play when he wrote in the *Irish Statesman*, 'I went away from the theatre hearing her voice (i.e., Nannie's voice) and remembering that learned Cardinal who spoke to John Inglesant about the virtue in passion released from all limits and how it followed in its motions a divinity than which there is none higher.'

Nor did the other critics dislike the play. The *Irish Times* mentioned that the house was packed and praised Sara Allgood's study of the outcast Nannie. The reviewer said that 'Nannie's Night Out' was not to be compared with either 'The Shadow' or 'Juno', 'but in some respects it surpasses the best in either. . . . In spite of its comedy, the tragedy of tenement life dominates the little play. . . . Nannie, herself, is a full expression of that tragedy, enforced again with the appearance of her little boy, half-starved and half-naked but knowing all about the day's runners. . . . "Nannie's Night Out" excites thought and pity as well as laughter.'

Reviewing the play for the *Irish Statesman*, Bertha Buggy had a similar point of view. 'Our sides ache, we laugh, we roar, we gasp – and then – a sudden feeling of discomfort, a queer, stupid feeling as if we wanted to cry. . . . He brings us to his plays and then he heaves life at us, with its sharp corners and its untidy jumble of laughter and tears. . . . And the worst of it is, that if we go on allowing him to make us laugh and cry together in this hysterical fashion, we may end by insisting that he is a genius.'

The *Irish Times* reviewer reported that the audience laughed appreciatively at the lines, about Nannie's son, 'It's a wonder they wouldn't do something for little kiddies like him, instead of thryin' to teach them Irish.' In his book, *Sean O'Casey, the Man I Knew*, Gabriel Fallon contradicts this, saying that the line earned O'Casey his first hisses although the hisses were countered by applause.

'Juno and the Paycock' was now doing well in London, making O'Casey dream of the comfortable life he could lead there as a successful writer. He wrote that only the cost of the journey held him back.

An American advertising executive has remarked that when James Joyce took to literature he missed a great career as an advertising copywriter. It could as truly be said of W. B. Yeats that he missed a great career in the allied field of public relations. His advance publicity for 'The Plough and the Stars' was masterly. He always professed to 'study hatred with great diligence' and to want 'strong unpopular plays' for the Abbey. But having a really strong play he was going to make it unpopular with as many people as possible. 'The Plough and the Stars' was that sort of play. He spent an unprecedented amount on posters and newspaper advertising. He hired men to carry sandwich-boards, such as had fired Joyce's imagination, through the streets. No advertising was needed to bring the Abbey's regular clientele to the theatre, they turned up religiously for every first night. But this time Yeats wanted more than the regular clientele. The campaign did not stop at advertising. All Dublin heard that this was O'Casey's strongest play.

The *Irish Independent* reported the false rumour that the play had been refused a London production by the Lord Chamberlain, and that the Irish Government was considering similar action. It was widely rumoured, again falsely, that Ria Mooney had refused to play the part of the prostitute. Literary Dublin knew that the Abbey manager, M. J. Dolan, disliked the play and wouldn't produce it; that Dolan had recently banned O'Casey from the Abbey green-room because he refused to restrain his scathing though well-intentioned criticisms of the players; that Eileen Crowe had refused to play Mrs Gogan because 'the part was not genteel'; that George O'Brien, the Government nominee to the Abbey board of directors, had objected to the play and secured two cuts from the original text.

One of these cuts, from the first act love scene between Nora and Clitheroe, has never been restored. The other, Rosie's song at the end of Act Two about 'bouncing about in the bed', was omitted from the first production but is now an accepted part of the play.

And, of course, all Dublin knew that Lennox Robinson, who was to produce the play, had just been sacked from the secretaryship of the Carnegie Trust for writing a short story which was considered to be obscene. Two weeks before the first night, at a party on the Curragh, Yeats hinted at what all this was leading to. As Gabriel Fallon recalls in his book, Yeats had been describing the riots over Synge's 'The Playboy of the Western World.' Actor Arthur Shields asked him if there would ever be another riot like that one. Yeats replied: 'I shall tell you that in a fortnight's time'.

Thus rumour wrote in invisible ink across all the black and saffron posters, 'the Abbey's most immoral play yet'. The result was Yeats' dream. All tickets were sold several nights before the premiere, and on the night itself, 8 February, 1926, a queue a quarter of a mile long coiled round the theatre waiting for seats in the gods.

O'Casey had so far been leading a charmed life as a dramatist. It is a measure of the Abbey's remoteness from Dublin life that his four satirical unromantic plays had evoked between them no more than a disapproving silence at one and some hissing at another. O'Casey broke down that remoteness at considerable cost to himself and, some believe, to the Abbey.

But in his early political writings and activities O'Casey had already angered the nationalists who were ignoring his plays. He had heretically approved of 'The Playboy of the Western World', while his comrades were joining demonstrations against the play. As a member of the Citizen Army he had opposed the alliance with the Volunteers which was to lead to the Easter Week Rising. He held that the Volunteers were controlled by capitalists and that the rights of Labour would be forgotten in the alliance. History has proved him right but his intransigence at the time, especially as it was always so ably expressed, earned him the enmity of the leaders of both parties. O'Casey added insult to injury in 1919 when he wrote *The Story of the Irish Citizen Army*. The book expressed his pacifist point of view. Its hero was Francis Sheehy Skeffington, who was murdered while leading his peace patrol around Dublin in Easter Week trying to stop the fighting and looting. Nationalists appealed to booksellers not to stock this book and to the public not to buy it.

This background of O'Casey's was recalled when Dublin heard he had written an anti-nationalist play. He was identified as an ally of the Protestant Ascendancy, represented by Yeats and Lady Gregory, and of the Free State Government, which was subsidising the Abbey. Yeats decided to rub in that he was a Senator of the Government. Before the play he had dinner with some members of the Cabinet and then brought them with him to the theatre. 'Bloody murderers', hissed Republican sympathiser

Joseph Holloway at them as they passed. 'It is an abominable play', wrote Holloway afterwards, 'there are no street-walkers in Dublin.'

The political overtones and the dispute with O'Casey did not help the players in their rehearsals. There was a feeling of tension which survived into the performance itself, and a reluctance to co-operate with the playwright. O'Casey's casting of the play was set aside, except for his choice of Barry Fitzgerald as Fluther Good. For O'Casey had realised Fitzgerald's comic talent before anyone in the Abbey, and insisted that he was the man for the part. Fitzgerald's brilliant performance was to make Fluther the central character of the play and establish Fitzgerald, then just a part-timer, as a star. The cast was finally as follows:

Jack Clitheroe	F. J. McCormick
Nora Clitheroe	Shelagh Richards
Peter Flynn	Eric Gorman
Young Covey	M. J. Dolan
Fluther Good	Barry Fitzgerald
Bessie Burgess	Maureen Delany
Mrs. Gogan	May Craig
Mollser	Kitty Curling
Lieut. Langan	Arthur Shields
Capt. Brennan	Gabriel Fallon
Cpl. Stoddart	P. J. Carolan
Sgt. Tinley	John Stephenson
Rosie Redmond	Ria Mooney
Barman	P. J. Carolan
Woman from Rathmines	Eileen Crowe
Voice	John Stephenson

The Abbey had little competition to meet on the first night. In the Gaiety Theatre the Dublin University Players were presenting 'Mrs Gorringe's Necklace' with what the *Irish Times* considered a 'competent cast'. There were revues in the Olympia and the Queen's. Cashing in on the latest rage, the Theatre Royal was billing 'the great wireless favourites, the Selma Four' as stars of its variety show.

In the Abbey foyer the theatre-goers were talking that night of the floods which were devastating the country and of the forthcoming by-elections in the constituencies of County Dublin and Leix-Offaly. A good conversational gambit was the Lenten pastorals of many Irish bishops, who deplored the increasing interest shown by the young in dances and other sinful amusements.

Despite all the fuss the first night went off quietly. The audience treated the play simply as a play, not as a piece of propaganda. The theatre was packed to the doors and many stood round the walls for the whole performance. Actors and audience were tense and expectant, ready for literally anything to happen. Nothing did. The audience applauded rapturously after every act and called at the end for the playwright. O'Casey made his usual shy, blinking, trench-coated appearance, wearing a cap to protect his pain-wracked eyes. The cap was always interpreted as a publicity gimmick and made the 'docker dramatist' the darling of the intellectual snobs.

The *Irish Times* reviewer found the play's motif in Mollser's line 'Is there no one with a titther of sense?' 'Great events are outlined only insofar as they have had reactions on the lives of the men and women Mr O'Casey recreates', wrote the reviewer. 'He hates human suffering and . . . he makes his audience feel that it (the Rising) was not worth it: that one drop of the milk of human kindness is worth more than the deepest draughts of the red wine of idealism.' He concluded, 'When these miniature speeches have been trimmed a little, "The Plough and the Stars" will be a better work.'

The *Irish Independent* succeeded in reviewing the play and praising Ria Mooney's performance as Rosie Redmond without mentioning Rosie's profession beyond terming it a 'difficult part'. The reviewer, J.W.G., predicted that it would be O'Casey's most popular play, but said there was no artistic advance on 'Juno and the Paycock'. He noted that O'Casey had not taken sides on the Rising: 'What the play drives home is the strength of the common ties that bind humanity'.

Both critics were unexcited about the value of the play. This was the common opinion of the newspaper critics. Not so Walter Starkie, a future director of the Abbey, who reviewed the play for the *Irish Statesman*. The last act, he said, was the biggest thing O'Casey had done yet; it had humanity, restraint and a 'true Aristotelian catharsis'. He compared O'Casey with leading contemporary dramatists: 'Sean O'Casey is not a social dramatist like most of the moderns, filled with a desire to expose some vice and correct by developing one thesis in his play. He looks at our society from all sides and his fund of sympathy is large enough to include all. But though he pardons all he never fails to expose hypocrites and evil to the gaze of humanity. . . . He leaves us at the end . . . with nothing but misery in our hearts. . . . There is no doubt that the audience . . . welcomed this new work of Mr O'Casey: we have rarely seen an audience more moved than in the last act. And yet many were the peals of laughter in the earlier acts at Fluther's sallies.'

Had Yeats' publicity failed? Was 'The Plough and the Stars' to be remembered as just another play, if a slightly better one than most? The weekly *Voice of Labour* hinted at what was to come. Its reviewer, 'An Lonndubh' (Gaelic for 'the blackbird') felt his loyalties divided by the play. He praised it eloquently for its indictment of war: 'Who gains by it all we do not know, nor do we want to. We only know that poverty pays the full price. In "The Plough and the Stars" humanity's cry against that price is a lyrical one.' He felt that much of the play was unforgettable, but that much also was unforgivable. The juxtaposition of nobility and degeneracy in Act Two he thought was unjustifiable. And he sounded a prophetic warning: 'The nationalism of Pearse may have fallen amongst strange companions in the days that witnessed its first manifestations, but it never lost its nobility. Mr O'Casey, whatever his purpose may be, takes away that, an unforgivable thing. An Irish audience may one day turn away from this play because of that. Our cynicism will not always last.' An Lonndubh's words were to be proved true before they appeared in print.

On Tuesday, the second night of the play's one-week run, half a dozen women in the pit stamped and hissed at intervals during the performance. No one paid any attention to them. On Wednesday night the same happened. The first act of Thursday night's performance was punctuated by similar interruptions, but that night the Republicans were there in force. A demonstration had been planned and organised in advance. One of the demonstrators was a Nurse Maguire who reported the night's events for *An Phoblacht*, the Republican weekly. In it she wrote 'a few nights ago I was asked to go see "The Plough and the Stars" at the Abbey Theatre and help to support the speakers who intended to make speeches protesting against the insults offered to the men of Easter Week throughout the whole play.'

There were more than speeches made. When the curtain rose for the second act on Rosie Redmond in the pub, pandemonium broke loose. Between howls and applause not a word of the act could be heard. 'I can still hear', wrote Gabriel Fallon, 'the

Joxer Daly-like accents of that fruity Dublin voice that wanted "that wumman taken offa th' stay-age".' The players carried on in dumb show to the end of the act. From the gallery a woman's voice shrieked against the defamation of the men of Easter Week. When the lights went up at the end of the act she was seen to be Mrs Sheehy Skeffington, widow of O'Casey's pacifist hero. 'You are a disgrace to your sex', a man shouted at her, and was led out by his friends. 'Send out O'Casey, O'Casey the coward', shouted a man in the pit. O'Casey was not yet in the theatre. Lady Gregory was at home in Coole. Lennox Robinson, the producer, was God only knows where. Yeats was in the *Irish Times* office handing in the text of a speech he planned to make.

During the interval a number of people left the theatre. When the curtain rose for the third act a dozen women rushed on to the stage and attacked the actors who tried to push them back. A young man hauled himself on to the stage and seemed to aim a blow at Maureen Delany. He was hurled into the orchestra pit by Barry Fitzgerald. On M. J. Dolan's orders the curtain was lowered and a young man and woman tried to tear it down altogether. Abbey attendants and some of the audience bundled demonstrators out of the theatre.

More people left. The curtain was raised again. After more hissing and booing, F. J. McCormick made himself heard: 'Please differentiate between the players and the author'. One hopes he appreciated the irony of the actors being assaulted for their parts in a play they disliked. Another young man jumped on to the stage but his speech could not be heard and he was pushed off, to cries of 'go on with the play'. McCormick continued, 'Everybody has a right to object. Please, do you think it is fair to come up and mob us? We play in all sorts of plays. We play in "Nan Kavanagh" by Miss Macardle.' Miss Macardle was the Republican historian, Dorothy Macardle, whom Joseph Holloway identified as one of the leaders of the protest. Perhaps McCormick had seen her too.

A voice shouted, 'Ask O'Casey to remove that scene and we will willingly look at the play. It is a disgrace in a Catholic country. It is a lie and a scandal.' More people rushed the stage and a fist-fight broke out between them and the actors. The curtain was lowered again.

Meanwhile O'Casey had arrived in the theatre and went straight to the secretary's office where he found Yeats enthroned. Yeats asked his permission to call the police. At first O'Casey was horrified by the idea but a roar from the theatre made him change his mind. His description of what followed is vivid and colourful but, unfortunately, wildly exaggerated. 'The whole place became a mass of moving, roaring people. . . . Rowdy, clenching, but well-groomed hands reached up to drag down the fading black-and-gold front curtain; others, snarling curiously, tried to tug up the very chairs from their roots . . . while some, in frenzy, pushed at the stout walls to force them down. Steamy fumes ascended here and there in the theatre, and a sickly stench crept all over the place, turning healthy faces pale.'

Yeats had the curtain raised and took the centre of the stage. As he spoke the police entered and quiet fell. Nurse Maguire was predictably, very unimpressed by Senator Yeats: 'On one occasion Mr Yeats had mounted the stage and struck an attitude – legs wide apart – hand well raised and bent over the head – result pandemonium!'

'Yeats is in his element at last', scribbled Holloway, 'it is really dirt for dirt's sake.'

Gabriel Fallon presents a different picture again. 'That night at the Abbey Theatre even the finest of players would have stood transfixed in admiration of Yeats' performance. Every gesture, every pause, every inflection, was geared to a tolerance calculated to meet an angry mob.'

Yeats' speech could scarcely be heard above the uproar. 'I thought you had got tired of this which commenced about fifteen years ago. But you have disgraced yourselves again. Is this going to be a recurring celebration of Irish genius? Synge first and then O'Casey! The news of the happenings of the last few minutes here will flash from country to country. Dublin has again rocked the cradle of a reputation. From such a scene in this theatre went forth the fame of Synge. Equally the fame of O'Casey is born here tonight. This is his apotheosis.'

'Up the Republic', shouted an undaunted one. 'We want the play', came the reply.

The police were now shoving people into the street, where they continued to make speeches. Demonstrators filtered into empty front seats. Two of them kept blowing a whistle till it broke. The curtain rose again and the play continued in comparative silence. There were occasional shouts and hisses. Some women sang *The Soldiers' Song* and were ejected by a few of the police who lined the walls. In the gallery Mrs Skeffington, who had taken no part in the violence, rose to make a speech.

'We are now leaving the hall under police protection. (Cheers and jeers.) I am one of the widows of Easter Week. It is no wonder that you do not remember the men of Easter Week, because none of you fought on either side. The play is going to London soon to be advertised there because it belies Ireland. We have no quarrel with the players – we realise that they at least have to earn their bread. But I say that if they were men they would refuse to play in some of the parts. All you need do now is sing *God Save the King*.' Mrs Skeffington then left the theatre. The actors had ignored her though one must have been hurt by her words. He was Arthur Shields, who had fought in the G.P.O. during the Easter Rising.

Snatches of other speeches could occasionally be heard: 'The Government is subsidising the Abbey to malign Pearse and Connolly.'

'We fought in 1916 and we did not frequent pubs nor associate with prostitutes.'

Despite these interruptions the play ended quietly. No arrests were made. No serious damage was done to the theatre. A double bass belonging to orchestra member Fred Deane lost its cover. A number of music sheets were torn. Two footlights were broken. Part of the curtain was torn. O'Casey's description of the night obviously over-indulges in hyperbole. Nearly all of the rioters were women and most of them looked like students. There were no gunmen involved. Holloway saw Dan Breen, the famous rebel fighter, there, but he did no more than argue with Yeats in the foyer. Many members of the audience complained at the spoiling of the play but no one seems to have feared any physical danger. O'Casey was not assaulted. As he left the theatre he met a number of the women demonstrators who abused him as a renegade and a friend of England. One told him there wasn't a prostitute in Ireland. O'Casey noticed no pretty faces among them and walked by. In *Inishfallen Fare Thee Well* he recalls how he felt at the time:

'Sean went home feeling no way exalted by his famous apotheosis. He was bewildered and felt sick rather than hilarious. . . . . Did these bawling fools think that their shouting would make him docile? He would leave them to their green hills of holy Ireland.' Before long he did.

The remaining performances of the play – one on Friday and two on Saturday – were booked out the next morning. The theatre was heavily guarded by police. Protests were confined to a few cat-calls during the last performances. Saturday night's was a triumph. One man walked out shouting about the terrible insult to Connolly and Pearse but there was a five-minute-long ovation for O'Casey at the end. Throughout the conflict there were more for him than against him, inside the theatre at least.

On the Saturday morning the Republicans made a last attempt to stop the play. Three teenagers with masks, slouched hats and revolvers arrived at the Clontarf home of Barry Fitzgerald's mother. They said they had orders to take him to a safe place to prevent his appearing on the stage. They were invited into the house but when severely scolded by Fitzgerald's sister, Mrs Mortished, their nervousness got the better of them and they ran to a waiting car without searching the house. Fitzgerald was in fact living in a flat on St Stephen's Green with Gabriel Fallon. He was not disturbed there.

Next to a funeral there is nothing the Irish like more than a post-mortem. The post-mortem on 'The Plough and the Stars' lasted for months, long after O'Casey had taken refuge in London. The *Irish Times* and *Irish Statesman* stood staunchly by O'Casey and the Abbey. *An Phoblacht* gloried in the riots. The *Irish Independent* and the *Evening Herald* dithered. After the riot the leader-writers were outraged that people who had paid for their seats should have their evening spoiled. The *Evening Herald* added a plea for theatre censorship: 'By far the worst kind of play is that which shows Irishmen up to the ridicule of foreigners. The scenes in this play are known to be sordid and by no means typical of the Irish.'

The *Irish Independent* had no sympathy for the methods of the Protestants and thanked the Abbey for having, in the past, wakened the nation from self-complacency. But 'there are some things that cannot be defended by invoking the name of Art. . . . It is known to every constant patron of the Abbey that in some plays words have been said and things have been shown that would make even a tolerant censor hesitate. Ireland may have sinned, but she has not become pagan.' Ten days later the same paper wanted a bigger subsidy for the Abbey because the theatre was qualified to undertake the 'elevating amusements' that the bishops were asking for.

The *Irish Times* saw the riot as proof that there had been no progress in education in thirty years – arguments were still answered with violence. No one answered the protests that there were no whores in Ireland by claiming to have slept with the real Rosie Redmond, one of Dublin's most famous prostitutes. But the *Irish Times* at least was honest: 'The young citizens of Dublin need not pay anything to see counterfeit prostitution on the stage of the Abbey Theatre. They can rub shoulders with the real thing on every night of the week in the central streets. There are few other cities in these islands where youth is more obvious to the moral and physical dangers of sexual vice.' There was no agitation, the paper said, until O'Casey had painted the conditions which create street-walkers. 'The things that defile Ireland today come not from without but from within.'

A.E.'s *Irish Statesman* expressed views similar to Yeats', for despite the rivalry between the two poets they would unite to face the common enemy – philistinism. The leading article hoped that the Abbey would continue to exasperate. 'If it received universal approbation, that could only mean that it had ceased to belong to the intellectual aristocracy and was on exactly the same level as the ordinary man.' The ordinary man goes to the Abbey 'with a kind of fearful pleasure' and loves the shaking up he gets there. The cry for censorship was idiotic.

The *Irish Statesman*'s columnist Spectator had attended the play on the night after the riot. He threw an interesting sidelight on the affair. He noticed the audience had listened with strained attention instead of with the senseless guffaws one usually heard in the Abbey. He thanked Mrs Skeffington for making a laughs-hunting public take a play seriously for a change: 'If his opponents did their best to spoil one night for Mr O'Casey, his admirers have marred a hundred.'

The *Statesman* also published an article entitled 'The Plough and the Stars, as a woman saw it' by Brigid O'Higgins, whose husband was Kevin O'Higgins, Minister for Justice. His assassination in a Dublin street on 10 July, 1927, was the last assassination of an Irish politician. Mrs O'Higgins praised O'Casey for his strength, sincerity and genius, but denied that the Tricolour could ever have been carried into a pub. Events had disproved O'Casey's view of the Rising, she said, 'and, hopefully and patiently, Ireland awaits her golden-voiced poet to sing the story of glorious '16.' She reproved those who treated O'Casey as a propagandist instead of as an artist. 'When is our impatience of criticism going to manifest itself in the production of constructive work?'

In other words, Mrs O'Higgins believed, like those she corrected, that the artist was at his best when being propagandist, for what else did she mean by 'constructive' art? This is a pernicious idea. How the artist is to be constructive without showing men to be both weak and strong perplexes everyone who tries to subordinate art to politics. The only answer for the politician is to treat the artist as the punter treats the horse: put his money on him and leave it to him to run the race.

An Phoblacht's leader-writer seized the opportunity to attack all the paper's enemies. Yeats and O'Casey, he said, were victims of the general demoralisation of a most degraded and cynical phase of public life. 'Naturally those whose traditions belong to the Planter, the Souper, the Emergency man, the Landlord and more venomous land-agent, have come to the surface again to celebrate their victory under the Treaty and the Free State.' The same issue carried a review, written after the riot, of 'The Plough and the Stars' by S.L. (the poet F. R. Higgins who was later the Abbey's first managing director). Higgins dismissed the play as a 'cheap farce, mixed with sentimentality . . . a technique based upon the revue structure . . . entirely lacks the sincerity of an artist . . . no sympathy with the progress of struggling life; he seems more concerned with its futility.' The play was written to pander to the Ascendancy.

Higgins was not the only poet to dismiss O'Casey, and the hint of snobbery and jealousy of this self-educated navvy was never very thickly veiled. But most of the attacks were a little fairer than this one. It is easy to understand how such vituperation made O'Casey forget the extent of his support.

Next it was the turn of the letter-writers. There were plenty of them. They dealt with the play and the riots in particular, and with O'Casey and the Abbey in general. Most had been deeply moved by the play, some with sympathy, others with disgust. To some the Abbey was the stronghold of the Ascendancy, to others that of intellectual freedom. Very few approved of the riot and fewer thought much of O'Casey as a dramatist.

What hurt O'Casey most was the attacks by the poets and intellectuals of Dublin. They dismissed his play on artistic and aesthetic grounds and they were men whose opinions on such matters he respected. F. R. Higgins repeated in the *Irish States-man* the remarks he had made in *An Phoblacht*. Austin Clarke, poet and university lecturer and as much a rebel as O'Casey, declared that 'several writers of the Irish school believe that Mr O'Casey's work is a crude exploitation of our poorer people in an Anglo-Irish tradition that is moribund.' Liam O'Flaherty the novelist, whom O'Casey looked on as a friend, seized the chance to attack Yeats through O'Casey, for he had that dislike of the Old Master common to most young writers of the period. He hurt O'Casey with a slighting remark that 'The Plough and the Stars' was a bad play, and that 'it would be quite in order for an audience to hiss it as a bad play'. Gabriel Fallon wrote to say that most of O'Flaherty's letter was irrelevant but he did not defend 'The Plough and the Stars'.

Years later O'Casey decided that the intellectuals of Dublin hadn't known what they were talking about. In *Inishfallen Fare Thee Well* he is as scathing of them as they were of him.

Lyle Donaghy, a young poet who was indefatigably loyal to O'Casey, wrote to the *Irish Statesman* that this was a great play with technical and artistic defects. The theme, he said, was universal. 'Had they (the men of 1916) lived to pass from ideal to deeper ideal, had they survived to survey the smoking ruins and assess the gains, I do not think that they would have been afraid to face the the facts; neither was Sean O'Casey; neither is any artist.'

The major controversy was between O'Casey and Mrs Sheehy Skeffington. Mrs Skeffington scorned the fashionable jousting ground of the *Statesman* and wrote to the *Irish Independent* instead. The demonstration, she said, was concerned only with the national, not with the moral, aspects of the play. This was the poorest of O'Casey's plays. It was an outrage that the Abbey, a supposedly national theatre, should deride the men of Easter Week.

O'Casey replied in the *Irish Times* that 'the author alone is responsible for the play, and he is willing to take it all.' People had demonstrated because 'some of the tinsel of sham was shaken from the body of truth'. Some of the rebels liked a bottle of stout and the bravest of them knew fear. All women feared for their men. 'The safety of her brood is the true morality of every woman.' He recalled the vanity of the Volunteers about the designing of their uniforms 'and how rich (to me) was the parade of the staid and stately uniformed men . . . serious, very human, but damnably funny.' He said he had seen the Tricolour in some very incongruous places, including one painted on the lavatory of a pub.

Again in the *Irish Independent*, Mrs Skeffington replied that indecent inscriptions in lavatories are not great literature. A play of 1916 without the glory was Hamlet without the Prince of Denmark.

O'Casey wrote to the *Independent* to declare 'there isn't a coward in the play'. What more could one expect of men than he had shown the rebels do? His parting shot was: 'The people that go to football matches are as much a part of Ireland as those that go to Bodenstown, and it would be wise for the Republican party to recognise this fact, unless they are determined to make of Ireland the terrible place of a land fit only for heroes to live in.'

The protagonists confronted each other in a debate held by the Universities' Republican Society. Mrs Skeffington repeated her charges. She was supported by Madame Maud Gomme McBride, Yeats' idol, and by Mrs McCarville. F. J. McCormick protested against mob censorship. Gabriel Fallon and Lyle Donaghy defended O'Casey. Although the audience was predominantly Republican, O'Casey's eloquent defence of his play and of the sincerity of his motives was enthusiastically applauded. Afterwards Mrs Skeffington shook hands with O'Casey with tears in her eyes. She had just read for the first time his *Story of the Irish Citizen Army* and his tribute in it to her husband as 'the purified soul of revolt against not only one nation's injustice to another, but . . . against man's inhumanity to man. And in this blazing pyre of national differences his beautiful nature, as far as this world is concerned, was consumed, leaving behind a hallowed and inspiring memory of the perfect love that casteth out fear, against which there can be no law.'

O'Casey was not mollified by her gesture. He returned home to 422 North Circular Road and discovered there a telegram from J. B. Fagan, the London producer of 'Juno and the Paycock', asking him to come and lend some publicity to the transfer of the play to a new theatre. A few days later O'Casey left. Although he had been contemplating this move for years he told Gabriel Fallon, who saw him off, that he would be back in a few days. He still loved Ireland, he said. Yet of his reaction to the riot in the Abbey he had written (in *Inishfallen Fare Thee Well*): 'For the first time in his life, Sean felt a surge of hatred for Cathleen Ni Houlihan sweeping over him. He saw that one who had the walk of a queen could be a bitch at times. She galled the hearts of her children who dared to be above the ordinary, and she often slew her best ones.'

He stayed away. He had decided Dublin had no more to

offer him as a writer except distractions. He had never been outside Ireland before. When he discovered London he could not face returning home. He explained why in a letter to Eileen Crowe. 'Here I'm being lionised. If I return to Dublin they'll tear me to pieces.'

He was lucky that he had not already been torn to pieces. He escaped because the controversy was not really about his play. It was an excuse for the women of the Republican party to attack the Free Staters. There was no reason why the Free Staters should not have been equally offended by 'The Plough and the Stars'. They could trace their descent as directly as could the Republicans to the men of Easter Week. But it was too much to expect of Dublin in the 1920s that it could be united about anything. Because the Free State Government had granted a subsidy to the Abbey the Republicans could blame the Government for everything the Abbey did. They did not miss their opportunity. O'Casey the scapegoat got out of it pretty lightly. The charges that this slum-dweller was the landlords' ally, that this Communist was a Government stooge, were telling in debate but could not have been very seriously meant.

O'Casey would not get off so lightly today. He would have to account for his words to both parties. The men of Easter Week were not so venerated forty years ago as they are today. In the 1920s it was remembered that it was the constitutional nation-wide movements of Parnell and Redmond that laid the foundations of independence. Five years of fighting by three thousand men had changed the constitutional form of independence; it had not created independence. Because only the romance and drama of Easter Week are remembered today, O'Casey would not be able to denigrate Easter Week with impunity.

'The Plough and the Stars' has stated its case. Because we are familiar with what it has to say we are no longer outraged though we do not agree. The last time the Abbey presented 'The Plough and the Stars', I heard one shout of 'Up the Republic' and several cheers for those brave acts and defiant words that the 1926 audiences had missed. But if the play were presented for the first time in 1966 it would still have the ability to shock and the iconoclasm alone would be noticed. And in the ensuing debates the same words would be used as were in fact used in 1926. 'The Plough and the Stars' could suffer the same fate as 'The Ginger Man' and 'The Rose Tattoo', which were both driven from the stage in recent years.

71

If the political content didn't finish it the moral content would. The biggest change that political independence has brought to Ireland is in the public face of morality. There was no censorship of books or films in 1926. There were no American TV serials telling the public that only queer people experience sexual passion. The men who defied the clergy had won the war; the influence of the clergy in public affairs was negligible. No cleric figured in the controversy over 'The Plough and the Stars'. Today the outward practice of religion is one of the trappings of middle-class success. We would tolerate the presence of a prostitute on stage. But could we tolerate it that a decent middle-aged Catholic like Fluther should lead her off to bed and that a publican should sympathise with her over the scarcity of clients?

It was necessary for O'Casey to leave Ireland when he did. The sole alternative was quiescence under an order he could never accept. Forty-six years is time enough to learn what there is to learn about Dublin.

5

PINK ICING

By Beatrice Coogan

THE first time that I met him he was sitting slumped in a chair in the Abbey green-room, his hands deep in his pocket and his peaked cap pulled down over his face.

I was dressed as an old woman for my part in Synge's 'Riders to the Sea'. Apart from the slightly intimidating figure in the chair there was no one else in the room. To kill time until my call I started to riff through the books on the little hanging book-shelves. I found that I had read them all.

I must have said so aloud. I must have forgotten that I wasn't alone because I jumped when a voice from under the peak of the cap asked me what kind of books did I like to read. I said that I read everything that I could lay my hands on. The peak rose up a bit, but the face was averted while the voice asked coldly if I had read anything by Anatole France. I said that I hadn't, and then Maureen Delaney, the famous Abbey comedienne, came in and ordered me to scratch her back.

Now it didn't occur to me that Sean O'Casey, or any other man, meeting me for the first time with my face covered with ochre and with black lines on my forehead to suggest age, and with my hair squeezed back under an old woman's shawl, would give me another thought.

But Sean, as he told me later, gave me all his thoughts; for the rest of the night and for all next day until it was time to go to the theatre again. There he was in the green-room next night with a copy of Anatole France's *The Gods are Athirst* under his arm; for me! Not just a loan, but a gift specially bought for me and with an inscription to me signed by him on the flyleaf. The shawl had not concealed my youth. It had accentuated it, he said, and when I turned from the bookshelves to answer him he had caught a flash of long hair that hung like an inner cloak of gold. The dramatist dramatising me, I thought!

When I opened the stage door to go home there was a thick fog coming up from the Liffey. Someone in front of me had stumbled over the step and a voice said 'Christ, what a night!' I drew back thinking it might be some rough character from the docks that led off the lane. But when I finally ventured out, there was the same figure, only it was recognisable now as Sean O'Casey. He was waiting for me and he wanted to know if he could see me home.

I was aghast. I was new to the Abbey; not long back from school. I had not come within the tumult of O'Casey's genius. All that I had seen of his efforts was his 'Nannie's Night Out' – that had been a flop. I saw a bit of it then from the wings. No sign of life came from the audience! Not a laugh. Not a clap. An actor came off-stage shrugging ruefully. A name will draw an audience as far as the proscenium. It cannot stir the emotions. I knew Sean had written much better plays. I was still a flapper – teenager to you – I appreciated genius on the stage and in books, but for an escort, my unformed appreciation tended towards charm and glamour. I saw neither the one nor the other in this oldish looking man – as old as my own father – in the shabby trench-coat, maroon pullover, crumpled tie and workman's cloth cap.

Today's teenager, in tousled jeans and hair like a bewitched barley stack, would have no such challenge to her social courage. The garb of shaggy genius is *de rigueur* with the cognoscenti of the pubs; and after the third long, black sinister pint everyone is a genius. Not, of course, that O'Casey was the vociferous Irish writer of the pub type. He spoke quietly. Low modulation lent dignity to his speech. He had none of the 'gurrier' accent of flat Dublinese. And pubs were not his milieu. With me he went always to cafes. He would talk and talk over endless cups of tea; but never pub talk; never bad language; not in my presence. He treated me to a gentle deference. But oh, if only he would take off that cap!

I hedged when he offered to see me home that first night. I said I preferred to walk and that Rathgar where I lived was much too far – for *him*.

I could see some people in evening dress making for my tram. Evening dress was a customary feature of theatre-going. In trams too; cars were not all that plentiful; taxis neither. I wasn't going to risk sitting in front of some girl whom I knew and she all decked out in a theatre cloak and escorted by some sheikh in evening clothes while I sat facing her with a shabby looking man with a cap down low over his eyes.

It was the snobbishness of being 'with it', just like today's snobbishness of Aran sweaters and long, rain-straight hair and scripts under the arm and the one who has the wavy hair is probably the male escort.

Sean was not to be put off. He loved walking he said; walked everywhere! 'Let us go in', he said 'and have a cup of tea and maybe the fog will lift later.'

We went to the Broadway and he took off the trench-coat, but he kept the cap on. I was mortified. I remember well I was wearing a French hat; sort of exotic. But in the presence of Sean's cap it became an incongruity.

He started to talk and I forgot the cap. I forgot the ephemera of fashion. How he talked! Incessantly, unfalteringly. Until I saw him on television about a year before his death, I had not seen him since he left Ireland; I had forgotten how he could talk, though his voice seemed to have acquired a higher and more strident pitch. I had forgotten too – or had I ever taken note? – the sweetness of his mouth set in the craggy strength of his face. When I knew him, it was an unsmiling mouth. Maybe that was because of his tendency to reminisce; and his reminiscences were bitter. He was still reminiscing when I hopped a passing tram.

Next night he resumed where he had left off, but first he handed me a copy of Thomas Hardy's *Under the Greenwood Tree*. I had told him the night before that I had read my first novel, Hardy's *Tess of the D'Urbervilles*, when I was nine years old. That had rocked him. To have read such books so young! He was well over sixteen himself before he could read or write, he said. He would listen, he said, to his brothers discussing history and arguing politics while he groped, frustrate, in the blind world of his own illiteracy. Then, the inarticulate genius stammering and hammering inside for release, drove him to buy a penny copybook.

He copied and scrawled until he could write the alphabet. Then he ventured on words like C-at and M-at and R-a-t. The three words that he finally attained sprawled across the full width of the two pages of his copybook. It was a revelation to me to hear him exult in the achievement of something that I accepted as I did the air that I breathed.

He asked me if I understood French and when I nodded casually and admitted that I had done a fair amount at school but that I was beginning to get rusty, he stopped dead on the pavement. 'Good God!' he exploded. 'Do you not realise what you possess? The key to a whole new field of literature. If only I possessed that key instead of having to stand at the gates peering longingly through the bars!'

On and on flowed the reminiscences through that first walk homeward. His early struggles walked with us through the lamplight of O'Connell Street and Grafton Street; his hunger and the torture of savoury smells from restaurant doors brought us through the dimmer lights of Harcourt Street and round Kelly's Corner and over Portobello Bridge until I was starving myself with the dint of walking and listening, and the sharp aperitif edge to the saga of his hunger. It rasped me when he came to telling of how he got his first job and still went foodless. At that stage, with my patent leather shoes full of feet and a persistent assault of mean splits of rain coming out of the north-west, and over in the other end of the sky a wisp of a moon not worth looking at; at that stage it would have comforted me to know that he had gorged himself with food out of his first wages. But no, he still went foodless. To buy the books for which he hungered still more.

When he couldn't afford to buy more he roved the free libraries, stuffing his unprepared mind with too rich and too varied fare. He studied authors rather than subjects. He seemed to be deeply impressed – and influenced – by the writings of Anatole France. He had devoured everything that author had ever written. By the time that I had caught up on reading the half-dozen volumes of France that he had given me I had the impression that O'Casey was almost a projection of Anatole France; the same religious bias, the socialism, the scepticism and all of these tinged by an unfailing quality of pity and of sympathy. I thought that France's treatment of romantic love was a bit rococo. I thought that Sean's was, too – at least in his application of it to myself. Now, when he first attempted to kiss me – but that is jumping ahead a bit. We are still walking me home.

We are on the last stretch and he is telling me about a play that the Abbey accepted from him. But what I did not know then was that 'Nannie's Night Out', that I had seen falling down, puerile and prostrate on the stage of Dublin's former Morgue, was the one that had brought him in touch with immortality. When the Abbey curtain had flown down the first night over the audience's silent dismissal of this play the actors came to him murmuring sympathy. With the insincerity of kindness they said that it was the audience that was bad; not the play. One could never judge by a first night! Tomorrow night would be different!

Sean shouldered away from their sympathy. He stumbled his way out through the stage door and down the lane and across streets and intersections, regardless of traffic. In that lonely tenement room he sat out his unrecorded vigil of disappointment and humiliation. Then suddenly he sat upright. He dug his elbows deeper into the little deal table that must now be a museum piece. Out through clamped jaws he gritted a prophecy, 'By Christ, Sean', he swore, 'you'll write a play that they *will* applaud.'

He reached out for the little steel 'n' pen and dipped it into the ink. He wrote through the night. And lo, as he wrote, 'The Plough and the Stars' fell across the pages.

Out of the arid void of that night's unmoved audience there burst forth with all the sudden maturity of a Nordic summer, the first scatterings of blossoms of the genius of Sean O'Casey. And, by his oath, 'they' did applaud! His prophecy was fulfilled.

He had started to talk about a play he was working on. The Church of the Three Patrons, Rathgar, loomed up, its door still open. 'I'm going in here', I said. A few yards round the corner was my home in Kenilworth Square. Every few moments my father would be out on the steps scanning all approaches. The church offered a strategic moment for parting from Sean. 'Are you coming in to say a prayer?' I quipped, thinking that he wouldn't, but wanting to soften my abruptness.

His answer surprised me. 'I'm not a Catholic' – I had assumed with a name like his that he was sure to be. 'I am an agnostic' he continued. 'I believe in Christ and I consider that St Augustine was the only Christian after Christ.' Then after that rather sententious remark his voice and even his face seemed to alter as he added, 'but if *you* want me to, I'll go inside and kneel with you while you pray.'

I found the words strangely humbling; they seemed to express an endearment. I think he meant them that way. For more than four miles of pavements his voice had rasped in reminiscences; now it had the huskiness of embarrassment, the warmth of a felt emotion. I turned from the church without entering. I did not feel like exercising subterfuge upon either the church or the man. Often during our subsequent association I was to find myself pulled up short by his quality of mental dignity.

We turned into the square and he halted abruptly. 'A bloomin'' rich man's square!' He was back in his cynicism. It was like a walled city around him. But he admired the houses and asked about the owners. When I indicated the one owned by Easons the bookseller of O'Connell Street, he stopped again. 'Easons!' Chippings gritted from his teeth.

It was at Easons that he had got his first job; six in the morning till eight at night for five bob a week. How eagerly he had queued for that first wage! At last he reached the cash desk. The pay clerk curtly ordered him to remove his cap. Sean had forgotten about it. His weak eyes had become so accustomed to the protection of its peak in lieu of the glasses that he could not afford. But Sean, as I have said, had more than his share of human dignity. He refused to remove the cap and was dismissed on the spot.

A light flashed in a top window in our house. He asked me what window was mine. I showed it to him and hurried in. On the top step I glanced back and there he was, a lonely figure standing exactly where I had left him.

It must have been an hour later. I had read a few chapters of the book he had given me and was dropping off asleep when my father came into my room followed by my mother. 'Don't turn on that light', my father hissed as I sat up and reached for the switch. Had the O'Casey outpourings staged a melodrama in my dreams? But no, my father, in full substance, was standing in the shadow of the curtains pointing out someone to my mother. 'He's been walking up and down there for three quarters of an hour and God knows *how* long before that.' My mother craned. 'He's a gunman', she gasped. 'He's watching this house. Phone the police quick. Look! he is looking straight up at this window!'

My father rushed from the room and I went to the window. Across the road, directly in front of the house in the shadow of the hedge that enclosed the park, a figure in a trench-coat, collar high over the back of his neck, cap low over his eyes, hands deep in his pockets; the conventional gunman image, was pacing up and down the length of our house. A chuck on my nightdress brought me to the floor. My mother's fierce whisper warned me that I was in the direct line of fire. By the time I got pelting down to where the phone was, my father had just got through and was saying something about 'a suspicious-looking character . . .'.

When I had succeeded in convincing him that it was no shadow of a gunman that menaced our home; just a troubadour silently dramatising the yet-to-be-written song 'On the Street where You Live', he was still disturbed. He started to recall the legend of his Presbyterian great-grandmother who had been fired at and wounded by a rejected poet-lover, as she emerged one Sunday from the Presbyterian church in Armagh.

Next morning bright and early I was out with my two dogs climbing the slopes of the Dublin mountains above Rathfarnham. There was a sparkle in the air. There was a lilt in the barking of the dogs with the dint of their excitement over the unexpected walk. There was a lilt in my own heart from the mountain air, following the excitement of that walk home to the beat of a great dramatist's life story that he had englamoured by his lonely vigil: even though that had frightened the wits out of my parents.

I threw a stick; for the dogs, for devilment, for the joy of having all that clear air and the mountains thrown in – all to myself. The stick misfired. It flew over the wall; the dogs followed. I whistled them back but I could hear them barking like mad across the field.

My foot found a crevice in the wall and I raised myself to peep over and as I did from somewhere beneath there came a groan. My blood chilled, but I forced myself to look down and there, on the grass under the shadow of the wall, lay the body of a man. A tramp, I thought in terror, and made to jump back. The ridiculous dread that attached in those days of unemployment to the spectacle of a poor tramp lying wherever he could find rest and shelter.

And suddenly I recognised the figure; the same trench-coat, the same cloth cap pulled down over the upper part of the face. The lower part was hidden in the crook of his arm. It was Sean O'Casey. He had not gone home. He had walked the night out until he had fallen asleep exhausted. I felt humble and guilty to be stealing upon him like that unawares. He looked so vulnerable lying there. A little wind sighed past. A peewit gave its lonely cry. In far parts of the world this eminent man was being acclaimed. From America students were arriving to write their academic theses on all that they could garner about this tramplike figure who lay at my feet. We were the only two people on the whole mountainside. One unaware of the other's presence and yet somehow, I knew that he was there because of me. Later I was to hear from Barry Fitzgerald that Sean had walked up and down in his flat most of one night talking about me unceasingly, how I was wasting the benefit of that store of reading that had for my age so amazed him, by writing shallow bits for newspapers. I should give it up. I should go away from all the restraint; starve; write until I could see the blood on the page.

He said that I would never write anything worthwhile until I had cleared out from the – to him – incredible restriction of my parents. It was a restriction, of course, that always rushed me from Sean's company too soon and too early for his liking.

He never knew how near my parents had come to putting himself under some slight police restriction. I never divulged to him that I had witnessed his mute serenade. There were others on subsequent occasions, but not for such duration; just a few pacings up and down before moving away.

The following night he brought me G. K. Chesterton's *Life of St Francis*. I suppose the choice was guided by our little interlude outside the church the previous night. He must have suspected St Francis of being a Christian, too, in spite of his statement about St Augustine. In fact, I had the impression that there was a basic spirituality always striving within O'Casey. Once, recalling some incident he said, inadvertently, 'I was teaching Sunday School at the time'. I was startled. 'Fancy you teaching Sunday School!' I exclaimed. The idea didn't seem to march with his brave, out-flinging part-pagan agnosticism. He looked as if he would like to have grabbed the words and pushed them back from where they had escaped. He never again alluded to Sunday School activities.

My bedroom was beginning to overflow with Sean's book gifts. They were becoming an embarrassment. So was the friendship; if that is how one would term the relationship. Anyway, his letters were advancing in warmth from 'Dear Miss Toal', to 'Dear Friend', and finally to 'My dear Friend'. They never got beyond that heat of ardour. I was beginning to feel hemmed in by his attentions. If I happened to be playing in the Abbey there was no escaping him. He would be there waiting for me except for a few nights when he stayed at home working on a play. He was going to dedicate it to me – which he never did. If I was not in the current cast he would write to me every day; often there would be a second letter in the evening's post. Then one night he pointed out the plough in the sky for me, and while I was gazing upwards and he was explaining about it and about how he came to call his play by that name, the peak of his cap suddenly overshadowed the great immensity of stars – plough and all. My shoulders were gripped in a steel vice and my face that was upturned – I assure

80

you – to his play's starry title, was assailed by a kiss that was meant for my lips, but landed on my cheek. An embarrassed kiss

Sean O'Casey – a young portrait

from an embarrassed man can be shattering to one's poise. It was not that he was really embarrassed. I think he expected that his eminence was sufficient to make his romantic overture acceptable.

He had talked a lot to me about his first love, Maire, and of how poverty and shabbiness had been a hopeless equipment for a suitor. He had formed other romantic attachments. I knew one girl whom he had fallen for. She had found his preoccupation with the severities of life and its inequalities, and this business of retaining the aura of poverty and shabbiness, rather offsetting. So, I thought, was this business of breaking off from some grave discourse to administer a kiss like a wallop. It was not my idea of how the white charger of romance should come galloping towards me.

I realise that had I seen O'Casey's masterpiece before I had met him I would never have written in this vein. I recall how I sat in the Abbey enthralled at 'The Plough and the Stars'. Here was a different O'Casey from the man who had walked and talked with me under the stars; the strength and the power of the language that he sent to the stage, compared to the primness of his words when he had snatched a kiss under the plough-shaped stars. 'You are being coquettish! You must not play the coquette with me.' Even then the term 'coquette' sounded square and dated; straight from his beloved Anatole France, or perhaps Proust; the same with his compliments. He would touch my long hair and say '. . . and bind up every wandering tress'. From his great contemporary Yeats who had eased the words, burning and lyrical, straight from his heart to the woman he loved! If only, I thought, O'Casey were content to mirror life; not cavil at it.

O'Casey the dramatist was a revelation to me. It was as though he had guarded the stuff of his genius as a shopkeeper guards the goods that are his stock-in-trade; and more so was the case with his stock of laughter.

Brendan Behan was prodigal of his laughter, of all his genius. But then Brendan was a personality genius; what reached the page was just the overflow.

Strolling homeward with O'Casey, the man, through streets or along the banks of the Dodder or sitting drinking tea in the Broadway Cafe in O'Connell Street, I was not conscious of any grandeur or sublimity of thought. He did not impress me as a great intellect, nor did he shed any pentecostal rays upon my mind. His wanderings and stumblings in a trackless forest of writers had left him print-dizzy. Until I had seen one of his successes I regarded him as a male 'bluestocking'.

The offerings of books maintained their steady flow. I would have welcomed the odd box of chocolates. But I suppose that, like myself, would have been too frivolous. I often wondered what the devil's father did he see in me.

There was a book at that time stealing, by labyrinthine ways, through Dublin. A dreadful book, a weird book. Banned too, if I remember aright.

People who possessed a copy gained sudden cachet. They were sought after. Its author was a crackpot, said the literary critics, ones who now accord him Homeric praise.

The author, it would seem, had discovered shock therapeutics before the medical profession. His readers seemed to have been subjected to high-voltage electricity. They emerged from the covers dazed, teeth shot out, hair on end, jangled, bewildered, but strangely stimulated. Never again would they return to the torpid standards of their literary judgement. I asked Sean about it, but he had not read it and what with all the murk and mystery about it he may have thought it was another bit of pornography sidling in from Paris like a yellow paperbacked Paul de Kock. And that was not the type of book that he purchased for me, though some of them did exhale the 'perfumed fragrance of perfumed sin'. To which, judging by our subsequent 'bedroom scene', Sean was not averse. Don't get het up in lascivious anticipation. It was a bedroom scene in the sense that Sean invited me to tea in the room that held his entire existence. It also held his iron bed. And, on the one occasion that I went there I brought a girl friend with me; one who claimed that Sean had been keen on herself for a space. Be that as it may he did not appear to be delirious with joy when I arrived with her in tow.

Meantime, at one of A.E.'s Thursday evenings, I came within nodding distance of this book. *Ulysses* I had been told it was called and it had been written by a man called James Joyce. A.E., otherwise George Russell, the statistician and editor of the *Statesman*, lived round the corner from our house. A man great in intellect and in girth. To sit and listen to the flow of his eloquence was like being laved and soothed in the cascade from some graceful fountain. The poet W. B. Yeats, his close friend and constant companion, was there. James Stephens, the poet, Patrick Tuohy, the leading portrait painter, who later committed suicide in America, and Joseph O'Neill, the author, who lived a few doors from us in Kenilworth Square. Sean O'Casey used to go there too. He was not there when I arrived but he was under discussion.

Joe Holloway, the famous first-nighter – he had never missed a single first night of an Abbey play – was asking the critic from one of the papers if he were still of the same opinion of O'Casey now that 'The Plough' was being played in New York and 'Juno' in London. This critic, it seems, had said to Joe during the tumult of 'The Plough's' first reception, that it would scarcely last the entire week. It was just a noise; and as for genius! He had scoffed at the idea. Now he declared that he was still of the same opinion. The plays would, no doubt, split the ears of the New York and London groundlings and then fizzle out. O'Casey would not live.

Having disposed of O'Casey he proceeded to dispose of this *Ulysses* book. He had just come on from a literary dinner where he had been asked to speak on it, and now he gave chapter and verse of his speech. He struck an attitude, threw back his shoulders and started to insert his thumb into the tiny pocket of his waist-coat before giving tongue about the absurdity that was *Ulysses* and about its cretinous creator. The book, he said, was the vapourings of a diseased brain. He went on in that vein for ten minutes still foosthering with his thumb. And then came his great *coup de grâce*, his curtain line. 'And then, I said to them, This, gentlemen, is a book that no decent wastepaper basket should be without a copy of.' He stood there waiting for the salvoes. You'd think he was the Lord Chancellor after giving orders to the common hangman to have *Ulysses* burned in the market place alongside of Molyneaux's *Case for Ireland* that became the Americans' text book for their rising against English rule. As *Ulysses* was to become their manual for their revolution against the established forms of literature.

There was no applause. He didn't even get a footing for his thumb in the pocket that was taut against the tight-packed drum of his Falstaffian belly. A woman columnist sent her pebble into the silence. She had, she said, tried to read *Ulysses* and at the part where Mr Bloom has his 'privy' soliloquy she had been eating a boiled egg. She got sick and had to give up. It was not clear whether it was the book or the egg that she gave up, but it was the book that I pleaded with her for the love of heaven to lend me. She promised that she would but when she went to confession, the priest warned her against giving scandal by lending it.

If all this about *Ulysses* seems irrelevant, I mention it because at the end of the evening Sean dropped in and on the way home he asked me to marry him; and *Ulysses* and wastepaper baskets and boiled eggs are interwoven with Sean O'Casey's proposal of marriage and are ensorcelled forever to its memory.

On the way home I told him what the newspaper critic had said about this *Ulysses* book. He didn't seem interested. He was preoccupied and moody; an angry moodiness. Instead of turning into the Square to my house he suggested as the night was so beautiful that we make a detour and stroll along the river.

The white glamour of the moonlight did nothing to soften his mood: there were many things wrong. He was going to seek wider horizons. He had decided to leave Dublin. 'I'm getting out of this bloomin' place.'

I didn't take him seriously. Dublin for the true Dubliner is more than a city. It is a sentience. The O'Casey mind had breathed in this quality in every pore and exhaled it in his plays.

I ventured into his outburst to suggest that it might be inadvisable to cut himself away from the scene of his inspiration.

His reply startled me. 'I won't go away if you marry me.' I ought to have realised that things were heading this way. But somehow I hadn't. I slowed and looked all around me. The setting was everything that one could wish for. The moon had attended to the lighting. Silver birch trees ranged along the banks like sheening candlesticks, their branches a chased filigree. The river was a silent torrent of moonbeams.

It seemed a pity to waste all that moonlight with the only answer that I could give. Soften it as I might the answer could only be 'No'. But a woman's interest will quicken to an unhappy man where it would not to a happy one. I tried temporising but he would have no perhaps-ing. Too much of his life had fretted itself away in uncertainties. It was easy for a young girl like me to talk of putting off decisions. Older people could not indulge in the luxury of postponement.

Young I may have been but not too young to sense that despite my obvious attraction for him, his sudden proposal had sprung from his angry hurt, his need for sympathy. He had spoken to me often about his first love and I suspected that even during my phase, and afterwards up to the time when he left Ireland and met the love that was to crown his life, he was still in love with the Maire to whom he had dedicated his first success. He told me that he would base a character in one of his plays on Maire and yet inconsistently he would tell me, repeatedly, that he was to dedicate a play to me. I think he liked the idea of carrying within him a shrine to first love. He was in love with love.

I knew two other girls whom he had been keen on before me and then I became for him love's embodiment. He rhapsodised

85

about my long hair that came well below my waist but his rhapsodies were all quotations. And when, more than a year after he had left Ireland, I was selected as a Beauty Queen and he saw my photo in a London paper he told a friend of mine that while he approved of the selection he considered that I had not been true to myself. He did not think that I would have entered such a contest.

I didn't actually. The paper I wrote for sent me to write up this competition, the first of its kind in Ireland. Not a Miss Ireland contest nor the subsequent annual Dawn Beauty Queen competition. Mine was a civic and State affair. It sought to embody Ireland as a beautiful woman, after the concept of the eighteenth-century poets. There were other qualities as essential as beauty.

When I heard of Sean's comment I was half tempted to write and explain how my selection had happened but I decided against it. He was no longer the Sean O'Casey who had walked for hours up and down 'the street where you live' and then on to sleep beneath the stars on a Dublin mountainside.

One of his missives arrived by the following afternoon's post. 'Had I considered the matter we had discussed?' The 'matter' being a proposal of marriage under a moon that could have generated more heat than a tropical sun at midday. Would I come to tea at his apartment next afternoon? (He didn't say apartment. He said 'room'.)

My mother would not hear of my going to his home. However, when I arranged to bring a friend she was satisfied. Sean was not satisfied.

As we stepped through the graceful Georgian doorway of the slum tenement that had once been a peer's mansion, a little girl sitting on the broken stairway jumped up and ran up to a room on the first floor shouting, 'Here they are'. It seemed out of character for Sean to have heralds waiting to proclaim our approach to the many inhabitants of that battered citadel.

Across the landing a section of a large family that lived in one room stood at their doorway and passed fair comment. 'Oh janey, there's a goudger!' 'Aye, Miss! Lend us your cape for a tent to go camping.' My friend had deemed that the occasion called for a long, dramatic looking cloak that swept the ground and any incidental cabbage stalks and similar garbage.

Sean's talk of tenements and early poverty had not prepared me for the room into which the child ushered us. It was accept-ble that the panels of its seeping walls may have been painted by Angelica Kauffman, that the high, shadowy ceiling was of the brothers Adam, that the mantel, the loveliest I had ever seen before – or since – was a Bossini: the chaste lines, the centre-piece basket of fruit and flowers, the mosaic trails of ivy on the slim side posts.

It was acceptable and indeed obvious that this bygone graci-ousness had communed through the keen interpreting senses of the aspiring dramatist, had whispered its mysteries to his expect-ant soul. But for me, for both of us girls, the room was an un-divulged mystery.

Why was O'Casey who was now in comfortable circumstances – even approaching the threshold of wealth – living in such a stark and frightening poverty? The only piece of furniture in the room was a bed whose sole covering was a man's torn overcoat. On the floor a piece of gaudy linoleum gazed up brazenly at the exquisitry of the ceiling. Out of a cloud of queer-smelling smoke a girl of about twenty-four rose to her feet. What was she doing here? Or why was she here, because as she turned from the fire it became obvious what she was doing. In the beautifully wrought grate under the beautiful mantlepiece she was burning an old boot. A saucepan rested on the boot. 'To heat milk for the baby and thank God you've come Miss, for that's the last sup of milk we have.' From under the old coat on the bed a baby's cry verified its existence.

The little gurrier girl had mistaken us for two members of the Infant Aid Society. The young mother told us that her husband was unemployed. When they got married he had been in a good job and they had bought nice furniture for the room. Wistfully she enumerated the treasured possessions that had been week by week pawned or sold to buy food since he lost his job. The arm-chairs, the Chesterfield, the little fancy china cabinet and all her china. I noticed that the essentials were the first to go. 'Last week', she said wistfully, 'we parted with the gramophone.'

Here was the stuff of O'Casey's plays. The starkness, the poverty and the gaiety of the inevitable gramophone: just such another, as I noticed later when it was redeemed from the Pawn Office, as the gramophone in 'Juno and the Paycock'.

But where was O'Casey? We must be in the wrong room. Mr O'Casey, we were told, had left here quite a good while. When we were starting out, Therese, my friend, had assured me that she knew where O'Casey lived and I had been content to tag along. I pulled out a few of his letters from my handbag; single sheets of cheap notepaper, some with no address, just the date. Together the two of us deciphered the scrawled row of figures and letters that formed the address on the one that contained the invitation. 422 N.C.R.

That perfectly harmless incident of the two of us scanning his letters for his address was to have drastic consequence.

We worked our way along the North Circular Road till we found 422. It was another multiple dwelling. A cut above the tenement socially, but far behind it architecturally. Lower middle class gone to seed, but never in its earliest most pristine blossoming would it have inspired the nascent genius of O'Casey.

Whatever characteristics the room may have had, if it had any, were dominated by the books. There were books everywhere. They overflowed on to the floor. In the centre stood a small deal table on which he normally wrote his plays, but this afternoon books and manuscripts were pushed to one end and a cloth was laid with tea things. In the centre was a pink iced cake piped with purple flowers. He seemed proud of the cake.

I had been told by someone who visited him frequently that the bed would not challenge the conventions, it would be covered with books. But this was not so. The iron bed dominated the room. Dominated the iced cake. Because it was covered with a palpably new pink satin eiderdown, with the price tag still blatantly peeping from one tufted corner. In that monastic setting the quilt was a bizarrerie. Whether the quilt represented the naïve fulfilment of a boyhood longing or a deliberately planned enticement I shall never know. As a little girl I used to plan that I would buy a sweet shop all for myself. Perhaps Sean, in his youth, sharing the inadequate bed-cover with his older brothers, may have envisioned the gorgeous quilt that some day he would buy. Or was it the Anatole France influence?

In one of the Anatole France novels that Sean had given me, there was a heroine who used to keep an afternoon tryst in her lover's bedroom and in intervals of ardour she would sit up 'in a crêpe de chine shift' and suck oranges. I looked around the room but there wasn't an orange in sight, not even a penny one.

We explained what had kept us late and when we spoke of the young woman burning the boot for fuel, he launched off into a tirade against the system that caused such things to be. Gasping for a cup of tea, we watched the kettle boil its substance over the gas cooker while Sean held forth on poverty and injustice.

Therese couldn't stand it any longer – the hunger I mean. She reached out and started buttering a currant bun. 'For God's sake, Sean', she exlaimed. 'What are you Ullagoaning about. It's no length since you tried to pawn your trousers for ten bob and you had to be content with five because the assistant thought you had stolen them. Now you are getting money galore.'

He lifted the kettle from the flame. 'I know', he said, 'but the money has come too late. I saw my sister dying of hunger on a heap of straw in the corner of a room such as the one you have seen back there. Her five little children were standing around her crying from want and misery. And I stood there looking at her. Out of work. Penniless. As helpless to relieve her as the youngest child.' He started to pour the water into the tea pot. It didn't hit the bottom with a lively hiss. I could never stand the flat sound made by water gone off the boil as it poured into a teapot. 'Sean', I pleaded, 'you should always bring the teapot to the kettle. Never the kettle to the teapot.' He burst out laughing and put the kettle back on the boil. 'You possess the divine gift of comedy,' he said. That was the last compliment I was to receive from Sean O'Casey.

The afternoon had for me all the constituents of O'Casey's plays. The poverty of the young mother in his previous home. The stark reminiscences that it had evoked from him. The teeming books. The lurking sensuality of the gaudy quilt, all puffed and beckoning like a bosomatique mistress! And the carnival of the iced cake.

For a few days I was preoccupied with the plight of that tenement household and didn't see Sean. My father drove me back there with provisions next day and I went hither and yon trying to get employment for her husband. No easy task then. At last I got him a job on a building scheme starting in Rathgar near my home.

I was delighted to be able to report this to Sean when I next met him in the Abbey green-room. But the information left him cold. He made some remark about my doing the Lady Bountiful. And then after a few laconic answers to my conversation, he walked out of the room. I couldn't believe my senses. It was a week before I got the explanation. Not from Sean. He never spoke to me again. He told someone, who told me, that I had made a mockery of him – I had shown his letters to my friends. In vain did I deny the accusation. I said it was an absolute lie. But there is, they say, a grain of truth in every lie. And in this one, there was the truth that I had taken his letters from my bag to scan them for his address when we had gone to the wrong house. My friend Therese had shuffled through them with me. Hence the pyramids! I could understand how it must have hurt him. A sensitive lonely man with a chip on his shoulder that festered afresh too readily. Had I done it consciously it would have been a mean thing. Not that they were any soul-revelations in those brief letters. No endearments – a few lines to say how much he had enjoyed our walk home; a few lines the following day asking me to meet him at the Broadway; again a few lines to say that he had bought me such and such a book. Would I read it soon and tell him what I thought of it? And so on; ending 'Yours sincerely' and progressing to 'your friend, Sean O'Casey'.

He was as obdurate with me as he was with the Abbey years later, when he withheld his consent to have his plays performed there.

Thomas Davis says that a man will modify his beliefs even in the act of defending them. There was no modification with Sean O'Casey. Not for the Abbey that had been his kind foster-mother, that had discerned with uncanny vision the mark upon his brow when they put on that first drab offering 'Nannie's Night Out'. Not for the Abbey audience that had endured it without asking for its money back. He glosses over that play as something unworthy of recall. As though it had not proved to be the evocation of his genius. And there was no yielding to those Abbey players who had matched his genius with their own. Shall I ever forget Ria Mooney's incomparable portrayal of the street woman? In the interval, I heard a lady whispering to her friend, that she had it on the strictest authority that Ria was the genuine article brought specially from 'Monto', Dublin's long-quenched red-light district. A compliment indeed to the dignified raven-haired girl who had risen so superbly to the challenge of that un-precedented role.

Sean went away without a word to me. I didn't go to the auc-tion of his few belongings. The ones who had decried him scrabbled for his books. The critic who had condemned Joyce to the wastepaper basket and O'Casey to oblivion, jostled to get bidding for the little deal table. It was knocked down to someone else for ten shillings and there was a brass plaque put in the centre. I wonder who got the brand new pink satin eiderdown? Passing through London on my honeymoon I rang Sean with some idea of clearing the misunderstanding. The first thing he said was 'What hotel are you staying at?' When I told him he said, 'A bloomin' rich man's hotel!' The very words that he had used about the square where I lived that first night he walked me home. I made no further effort to convince him. It would have been no use. Sean had not changed.

6

THE ABBEY DAZE

By Anthony Butler

ON 25 November 1921 Lady Gregory recorded in her journal that she had read 'The Crimson and the Tricolour' a play submitted by Sean O'Casey. It was the first hard evidence that the playwright was making an impression on the tough literary fortress of the Abbey Theatre. Although she felt it had many faults, her inclination was to try it on the stage so that the author might gain a little experience. But Mr Yeats was the decisive force and Mr Yeats was firm that it would not do and so the drama postulant had to retire and start again.

They had need of him. The Abbey Theatre for many years had been scarcely able to keep its box-office afloat in very rough financial waters. It was true that civil war and a politically disturbed community did not provide an ideal environment for the arts, but this was only half the story. Wretched management and a poor sense of play selection helped to drive the audience away. As Micheal MacLiammóir wrote in later years: 'Yeats thinned the stalls down to a few ecstatic readers of poetry.' Exaggerated, perhaps, but the stuff of truth.

Three individuals, in varying degrees, exercised control over the Abbey's theatrical fortunes, William Butler Yeats, Lady Gregory and Lennox Robinson. Each was to play an important role in the life of Sean O'Casey, and it will be useful to take a swift look at this strange trinity.

It is perhaps best to start in order of unimportance with Esme Stuart Lennox Robinson, an unlikely product of County Cork who managed to conceal beneath a vague and languid manner what his biographer Michael J. O'Neill called 'an instinctive shrewdness'.

He was the son of a stockbroker who, with graceful ease, abandoned Stock Exchange quotations for those of the Bible when he became a Church of Ireland curate. As a boy Esme Stuart Lennox was dressed for many years in a black velvet suit and lace collar – a traumatic experience which was not without effect on his character. Psychologically he was to wear them for the rest of his life.

One story of his employment with the Abbey Theatre is told by himself in his book *Curtains Up*. W. B. Yeats is alleged to have sat behind him in the theatre and fascinated by the shape of Robinson's skull declared, 'the man with that head must be our manager'. It probably justified the decision as much as anything else.

From the beginning he was a creature of the poet and as Robinson himself recorded: 'From the day I met him to the day of his death he was the dominant personality in my life'. One illustration of this influence is worth mentioning. In 1910 Yeats stormed at him for being late at a rehearsal of 'Thomas Muskerry'. The effect was so great that it frightened him into punctuality for the rest of his life. He had more than a passing interest in spirits but they were of a more tangible nature than those alleged to haunt Yeats. All in all his father's prayer when Lennox left home for the first time seems to have been heard: '. . . but I trust by God's grace you will be kept in the way of religion and goodness'. Only Lady Gregory found him less than charming and after her death he wrote sadly, 'She had never liked me very much . . .'

Second in the Abbey scale of authority was one who merits generous adjectival description – the good, buxom, kindly, naïve and simple Lady Gregory. She was born Isabella Augusta Persse of Galway and when she was twenty-eight and reconciled to placid spinsterhood her family became alerted to the possibility of a marriage with Sir William Gregory of Coole; a widower, a reformed gambler, a former M.P., an ex-Governor of Ceylon and a man of sixty-three years.

We may speculate that Sir William took the hint when he found Isabella Augusta herded into his presence at regular intervals and on one occasion even anticipating his arrival in Rome. In any event he yielded like a gentleman and married her on 4 March, 1880 – the same month and the same year in which John Casey came into the world.

Sir William died in 1892 and Lady Gregory went into mourning which she never completely discarded for the rest of her life. She met Yeats in Galway in 1896 when he was a handsome thirty-one and she a matronly forty-four. The following year they met again and he discussed with her a plan for an Irish Theatre. From that time forward she took him under her wing, giving him generous accommodation at Coole and sending him gifts of port, food and other comforts when he was away.

The malicious have not allowed their relationship to pass without question, but there is not a shred of evidence that it was anything more on her part than a warm maternal affection and admiration and on his the stunned happy joy of an Israelite when the skies rained manna. The local people at Coole called her Mrs Yeats but this may be dismissed as the ribald humour of peasants. When Yeats writes from London in March 1900: 'My dear Lady Gregory, I have measured the breadth of the wire mattress part of the bed – it is $41\frac{1}{2}$ inches', we need not misinterpret. It was less a prudent statistical preliminary to middle-aged passion than an attempt to cadge a palliasse.

Her generosity was boundless and she gave without ostentation or a sense of doing anything extraordinary. She was the heart and soul of the Abbey from the time she became associated with it, and it was her courage and fighting qualities that kept it going in difficult times. Time and time again she had to fight the willingness of Yeats to abandon the whole thing. She would do anything to serve it and even took over the part of 'Cathleen ni Houlihan' in 1919 although she was subject to nervousness. Her plays were not always successful and when one drama failed she could console herself with the thought that it '. . . required nothing new but an india-rubber ball and a coconut'. Only a small mind would deny her right to these.

She made many contributions of energy and money to the Abbey but she also nourished it with Gort cakes. These were monstrous barmbracks which she ferried from Galway in vast quantities for the green-room. They are frequently mentioned in her journals.

The last of the Abbey triumvirate and the most powerful, is also the most difficult to sketch in general terms. Elizabeth Coxhead, the biographer of Lady Gregory, wrote that the generous and the insincere were intimately bound up in W. B. Yeats, and she added that in him all the human qualities were heightened, the good as well as the bad.

He was in many ways an idealist but there was much in him of the charlatan; he could be the epitome of dignity at one time and approach the level of the buffoon at another. Even in the period since his death a definitive judgement of his work has been difficult because the Barnum-like projection of his ego still clouds the scholarship devoted to him. Certainly he applied the theory of the Mask to his own life with consistency and profit.

He was a superb literary politician and it was unfortunate that his entry to real statesmanship as a Senator should have been so late in life when his energies had ebbed. Yet he managed to obtain a Nobel prize – given partly in tribute to his work and partly in tribute to the new Irish state – and politics as well as poetry played their part.

The interest of W. B. Yeats in the Abbey Theatre had been waning for some time before O'Casey arrived on the scene, and he was anxious to hand it over to the Irish Free State when the nation achieved some independence. No doubt he fancied he would be taken over with the building and the company as a national literary monument and honoured accordingly. Although he failed in this objective he did succeed in obtaining a subsidy for the theatre.

O'Casey has little to say in his Autobiographies about the acceptance of his play 'The Shadow of a Gunman' or its reception in 1923. It was a success, much to the delight of Lady Gregory who was elated to find the house full and the audience enjoying the lines. She kept Sean near her and he poured out his automatic tale of woe and poverty. He told her of his father dying when he was three and impressed her with an account of his desperate efforts to acquire an education.

The playwright's one-act plays at the Abbey were failures but in 'Juno and the Paycock' he revealed that he had climbed to where his dramatic genius could be displayed. Again he continued to impress Lady Gregory with highly inaccurate stories of how he taught himself to read at the age of fourteen and gave his standard and almost fictional account of his mother's death and funeral. The old lady of the theatre could hardly wait to record his vapourings in her journal.

He was also prepared to repudiate his Labour past and he could tell her: 'I have helped strikers and revolution according to what were then my lights. I was a Socialist then.' The use of the past tense was significant when one considers how ridiculous he made Socialism in the character of 'The Covey' in the 'Plough'.

Although he never attacked Lady Gregory – or Blessed Bridget O'Coole as he called her in his books – he did purge himself of his resentments in his collection of essays and stories, *The Green Crow*. He wrote of himself in those days as 'The timid drama-postulant knocking at the temple door, ready to wear any habit offered to him, and take any vow required.' Whatever else this sentence reveals it does something to prove the accuracy of Lady Gregory's diary. Inconsistency was nothing new to him and he had been in turn a Gaelic Nationalist, an international Socialist, a pacifist and a militant revolutionary.

But his real aggressive domineering character was coming to the surface and when he brought 'Juno and the Paycock' to the Abbey he could demand Barry Fitzgerald for the chief comic part without regard for the feelings of F. J. McCormick who had been originally selected for the role. That O'Casey was right need not be denied, but his tactless approach could be questioned.

With the acceptance of 'The Plough and the Stars' O'Casey not alone stepped into the front rank of Irish playwrights but reached out for international stature. It was and is a play that storms with all the energy of mighty experience. So far as Ireland was concerned it was the last real triumph of his career.

Even before it was produced he aroused distrust, hate and hostility in many people. In particular he had many enemies in the Abbey company, including M. J. Dolan, the actor-manager, a dour, tough, bitter man. He and some other members of the cast had a heated argument with O'Casey over a production of 'Man and Superman' and it was an incident which was not forgotten.

Indeed a great deal was done to keep 'The Plough and the Stars' off the stage. One instance shows how far Dolan was prepared to go to sabotage the playwright. The Government nominee on the Abbey board, George O'Brien, was convinced the play was 'excellent' but half an hour with the disgruntled manager changed his mind and he demanded considerable alteration in the script. Dolan went so far as to write to Lady Gregory and tell her that the language of the writer was 'beyond the beyond'. He even hinted that the cast might refuse to accept parts in it.

The worst was not past and Lennox Robinson, Gabriel Fallon suggests, miscast the play which in view of his capacity for envy would not have been surprising. Some of the actors objected to their lines. O'Casey had words with the producer and he recalled later 'an odd coldness and an irritant nervousness in the manner of the cast'.

In any event his intimate associations with the theatre were ending, largely one feels because of his extraordinary talent for harsh and unfeeling criticism. With drooling self-pity he expresses naïve wonder at these reactions in *Inishfallen Fare Thee Well* but he need not have been surprised. It had been happening to him all his life with one group or another.

One night when he was going backstage he was stopped by Seaghan Barlow, the Abbey stage chief and general handyman. As O'Casey recalled it the dialogue was as follows: 'There's none but the actors and officials allowed on the stage', said the bold Barlow, with a dominant note in his voice: 'and we'd be glad if you come this way no more.'

The playwright says it was a decisive moment in his life which convinced him he should go to England.

In Lennox Robinson's history of the Abbey, Barlow says nothing about the incident although he recalls many trivial items which remained in his mind over the years. In order to find some answer to the riddle I called to see him one day in the scene dock of the theatre in the C.I.E. stores at Amiens Street. At eighty years he was trim, neat and surprisingly youthful as he stood surrounded by all the naked and exposed illusion of the stage. On a bench was a gilt goblet for the pantomime and behind him stacked spears and scenery. An ancient and faded poster on the wall in Polish and Russian recalled the Warsaw presentation of 'Riders to the Sea' in the far distant past. His own paintings hung not far from it – a row of bright but talented sketches.

No, he had never read what O'Casey said about him although he had heard of it. He couldn't give an interview but in any case he couldn't remember the incident described by the playwright and he had too much to do in the old days to watch every word he said. And that was all. Was it the full story? No one can tell what time has eroded from memories and we must accept it.

But O'Casey went to England and like a sponge absorbed the adulation, the interviews and the publicity to which he was exposed. It was wonderful; and on the opening night of 'Juno and the Paycock' in London in March 1926 he told the audience how kind he thought their city had been and how it would be hard to dig him out of it again. He was to sink even deeper roots in British soil when 'The Silver Tassie' was rejected.

Hone in his biography of Yeats has one comment which he does nothing to illustrate: 'There was more to the rejection of 'The Silver Tassie' than the simple fact of defective construction.' We may never know the exact truth as Yeats, with his prudent regard for the judgement of history, does not appear to have left any detailed material by which we might assess his real motives.

97

We can, however, agree with Krause when he writes: 'When Yeats rejected "The Silver Tassie" he administered a serious blow to the future of the Abbey Theatre as well as the future of Sean O'Casey.'

The author at least had a high opinion of the drama: 'Personally I think it is the best work I have yet done. I have certainly put my best into it, and have written the work solely because of love and a deep feeling that what I have written should have been written.'

When submitted, the play was first read by Lennox Robinson and then passed to Lady Gregory at the end of March, 1928. Robinson was not enthusiastic but he took it for granted that with amendment it would be staged. Since he was to bear the blame for the rejection, this primary reaction is important and his exact words to her in a letter were: '. . . Sean will have time to think over his last two acts before July and August'.

But before this there had been incidents which suggested to O'Casey that 'The Silver Tassie' might not have an easy passage. Lennox Robinson and Yeats had called on him at different times to obtain an assurance that the play would be offered to them. Yeats, in fact, was given a detailed outline of the play which he appears to have absorbed without comment.

The playwright was later to imply that this was a plot to discredit him, but it was true that he had been negotiating with another management. He promised the first glimpse of the script to Sir Barry Jackson which was unfair to all concerned as C. B. Cochran told him.

On 27 April, 1928, Lady Gregory received Yeats' rejection of 'The Silver Tassie' outlined in two letters; one for her own eye and the other for dispatch to O'Casey. A third letter came from the poet on 28 April, one that was to add fuel to the bonfire to come. In her journal for the 28th she recorded that she sent on the letters to Sean because: '. . . he had written he was "correcting proofs" for publication.'

This entry is a little misleading as it suggests she had acted on her own initiative in sending on the correspondence when in fact she had followed – in her own way – the instructions of Yeats. In his first communication which accompanied the rejection he wrote: '. . . O'Casey has told various journalists that he has sent the play to us and may go on doing so; it seems wrong to allow him to deceive himself. . . . I am afraid our refusal will be a very great blow to him but if anybody can soften the blow you can.'

Lady Gregory did send more than the poet intended when she included his two private letters to herself. It is well she did as they give us some opportunity of examining his approach to the matter. In spite of Yeats' definite rejection Lady Gregory still had hopes that the play might go on and she was obviously confused. When O'Casey did not reply to her letters she recorded: 'But he may shrink from a rewriting. . . '. The playwright, however, recognised that a mortal blow had been aimed at him and when eventually he did reply it was with unrestrained bitterness.

It would serve no purpose to deal with the correspondence in detail; it has been published many times and it is – with little exception – all sound and fury. Yeats' letter to O'Casey was a verbal bubble – delicately exuded, highly coloured and as substantial. He told the author that he was not deeply interested in the Great War and producing a typical piece of prose tartan he wrote, 'the whole history of the world must be reduced to wallpaper in front of which the characters must pose and speak.'

O'Casey burst the bubble and rent the tartan but failed to deal with the key point in Yeats' letter: '. . . I cannot advise you to amend it.' Another will-o'-the wisp which attracted the wrath of the playwright was a suggestion contained in the second private letter of the poet to Lady Gregory. This urged her to ask O'Casey to withdraw 'The Silver Tassie' himself and then inform the press that he wanted to make revisions in it. It was an idea which might have occurred to the mind of an ignorant, unscrupulous and venial county councillor, but it was one unlikely to win the acceptance of the playwright.

Certainly it would have suited Yeats to rid himself so quietly and so easily of O'Casey, but he under-estimated the happy self-pity of the man who revelled in situations of this kind. It was the type of emotional orgasm which – next to adulation – he enjoyed most. On this occasion O'Casey had the additional and unusual pleasure of being right – he had suffered a real injustice.

His threat to publish the correspondence disturbed Yeats and in late May, 1928, he wrote to Olivia Shakespeare that his head was frozen with mystic geometry. He was able to assure her before the end of the letter that one chapter of a detective story melted his head: 'My blood-pressure was normal three weeks ago and though Casey and late hours have sent it up a bit I am really well.'

One director of the Abbey, Walter Starkie, was in favour of accepting 'The Silver Tassie', but this was of little account since his opinion was only considered after the play had been rejected. Starkie was annoyed that the correspondence was sent to O'Casey before he had been consulted, and Lady Gregory tried to appease him.

In the course of this letter she told him that she had made an effort to revise the decision to reject the 'Tassie': '. . . I asked

The old Abbey Theatre – scene of the O'Casey first productions. This building was burned out in 1951

Yeats and Lennox Robinson . . . if we might consider putting it on. Yeats inclined to it but L.R. said "No".'

I doubt it we need give much credit to the poet for this sign of wavering. It was, I feel, the pseudo-hesitation of a ventriloquist who knows that he can make his dummy persuade him to any desired course of action and Lennox Robinson was nothing more than a manipulated puppet. It may be noted that the following day the play was returned with a formal notice, so that the moment of doubt was of very brief duration.

That it was unjust to reject 'The Silver Tassie' so ruthlessly and so lightly need not be doubted. The refusal was arrived at with indecent haste and without a formal meeting of the Abbey board – one factor, it would seem, in Walter Starkie's protest. It arrived at the Abbey around the last week in March and after a very brief examination by Yeats his opinion was dictated on 20 April. This was not the consideration to which a playwright of O'Casey's repute and achievement was entitled. He brought something to the Abbey Theatre which it was not to see again for a very long time. He brought it fresh affluence; fresh energy and new audiences. Not only was he entitled to every courtesy but he also deserved the benefit of every possible doubt. He had earned the right to the performance of any play of his that was not hopelessly and obviously inadequate and no one suggested that the 'Tassie' could be so described.

In the end he was treated as if he were a newcomer to the stage, a beginner without any claims or rights. Above all, he was not given a chance to amend and alter the play which was the very least he might have expected.

'. . . I cannot advise you to amend it.' Yeats meant it to be absolute and final.

And yet he and Robinson admitted that it contained some of the best things that O'Casey had ever produced and nothing in their letters suggest that it was beyond remedy. A discussion with the writer might have been arranged and re-writing proposed, and this was clearly in the minds of both Robinson and Lady Gregory at various times.

Everything about Yeats' rejection indicates that it was to be without appeal. He is pompous, pretentious and obscure when writing to O'Casey, but his letters to Lady Gregory are sharp and practical in their handling of the situation. She is to send the refusal without delay as the playwright is talking to journalists and this, of course, demands haste. Too much publicity would create a certainty in the public mind that the play would go on and make the position of the Abbey board peculiarly difficult; it might also create a faction for O'Casey.

If possible Lady Gregory must try to soften the blow and she was the dupe who was expected to wrap the weapon in velvet cloth. She was also to try and fool O'Casey into withdrawing 'The Silver Tassie' himself. But these were only the trappings by which Yeats hoped to conceal the simple stiletto mentality of a

Renaissance assassin. The cloak was to be employed if possible but nothing was to divert the dagger.

Poor O'Casey, it was quite hopeless for him. He could rant and debate and write to the poet: '. . . . there seem to be shallows in you of which no one ever dreamed.' It was the wrong word. Shallows there were, without doubt, but there were also depths. . . .

There can be no question of the responsibility of Yeats for the rejection of 'The Silver Tassie'. The decision was his and almost his alone. Reading the correspondence now one can observe that Lennox Robinson's letter does not reject: he adopts a vague position which could be shifted as he saw the situation develop. Lady Gregory's notes are not available to us but from her journal it would seem that she did not differ greatly with Robinson.

The secret of that decision lay somewhere in the shifting psyche of Yeats which today can only be partially glimpsed behind the opalescent shimmer of his historical mask. What was it?

Superficially there was not a single reason why Yeats should have objected to the staging of the 'Tassie'. It might have been expected at that period that a certain mellowness would mould his outlook. He was at the height of his fame; he was the winner of a Nobel Prize and could afford silver buckles for his shoes and wider ribbons for his big tortoiseshell glasses and he was a Free State Senator. Indeed he was growing fat with prosperity and had to do Swedish exercises – Swedish because he had certain obligations to that country.

He was no longer deeply interested in the Abbey Theatre even though he attended all the board meetings whenever possible. At the same time, as Hone points out, he exercised '. . . when he wished to do so, the decisive influence on policy.' For some reason which I shall try to probe he elected to exercise that decisive influence against Sean O'Casey and 'The Silver Tassie'.

The mystery centres on his obvious determination to reject it. As I have stressed, O'Casey deserved acceptance; he had been right in the past when the Abbey was wrong and he might be so again. His repute would guarantee a box-office success so there was no need for fear on that score. Even Yeats admitted that it had something; much more than most of the rubbish that was produced without protest before and after the rejection. But then the poet had nothing to fear from rubbish.

In fact I believe 'The Silver Tassie' touched the soul of the poet with a moment of apprehension, if fear is too strong a word. We may see him for what he was at that hour – the greatest literary repute in Ireland and possessed of international recognition. The pale planet of Joyce was still too low on the horizon to eclipse any portion of that disc of glory. Yeats was literary lord of all he surveyed. Or almost lord . . . for Sean O'Casey was blazing in the astronomy of letters.

His light was dazzling London and in a little time a statement of intellectual and artistic Ireland might conceivably demand a certain linking of names – Yeats and O'Casey or, even greater horror, O'Casey and Yeats. If, however, the playwright could be revealed, not as a planet or star, but as a comet that flared and died, all might yet be well.

Yeats could, of course, separate himself as poet from comparison with a dramatist but even this last protection was under attack. As he read 'The Silver Tassie' he must have realised that O'Casey, with creative impudence, was challenging him on his own ground and at the point where he, Yeats, was weakest. The play was dramatic poetry of extraordinary power and this was the field in which Yeats had been a failure – in spite of his ambitions.

He, at least, may have noticed what many drama critics have failed to emphasise, that the second act of the 'Tassie' is an autonomous piece of intense lyrical verse which as a one-act play would be superb – perfect. Yeats was sufficiently shrewd to know that he faced a major challenge. He had always been wary of this strange man as O'Casey himself noted. 'Friendship with Yeats was something Sean couldn't reach yet.'

It was easy to say that the 'Tassie' could not succeed; that the public might reject it; but then O'Casey had an uncanny talent for success. He had gone from strength to strength with 'The Shadow of a Gunman', 'Juno and the Paycock' and 'The Plough and the Stars'. What if the 'Tassie' should prove another step forward? Then nothing could ever be the same again. It would inevitably be Yeats and O'Casey or O'Casey and Yeats.

And yet, as he read, Yeats must have been aware that the answer to the threat lay in his own hands. The damnation of a rejection would suffice to eliminate the threat: to end it for all time. The stiletto was to hand and he had the courage to use it.

All this is but speculation, theory and analysis, but it does answer some of the questions and solves puzzles. We must bear in mind several things; the absolute responsibility of Yeats for the rejection of 'The Silver Tassie'; the speed with which it was thrown back at O'Casey; the poet's determination to refuse it; the failure to hold a proper board meeting to consider it; the unwillingness to seek a compromise and finally the cryptic phrase of Hone: 'There were more reasons behind Yeats' rejection of "The Silver Tassie" than the simple fact of its defective construction.'

It will be pointed out that Yeats did allow the production of the play at the Abbey in 1935 after his reconciliation with O'Casey, but this need weigh very lightly in the scales. By that time it had failed in London, it had no international success and Yeats could afford to be generous. It is emotionally extravagant to twist stilettoes in mortal wounds, and the poet always practised psychological economy.

I agree with those who hold that the rejection of the 'Tassie' destroyed some dynamic force in O'Casey. Never again was he to touch the heart of a major audience as he did with 'The Plough and the Stars', and his theatrical appeal declined with the later plays.

In view of the enduring nature of the playwright's hate it may puzzle some why he should have forgiven Yeats. The blow to his pride and fortunes had been great and he never forgot the rejection. What is even more surprising is the fact that the first direct overtures to end the rift should have been made by O'Casey, although he gives a misleading account in *Rose and Crown*: ' . . . one day a letter came to him from W. B. Yeats. He was bade to take dinner with the poet. . . '.

No mention was made of the fact that it was he who wrote first to the poet to offer sympathy after an illness. As the published letters of her husband were ambiguous I wrote to Mrs Yeats to confirm what had happened. She replied that Sean O'Casey wrote first telling how glad he was to hear of the poet's recovery.

In an earlier chapter I suggested that the playwright was paranoid to some degree and this would explain his uncharacteristic behaviour in this instance. Certain people were essential psychological furniture to him – Yeats, Shaw and Nathan. Even when they offended he could rationalise their conduct to fit his private world of near-illusion. The obvious guilt of Yeats was projected on to Lennox Robinson, even though this was contrary to every known fact, but the device restored the poet to his pedestal in the psyche of O'Casey. In a letter to Dublin's *Irish*

Times in 1962 he could write: 'I have long known that the head and front of "The Silver Tassie" 's rejection was not W. B. Yeats but Dr Lennox Robinson.'

For Yeats reconciliation was a useful elimination of a dangerous and unnecessary enmity. His repute was safe and he could afford to smile warmly on the ambitions and the genius he had crippled with one simple, brutal thrust. As we contemplate the cruel and terrible waste of that act we may consider with him the problem he once raised in a letter to Dorothy Wellesley: ' . . . I spent a gloomy evening wondering whether I am, as my wife sometimes says, "ruthless".'

7

THE EXILE

By Tim Pat Coogan

'I WILL not serve', said Joyce and, artistic integrity revolting at the thought of staying in Ireland to render unto Christ the things that were Caesar's, he stepped gladly on to the boat that took him into a life of 'silence, cunning and exile'. Stepping reluctantly on to another boat some years later Sean O'Casey said to the friend who saw him off, 'I'll see you to-morrow night'. But he too was to become a world-famous symbol of exile, showing nothing of silence and very little of cunning.

Three quotations (from *Sean O'Casey, the Man Behind the Plays* by Saros Cowasjee) outline the generally held opinions of those interested in the subject as to why he should have done this. They have the merit of coming from three distinguished men of letters:

Sean O Faolain says the exile 'was an error, not of the judgement, but of the emotions'. He blames O'Casey for mistaking 'two theatre directors for a whole people' and thereby depriving himself of 'an inspiration, of an audience and of a home'.

Frederick Lumley avers that 'in his new home his genius turned to bitterness, his poetry to politics, his nationalistic hopes became hopes for a Communist International and his darlin' son was born a Red Commissar'.

Richard Findlater judged that: 'With his departure the holy fire abated in O'Casey's work, and his subsequent plays – whatever their streaks of genius – are ultimately unsuccessful. For he was trying to create a new drama in an alien country out of his own head, and he had the imagination, but not the intellect to do so'.

Apart from their similarity of viewpoint I feel, with all due respect to the men from whom they emanate, that the three quotations share another common thread – inaccuracy.

Taking Mr O Faolain first. If O'Casey had been a non-Irish flip writer in an English posh paper supplement he might have been accused of 'putting two theatre directors in place of a nation', after the Abbey directorate had turned down 'The Silver Tassie' and after some sort of malicious stupidity apparently began, as a matter of policy, to cloud O'Casey's subsequent dealing with the 'Cradle of Genius'. But he was Irish and furthermore he was forty-six years of age when he left Ireland after experiences in politics and in the constant struggle against adversity which had given him an insight into Ireland, which had enabled him to write two of the greatest plays ever to be performed not alone in Ireland but anywhere: 'Juno and the Paycock' and 'The Plough and the Stars'.

Mr Lumley is wrong in as much as O'Casey was 'bitter' and full of savage indignation at the injustices of life, long before he ever left Ireland, and it was his politics which turned to poetry, not vice versa. Nor did his nationalist hopes transmute into communism. His break with the Irish Citizen Army, of which he was secretary, was caused by his objecting to the I.C.A. involving itself with the Irish Volunteers, whom he considered to be controlled by bourgeois Nationalists whose aims would submerge the Socialist objectives of the I.C.A.

Mr Findlater's assertion that the 'holy fire abated in O'Casey's work' does not stand examination in the light of the playwright's Autobiographies. It is the 'holy fire' that makes them so readable. However Mr Findlater is correct in saying that the plays are in a sense unsuccessful. They contain writing of great beauty, but plays are intended for production, not reading solely – who for instance would fancy attempting to produce 'Cock-a-Doodle Dandy' on stage? (Though it might be made to work on television.) Insofar as playwriting was concerned, the years of exile, although not a failure, certainly did not produce anything to equal 'Juno' and 'The Plough'. But apart from the fact that they were a success by any standard where prose writing is concerned, it doesn't appear to have dawned on anyone that O'Casey might not have written anything to equal the Big Two, or Three, if he *had* stayed in Ireland, and that in fact all the available evidence seems to indicate that he would not have done so.

O'Casey's Big Three were all written out of the major traumas of Ireland's development as a nation. Two, 'The Shadow' and 'The Plough', dealt with conflict between Ireland and England. 'Juno' came out of the torment of the Civil War. Take away the basic currents of conflict and death and 'The Shadow' and 'The Plough' would hardly have been written; 'Juno' would simply have been a good Dublin mother.

Let us examine the position on 5 March 1926 as O'Casey sailed away into public acrimony and private happiness. Out of 'The Troubles' a new State had been born, four years earlier, following the 1916 uprising and a period of guerrilla warfare. The afterbirth had been Civil War in the predominantly Catholic south, with partition, pogrom and riot in the Protestant dominated North. Unemployment and destruction were everywhere and an occasional shot could still be heard ringing in Cathleen ni Houlihan's ears. Nowhere did the institutions of State seem to have completely solid foundation. At a superficial glance one might agree with the psychiatrist who after examining both Oedipus and his daughter turned again to Oedipus and said; 'and I thought *you* had troubles. . . .'

But permanency *had* been achieved, despite all appearances to the contrary. In the North a handful of Nationalist, Catholic M.P.s had begun to trickle into the hated Stormont Parliament. In the South, de Valera was announcing the creation of the Fianna Fail party from the ranks of those who were defeated in the Civil War. The growth of parliamentary democracy was under way. But north and south the same thing was happening to Labour, it was being squeezed off the stage. In the North by religious bigotry between Catholics and Protestants, in the South between the two halves of a sundered nationalist movement. And so we come to the first really significant note of O'Casey's Triad of Estrangement – politics.

Undoubtedly O'Casey, as a politician, was one of those who allow their bleeding hearts to run away with their bloody heads; equally indisputable, however, is the fact that his heart bled in the cause of the Left. What cause was there for a man of the extreme Left in the Ireland of 1926? On the face of it there was a most obvious one.

The 1916 Rising had taken the life of one of the two giants of Irish labour, James Connolly, but the second one, James Larkin, was back from America (where he had been when the Rising broke out) trying to get his Irish Workers Union off the ground and feuding mightily with William O'Brien who had succeeded Connolly as leader of the Irish Transport and General Workers Union. The fight was to wreck the chances of Labour forming a Government in Ireland for the next fifty years and possibly even longer. The issue was fundamentally the personality difference between Larkin and O'Brien. But the question resolved was whether Larkin's flaming radicalism, or O'Brien's cautious pragmatism were to be the dominant policies of the Irish Labour movement. Given O'Casey's high regard for Larkin, the proto-type of 'Red Jim' in 'The Star Turns Red', one might have expected to find him in the van of this struggle. In fact he seems to have taken little or no part in it. Certainly if he did Larkin's biographers R. M. Fox and Emmet Larkin (no relation) did not consider his efforts at this stage to be worth chronicling.

O'Casey himself did claim in a letter to Saros Cowasjee (dated 23 October 1958) that he 'worked in Langrishe Place mainly to see how best funds could be gathered for Jim Larkin when he returned. . . . we knew the opposition Jim would meet when he came home from the self-centred, conventional, 'horo-frightened' leaders of the Irish Labour movement'. During O'Casey's six-month spell of employment at Langrishe Place (during 1920) a hall taken by Delia, Larkin's sister, he worked as a cleaner for thirty shillings a week. But this spell of employ-ment was followed by more broken time and insecurity which continued until the first production of 'Juno' in 1924, when the strong nourishing smell of success induced him to give up labouring and become a full-time writer.

As he said himself, 'One job is enough for any man' (quoted in *No Phanthoms Here*, by J. L. Hodson, page 151). But why was that job to be playwriting and not politics? The short answer, of course, is that O'Casey was a dramatic genius whose muse was geared to the birth pangs of his country and the genius and the pangs were now combining to force him to write his master-pieces. But the more complete answer takes one back again to his political evolution.

Trying to change things, the hellish Dublin slums, the British overlordship that was stifling the country, he joined a number of societies bound up with the struggles of the day. The Gaelic League, the Gaelic Athletic Association, The Irish Republican Brotherhood, the Labour movement (that is to say he did what he could for the cause on Larkin's side during the great lock-out of 1913), the Irish Citizen Army and the Irish Socialist Party. He spent approximately fifteen years in the service of these bodies and though he worked for all of them with a marvellous courage and energy he also outgrew all of them without any great achievement to show for his trouble, barring a change in his name from Johnny to Sean.

Like many another young man of his time, the Gaelic League and the Gaelic Athletic Association brought him into contact with the Irish Republican Brotherhood, or Fenian movement, which was quietly infiltrating every movement it could in a communist-style revolutionary bent tactic. He worked for the I.R.B. with a vigour which may be gauged from Desmond Ryan's description of him being a 'Jacobin of Jacobins', a man imbued with 'anti-English Nationalism of the most uncompromising style' (*Remembering Sion*, page 82). But O'Casey was to break with the I.R.B. because of his fierce championing of 'Union between the separatist and the railway labourer, the factory hand and the transport worker'. (O'Casey's article in *Irish Freedom*, the I.R.B. journal, in March 1913). He felt that the I.R.B. were not sufficiently aware of the working man's problems. In his usual style he annoyed people with his criticism and refused to pull in his horns when asked to do so by the I.R.B.

Ironically, when the I.R.B. did link up with the workers, O'Casey left the militant, working-class Irish Citizen Army, of which he was secretary, in protest! He had joined the I.C.A. after leaving the I.R.B. It was on the face of it a more congenial organisation for him, having been formed to protect the workers from police brutality during the great lock-out of 1913. The lock-out, during which Larkin led the workers against the forces of capitalism led by William Martin Murphy, was the highest point the class war was to reach in Europe until the Bolshevik revolution of 1917. After Larkin went to America following the workers' defeat, James Connolly controlled the I.C.A.

When a policy began to develop within the I.C.A. of having closer links with the Irish Volunteers, O'Casey objected. He disliked the Volunteers, because he regarded them as bourgeois nationalists, antipathetic towards the workers. The Volunteers were the South's reply to Carson's Ulster Volunteers in the North, who were formed to defy the Liberal Government's plans to give Home Rule to Ireland under a Dublin parliament. When the I.C.A. Executive refused to adopt a resolution which he tabled calling on the prominent Citizen Army leader, Countess Markievicz, to disassociate herself from the Volunteers, O'Casey resigned in protest.

What O'Casey did not know at this stage was that the I.R.B. had infiltrated the Volunteers' Executive and that, though respectable bourgeois figures like Professor Eoin MacNeill, the Volunteers' creator, were apparently running the force the I.R.B. controlled key posts. Nor did he realise that earlier when he had been urging the Brotherhood to throw in its lot with the workers he was going too fast for them. At that stage of development the I.R.B. were not willing to run the risk of losing strength through becoming identified with a purely sectional interest. The I.R.B.'s attitude towards this queer, peering 'Jacobin of Jacobins' may be imagined from the following quotation from a letter of the great Fenian leader, Tom Clarke:

'Larkin's people for some time have been making war on the Irish Volunteers. I think this is largely inspired by a disgruntled fellow named O'Casey'. (Letter to John Devoy, 14 May 1914.)

The 'war' ended with O'Casey's departure from the I.C.A. but the I.C.A. and the Volunteers continued to co-exist independently until the early part of 1916, when around 19th January the I.R.B. (alarmed at Connolly's apparent determination to rise in revolt himself, while England was preoccupied with the Great War, and for the sake of causing nothing but a 'riot in the streets' as Pearse termed it, spoil their plans for a Rising later that year) induced Connolly to a three-day meeting with the I.R.B. leader, Padraig Pearse.

One of the induction party, Frank Daly, is still alive. Frank told me:

'We all regarded Jim Connolly as a Red. But after he met Pearse no one ever heard a word of Communism out of him again.'

Connolly's apparent political conversion was due less to Pearse's religious influence than to the fact that Connolly had decided to throw in the Citizen Army's lot with the Volunteers when the Rising came. He was a Marxist in the sense that he believed that the workers should use force to take control of the means of production, but he was not an atheist and died in the arms of the Church. However, Daly was right in one respect. No one ever heard a word of communism out of the Irish Revolution thereafter. Following the 1916 Rising and the emotional climate created by the execution of the Irish leaders, nationalism became the dominating force in Irish political life.

In his first published book *The Story of the Irish Citizen Army*, O'Casey wrote:

'Jim Connolly had stepped from the narrow byway of Irish socialism on to the broad and crowded highway of Irish nationalism . . . the appeal of Caitlin Ni hUllachain (his spelling) was in his ears a louder cry than the appeal of the Internationale.'

111

Labour, said O'Casey, had 'laid its precious gift of independence on the altar of Irish nationalism'. To add to his chagrin over these developments one should bear in mind the fact that for the period of the 1913 lock-out he lived on dry bread and tea purchased on his mother's pension, which was the only income they had, and contracted paralysis of the legs and a tubercular swelling of the neck which took him two years to get over and left him if anything fuller of 'holy fire' than ever. During his stay in St Vincent's Hospital with the tubercular complaint he heard a nun criticise Larkin and immediately got up and left.

Nevertheless the 'holy fire' had left itself without a fireplace by the time the 1916 Rising broke out. O'Casey was estranged from all his former political groups and he knew that the tiny Irish Socialist Party which he joined after 1916 was an irrelevance in post-Rising Ireland. This didn't prevent him working loyally and industriously for causes like meals for school children, but with the country going up in flames, no one took much notice politically of a fire-eater who had apparently contrived to be missing when the fires of Easter Week blazed. To keep himself alive he took a variety of nondescript jobs and lost or threw them up as soon as he got them.

In so far as effective, practical politics were concerned O'Casey was wasting his time. By the time he stepped on the boat he was a political rebel, not without a cause, but without a platform. Once abroad the logical platform for him was communism. It was consistent with his Irish political activities but no more successful. The main benefit he conferred on the cause of Marxism was the profit the communists derived from linking his name with red front causes. The *Daily Worker* could always rely on him for a quote when need arose, and he was on that paper's board of directors.

In his book *I Believed*, Douglas Hyde, the former news editor of the *Daily Worker*, who turned noisily Catholic in 1948, said of this board:

'It had neither administrative, nor policy-making powers. It could have ceased to exist at any moment and not an ounce of difference would have been made to the running of the paper. It was and is a stuffed shirt body.' Communism did nothing memorable for O'Casey either, although one might argue that it conferred on him the demerit of infusing 'The Star Turns Red' with too ruddy a tint for artistic satisfaction, and to the end of his life it left him with an uncritical sympathy towards Russia which caused in him a certain diseased clarity of vision when he looked at the West and particularly at Ireland.

The second and in many ways the most important although least complicated note in the O'Casey Triad of Estrangement was the simple factor of economics. It has always seemed to me that discussion of O'Casey has never given this circumstance the weight it deserves. Even today it is not possible for a serious writer to live solely on the Irish market, composed as it is of a total of only a little over four million people (including both North and South of the Border) and O'Casey, as we have seen, was forty years of age before an income of thirty shillings a week as a labourer enabled him to eat regularly. When he started to make money from the Abbey his earnings were still trifling compared to what the London stage offered – something of the order of £80 a week during a good run in London, compared to about a quarter of that at the best of times at home. There was also the money to be picked up from writing articles, essays and so on. At a rough estimate O'Casey could expect £30 for the article which in Dublin would fetch £3.

Even though he was to know poverty in England which caused him to sell the amateur rights of the Big Three for a paltry £300 (which with the upsurge of the amateur dramatic movement in Ireland after the Second World War he would have received in royalties from Ireland alone in one year) his poverty in England was to be luxurious compared to his existence in Dublin. Such things as 'bungalows' and 'nannies' entered O'Casey's life and he, of course, acquired also his beautiful and talented wife, Eileen Carey. An actress by profession, she too was able to bring in money through her art and by bringing him a family into the bargain she gave him further roots in England. England's own economic circumstances also gave O'Casey access to a wider world of art galleries, theatres, films, than flourished in the poorer and more provincial cultural climate of Dublin. The impact of these things on O'Casey's mind and the standards of comparison which a poor but renowned playwright in England might make with his former existence as a habitually unemployed builder's labourer in Dublin, would unquestionably have left a mark also. But there is a less tangible thing, an aspect of the Irish character, which when it becomes affected by emigration turns to distaste for the country that has failed to support it, and adopts the cause of its country's misfortunes, England, un-equivocally.

113

Shaw, that other Protestant exile from Dublin, caught the feeling very well in 'Man and Superman' (Act Four).

Says the millionaire, HECTOR MALONE: My father died of starvation in Ireland in the black '47.

VIOLET: The Famine?

MALONE: No, the starvation. When a country is full of food and exporting it there can be no famine. My father was starved dead and I was starved out to America in me mother's arms. English rule drove me and mine out of Ireland. Well, you can keep Ireland. Me and my kind are coming back to buy England and we'll buy the best of it . . .

Economically O'Casey said amen to Hector Malone's philosophy, but intellectually he kept letting Ireland get under his skin, and as we shall see few writers ever got under their country's skin to quite the same extent as O'Casey did, in the third note of the Triad, the intertwined artistic, religious and social rejection. There are two main elements in the final note. One, the feeling of O'Casey for Ireland and the other the feeling of Ireland for O'Casey. O'Casey's feeling may be gauged from the Autobiographies, but I don't think that the depths of feeling which his love-hate relationship with his country aroused in some of his countrymen, has ever been fully appreciated outside the country.

The following conversation took place between myself and a friendly decent young mechanic, the day after 'Bishop's Bonfire' opened in Dublin:

Self: What do you think of O'Casey?

F.D.Y.M.: I've no time for a fellow like that.

Self: Did you read much of his work?

F.D.Y.M.: I wouldn't dirty my mind by reading filth like that. You don't have to read books to know his type. He soiled his own nest.

Self: Silence and cunning, followed by more silence.

To understand the young man's reaction it should be remembered that as nationalism had won out, the protagonists of both major Irish political parties tended to respond to all outside criticism (or to inside criticism for that matter) with an injured air of patriotism. An attitude of 'How dare you hit me now with Cathleen ni Houlihan in my arms'. Inevitably this political attitude became a popular one also. As late as 1961, for instance, Ireland's county councillors were in uproar as throughout the

114

country resolutions were passed condemning *Vogue* magazine for carrying a slighting and inaccurate (but utterly trivial) article about Ireland. Two years later, in 1963, the public consciousness was deeply disturbed when in a series of house collapses throughout Dublin, a number of people were killed as heavy rains undermined tenement properties which had pretty obviously been in need of repair for several years beforehand. There was no thunder from the county councils on this occasion however. That sort of thing would be 'a reflection on the country'. There was also the effect of the censorship of films and books which while on the one hand through a fatuous preoccupation with sex as the deadliest deadly sin assembled a list of books and films which contained the very flower of what the twentieth century has to offer in both mediums, on the other naturally created a distinctly unenlightened public taste.

Remembering that Sean O'Casey himself admitted that he 'had always had a bent for criticism' it is not hard to imagine how his barbed comments affected some people. Even before his break with the Citizen Army he had been known as a member of the 'Step Committee' from his habit of standing outside Liberty Hall, the I.C.A.'s headquarters, on the steps and delivering his criticisms of whatever the Army's executive happened to be doing at the moment. The fact that in his exile from Ireland he became not alone a member of the National Step Committee, but its chairman, did nothing to endear him to his own people.

Criticisms by emigre writers were normally condemned as being 'anti-national' or irreligious whether they were or not. And O'Casey's most certainly were both. Few writers ever kicked their country's most cherished beliefs so firmly in the national testicles, so accurately or so often. In view of the fact that the blood-obsessed chauvinist (The Speaker) of 'The Plough and the Stars' was Padraig Pearse it was no wonder that the last outraged residue of this injured pride led the National Committee, set up to commemorate the 50th Anniversary of the 1916 Rising, to 'ask' the Abbey, dependent on State funds, to refrain from desecrating the occasion by staging a play by Sean during the anniversary celebration.

However not alone did O'Casey separate himself from the Nationalist element who controlled the country, he also cut himself off from the intellectuals and from enlightened people who, while deploring what the censors and the extremist Gaelic League elements were doing to the mental climate of Ireland, were equally repelled by his incessant shrillness. Anna Livia Plurabelle is not a stagnant stream, after all it does flow, even though the flow was sluggish in the extreme for more than four-fifths of the years of Ireland's independent statehood, and those living at home were not all reactionary time-servers blindly shelling out to Christ and Caesar, some just happened to like living in Ireland. From being conscious that some improvements were being effected and that all O'Casey's criticisms were not quite fair it was a short step from saying 'I don't think the bottle is half empty. To me it seems half full' to the less defensible 'the bottle is beautifully full'. But O'Casey's non-stop attack, his refusal to look for any improvements anywhere, but to keep on picking on blemishes which proved the thesis he never abandoned – 'Ireland was in a terrible state of chassis' – lost him allies where he might have looked for them, among the sentient classes. He never allowed for the fact that the average Dubliner always looked with some envy on 'the one who got away'.

With the best will in the world no emigre writer can escape the effects of this difficulty. I had a sample of it recently when a friend of mine wrote a number of articles about Ireland for an English newspaper. In the course of a letter to him praising three of the four articles I said that I felt one of them was a 'little out of touch'. The friend, who normally only corresponds in short notes, replied to my 'out of touch' remark with four closely typed pages of equally closely argued rebuttal. Yet had someone from another country made the same observation he would in all probability have either accepted it or mildy disputed it. But even a well-disposed fellow countryman seems to be an apologist for the Establishment when he replies to a foreign-based Irishman's criticism. My particular disagreement didn't affect the friendship, partially because of the good sense of my friend, but partially also because he is a frequent visitor to Dublin and we soon had the opportunity of pouring a few soothing pints on the argument.

However, apart from the paucity of his visits O'Casey would also have had to contend with the fact that few of his countrymen, certainly very few indeed among the upper classes, would have been willing to have a drink with him. Ireland likes her iconoclasts to be well-connected. For instance, Dr Conor Cruise O'Brien, who to my mind is one of the few living emigre writers of O'Casey-like stature (I exempt Beckett, who does not concern himself with Irish affairs, at least insofar as commenting on

116

them is concerned) occasionally delivers himself of observations about Irish foreign policy and the Irish Church which are at least as abrasive as anything O'Casey ever said. Granted that he only makes such remarks occasionally, he nevertheless does make them; but *vive la différence*, Dr Cruise O'Brien would be one of the most welcome catches any Dublin socialite hostess could hope to land for a dinner party. Even immediately after the Katanga debacle a party he gave was the best attended social gathering for months. The fact of his standing as a historian and literary critic has only a small bearing on this welcome. Cruise O'Brien looks and talks like what he is, an eminent diplomat turned academician. Sean O'Casey looked like what he was, and though the nature of his speech was light years away from his accent, the accent was still that of a Dublin slum dweller. This was something Dublin would not readily tolerate. 'The trouble with O'Casey was that he lacked a formal education. He learned to read, but not *how* to read. The impact of undirected reading on his uncultivated mind was too much for him.' So sniffed a middle-aged academic friend of mine as we discussed O'Casey at the interval of a worthless play at the Gaiety Theatre one evening. To such a man O'Casey had no business criticising his betters.

En passant one may wonder how much of a factor was this class-consciousness in Yeats's rejection of 'The Silver Tassie'? The idea of O'Casey writing about Dublin slum dwellers was all very well. He was good at that. But to have him turning his pen on the Great War was another matter.

The final note in the Triad of Estrangement was, of course, O'Casey versus the Church. Ireland being Ireland and O'Casey being O'Casey this was a scheduled bout from the moment of his birth. Given O'Casey's militant belief in artistic freedom and his egoism (what ever about rendering unto Caesar, nobody except Caesar himself rendered so much of himself in the third person) his rejection of both the terrors and consolations of Christianity was to be expected. But why having rejected the Christian religion *en bloc* did he keep harping on the Irish Catholic Church in particular? He continued throughout his life to present it as being organised on the principle that each parish priest had his own hot line to Christ with the bishops controlling the heavenly telephone exchange so as to ensure that the people were kept plentifully supplied with wrong numbers.

The reason for this, I believe, was a combination of his

Protestant upbringing and the fact that every political movement he had joined in Ireland had been to a greater or less
extent viewed with suspicion and even hostility by the Church.
O'Casey's incandescent intelligence was certainly capable of
understanding the motives which lay behind the Church's
attitudes to these bodies, but the Protestant streak in him kept
him from *wanting* to understand them. By 'understanding' I do
not mean that he should have fallen in dumb acquiescence
behind the banners of the Irish clergy, but in more Shaw-like
fashion by setting out the causes for the actions he might have
been able to show those involved what they were doing and where
they were going, and possibly have helped to bring about the
change of direction which in the event we had to wait for Pope
John to achieve. In O'Casey's time in Dublin, however, it was
inconceivable that a time would ever come in which a Roman
pontiff (Pope Paul) would say that at some stages in the past
and at all times in the future the attitude of the Church towards
the artist would have to be reconsidered. Criticism of O'Casey
in this regard must after all take into consideration what happened
to Christ. And Christ died for love. Savage old Sean derived a
considerable enjoyment from life through taking the skin off the
Catholics of Ireland.

Sean's father's deep religious convictions caused him to suffer
the fate all laymen undergo who work in the service of any
Church – poverty, in the service of the Irish Church Missions.
The Irish Church Missions were either a proselytising society,
who during the famine had endeavoured to wean starving Irish
peasants from their strong ignorant faith by the offer of ladlefuls
of hot nourishing Christian soup, or an effective missionary
society, depending on whether you examined their activities from
a papist or a 'proddy' viewpoint. At all events 'souper' today
far outweighs 'landgrabber' in the Irish national vocabulary of
invective.

There is no statistical method of measuring the effect of
O'Casey *père* on young Cassidie. With filial anti-popery, however, Sean's castigations become understandable, tolerable:
without they would be just pub talk. And one thing which could
never be said about O'Casey was that he needed alcohol to make
him tick. The turns of history which in the seventeenth and
eighteenth centuries had made Irish Catholicism and Irish nation-
hood synonymous had created a division of interest between
Church and Nationalism at the opening of the twentieth. The

opening of Maynooth in 1795, the easing of the Penal Sanctions and Catholic emancipation in 1829 had created a situation wherein the Church's interest was best served by the maintenance of British suzerainty and the status quo. The continuing undertow of French-inspired Republicanism, stemming from the days of Wolfe Tone's 1798 Rebellion, of which the Irish Republican Brotherhood were the inheritors, was correctly seen as a threat to British rule, and less justifiably as a force which would swamp Ireland in godless French Republicanism.

The Gaelic League was viewed with suspicion by the Hierarchy and senior clergy also. The fact that English was the sole medium of instruction in the Church-controlled National schools meant that the Irish missionary effort, resulting in a great increase in the strength of the church in other countries, was far in advance of, say, that of Poland, a much larger nation, simply because the English-speaking Irish emigrants were so easily able to adapt themselves to other cultures in the English-speaking world. For the doubtful benefit of reviving a dying language, the Gaelic League was, it was feared, jeopardising this great effort. It required unusual tact and diplomacy on the part of the League's senior figures, like Eoin MacNeill and Douglas Hyde, to overcome such understandable fear. These were two qualities O'Casey lacked.

The Socialistic principles of the Irish Citizen Army, their implied threat to property and the possibility of the use of force, inevitably made Church authorities suspicious of the I.C.A. In those days socialism was the most revolutionary force in Europe, correspondingly hated and admired by its supporters and opponents. And in Dublin in 1913, socialism had no more fervent disciple than Sean O'Casey, wedded to Jim Larkin's heroic cause of leading the starving poor out of the excreta-smeared slums of Dublin.

In those slums 87,000 people lived in 5,000 tenement dwellings, suffering conditions which in our day are hardly equalled in either Hong Kong or Calcutta. It is a fact that the part played by some members of the Irish clergy in opposing Larkin's effort was, we can see with the benefit of hindsight, not a part to be proud of. A young Dublin priest who was attached to the Dublin Institute of Catholic Sociology, told me that as a result of Archbishop Walsh's condemnation of the strikers during the 1913 lock-out, he had found in his experience that some men with memories of those grim days had only returned to the arms of the

119

church on their death beds. Given all these circumstances, and bearing in mind that Darwin's *Descent of Man* was one of his bibles, it is hardly surprising that Sean O'Casey should have had strong feelings concerning the Church. But it was hardly to be expected of a genius of his powers of perception that he should have used the examples he did to find outlet for those feelings.

For instance, readers of *Inishfallen Fare Thee Well* will be familiar with the fact that O'Casey dedicated this volume of the Autobiographies to Dr Walter McDonald, professor of Moral Theology at Maynooth, whose writings he admired. Father McDonald was not allowed to publish some of his theological writings, which were considered to be ahead of their time, but he was never removed from his Chair at Maynooth, thus faring rather better than did Père Teilhard de Chardin in our time. Dr McDonald was a friend and adviser to another Maynooth man, the turbulent Father O'Hickey, holder of the Chair of Irish at Maynooth. This chair had been viewed with a somewhat apathetic regard by the College authorities prior to O'Hickey's advent, being oftener vacant than filled and then by men who made no memorable contribution to the language movement. However, O'Hickey by dint of some brisk lobbying had himself installed, until his downfall which is also cited in the Autobiographies as being that of a decent man unjustly done down by the obscurantist hierarchy.

Now I have no intention of trying to prove or disprove charges of obscurantism, whether founded or unfounded, against the Irish Hierarchy. To my mind one of the inhibiting factors in creating a healthy climate of discussion in my country has been the marked tendency of many loud-mouthed people in Ireland to imagine that the doctrine of papal infallibility extends not alone to the Pope but also to the bishops and parish priests of Ireland, and so, by stifling all attempts at fruitful criticism, creating sitting targets for the Sean O'Caseys and for lesser men.

Were it not for this circumstance I have a feeling that the Hierarchy would have got a better press than they have done. It is not their enemies but their friends who have done them most harm. However, it would be outside the scope of this discussion to attempt to prove this point and outside the scope of my theological competence to pass judgement on the banning of Dr McDonald's work. But I think it can be shown that decent though Fr O'Hickey undoubtedly was, the amount of injustice involved in his case is at least a matter of opinion.

In 1908 O'Hickey was to the fore in the campaign to have Irish made a compulsory subject on the matriculation course for the new university which was to be set up the following year.

The doorway of his home at North Circular Road – his last permanent Dublin address

The compulsory Irish issue was a burning one. The more diplomatic members of the Gaelic League had succeeded in calming the worst fears of those opposed to the move, but there was still a strong residual objection that the introduction of Irish might have the effect of throwing some Catholics into the arms of Protestantism, by causing those who failed to enter the new university through lack of Irish to turn instead to Trinity College, at which there was little of Gaelic but much of Anglicanism. However, O'Hickey's headlong attitude to the question may be judged from this speech which he delivered to a public meeting called to discuss the question:

'The treachery of those who show themselves false to Ireland at this juncture must never be forgotten', he said. He wished that the names of those who voted against the proposal should be remembered to posterity in the same category as those who voted for the Act of Union, base hearts who:

> '*By perjury and fraud*
> *By slaves who sold their land for gold,*
> *As Judas sold his God.*'

Fr O'Hickey wished that the names of the nationalist members of the Senate of the proposed new university (who included representatives of the Hierarchy) might be remembered so that 'in after times all men may know who were the false and vile in a supreme crisis of Ireland's fortune and who the loyal and true'. His tone was one with which those who have had occasion to differ from aspects of the language revivalist's policy, were to become distressingly familiar in the years which followed. But his speech was delivered to an audience largely composed of students and in the presence of senior clergy and representatives of the Hierarchy.

The Hierarchy issued a public warning to O'Hickey on the necessity of desisting from unfair controversy, but took no other action against him until O'Hickey replied publicly to this rebuke in such provocative terms that the Hierarchy apparently felt he had gone too far and removed him from the Chair of Irish. A public testimonial taken up for O'Hickey by language enthusiasts was a flop and into the bargain the unfortunate O'Hickey lost his case when he took it to Rome. He died, an unhappy man, less than ten years after his removal.

For an independent view of the affair from a source which might be expected to be sympathetic to O'Hickey here is an extract from an article (admittedly in the Jesuit edited *Studies*) written by one of Ireland's most enthusiastic Gaelic Revivalists, Leon O'Broin, secretary to the Irish Department of Posts and

Telegraphs: 'The bishops do not seem to have anything to answer. Whether they were right or wrong in their attitude to the question of essential Irish, whether they were hurt or not by the rejection of their point of view at the insistence of the Gaelic League, they were entitled to be aggrieved at the leading part one of the priests took against them and at the intemperate language he used in the course of the debate. In particular, they could not have been expected to tolerate his address to a highly inflammable group of students. That they dealt drastically with him under provocation is defensible in the light of what would be done even today in similar circumstances, both within the church and elsewhere.'

O'Casey, who witnessed the affair first hand, must have been as well aware of all the facts as O'Broin; his refusal, therefore, to take the same detached view, could be either attributable to partisanship, or to a blind spot caused by his Protestant origins or by a growing anti-clericalism, but whatever the reason they do add up to a desire to seize any stick that came to hand to wallop the 'Clergy', which is hardly a fruitful attitude where prospects of procuring reform are concerned. However it must be conceded that in O'Casey's declining years when he might have been expected to mellow somewhat – the years of *Rose and Crown* (1952) and *Sunset and Evening Star* (1954) – it would be impossible to defend Irish Catholicism from a charge of reaction which, coupled with his bitterness, precluded any prospect of ecumenical reapproachment, if not between O'Casey and Rome, at least between him and Dublin.

Even though Ireland was the only Catholic state in Europe not to be overwhelmed by fascism (albeit this was due less to an enlightened Church than to de Valera's crushing of the neo-fascist Blueshirt movement in the early 'thirties), some of the voices raised in Ireland between the ending of the war and the last years of the 1950s were well to the right of the Roman curia. Looking back we can see why. The Iron Curtain had clanged down across Europe. In 1948 de Gasperi only barely made it for the Italian premiership in the face of a strong Italian Communist Party threat. Pro- and anti-communists everywhere were at their most virulent. It was the decade of the Berlin airlift, the Korean war, Senator Joseph McCarthy and the crushing of the Hungarian Uprising. This last was to Sean O'Casey 'a sad necessity'.

Reacting to the world situation, Irish Catholicism took on a somewhat intolerant hue, which was reflected in a number of developments like the uprise of the extremist Catholic Action group, the Maria Duce Society which was to form the most vocal part of the lunatic fringe which protested outside the Gaiety Theatre on the night that 'The Bishop's Bonfire' was first produced. But more important insofar as O'Casey was concerned was the change in tone which the world crisis produced in the *Catholic Standard*. Up to the early 'fifties this was quite a worthy Catholic paper, but it changed around this time to become a hysterical witch-hunting rag. At the time of writing this line of thinking has given away to such a preoccupation with reviewing books about the 'pill' and discussions about contraception that a colleague of mine has now conjoined it with the *News of the World* as being unsuitable for entrance to his home.

O'Casey was not to see this metamorphosis. All he was to be aware of was the fact that along with its other activities such as trying to get a group of Irish trade unionists dismissed because they paid a visit to Russia, calling for an intensification of censorship and generally making a shrieking nuisance of itself, the *Standard* was inciting Dubliners to extinguish his 'Bonfire'. On 25 February 1955, for example, this Christian organ wrote:

'O'Casey has prostituted his undoubted ability in the cause of anti-God and anti-clericalism . . . it is one of the contradictions of our modern life that he should be offered a stage in the capital city of the country most steadfastly ranged against the enemies who are his friends.' Both the subsequent 'Bonfire' uproar and the reaction of my young mechanic friend should be judged in the light of that and similar utterances from the largest Catholic paper in the country.

I think that Gabriel Fallon is expecting too much of human nature when he writes (in *Sean O'Casey, the Man I Knew*, page 174) that Seamus Byrne, the *Standard's* critic for the occasion, could not be accused of pro-clericalism because a play that Byrne had written some time earlier, 'Design for a Head Stone', had almost created a theatre riot because it was thought anti-clerical. If Stark Young had come back on earth and written a critical notice of 'The Bonfire' neither O'Casey nor anyone else could have been expected to take it at its face value, given the headline treatment and yellow press journalism techniques used by the *Standard* in presenting the critique. Seen from Devon, not alone the *Standard's* knocking reception of the play but that of all the other Dublin critics could be lumped together in chauvinistic pietas.

'The Bonfire' blazed up in March. The following May Grahame Greene came under fire both from Mr Fallon and Seamus Byrne, neither of whom thought much of 'The Living Room'.

On 14 May Gabriel Fallon, writing in the *Evening Press*, advised Grahame Greene that when next embarking 'on the hazardous voyage between God and evil' he should 'take with him and read with more humility, a copy of the Catechism'. His article was headed 'Read your Catechism Mr Greene'.

The previous day, 13 May, Seamus Byrne had written in the *Standard* that the crippled priest, anti-hero of 'The Living Room' was a 'phoney in a Roman collar', and the *Standard's* lead story on page one, devoted to attacking Grahame Greene and those who staged his play, was headlined 'The enemy within the gates'. Given the climate of the time O'Casey would have had to have an extra portion of Christian charity to believe that both men were separately arriving at judgements based on religious conviction and not merely acting as Irish Catholic apologists. And yet, as it happens, both men were sincere. A few years later Mr Fallon resigned as patron of the Amateur Drama Movement of Ireland in protest at the number of priests who were holding positions of influence with the movement. As the Irish clergy have always regarded Mr Fallon as the one pillar of respectability within the puzzling and disturbing world of the theatre, his resignation fell on many of them with the force almost of the announcement of a papal elopement. That year, at the annual diocesan examination which young priests are required to undergo for the first five years after ordination, the young clerics of Dublin were asked to give their opinions as to what the resignation signified.

It signified nothing except that Mr Fallon was acting according to his conscience, just as did Mr Byrne who a little later was involved in controversy when he wrote a truthful play (about abortion) and was the victim of many venomous newspaper correspondents' attacks. But to those who go abroad Anna Livia Plurabelle is always thick with clericalism and sluggish with obscurantism. Were Galileo an Irishman he would probably when shown the instruments have muttered under his breath 'But it *doesn't* move!' In retrospect, then, it seems remarkable not that the 'Drums of Father Ned' controversy which killed the 1958 Theatre Festival should have happened, but that anyone should have imagined that it could be avoided.

Having asked O'Casey for a play for the Festival, which was

also scheduled to contain a play by Beckett and a dramatisation of *Ulysses*, the organisers of the Festival then asked the Roman Catholic Archbishop of Dublin, Dr McQuaid, for permission to have a Mass said to open the Festival. His Grace at first gave permission, but later withdrew it when he learned that the work of Joyce and O'Casey was to be included in the Festival. This threw the entire proceedings into a fog of uproar and uncertainty which ended in the collapse of the Festival, the withdrawal of the Beckett play by its author and of 'The Drums of Father Ned' by *its* author. O'Casey followed this up by putting a ban on the production of any of his plays in Ireland. In practice this only extended to the professional stage, as he had sold the amateur rights of the Big Three, as we saw.

And so in a futile uproar over a hopeless effort to render unto Christ the things that were Thespis's the curtain fell on the last act of a drama that had been going on since O'Casey stepped on the boat in 1926; the efforts of two irreconcilable elements to come to terms with each other on a basis whereby each demanded unconditional surrender from the other. The truth was that neither O'Casey nor Ireland had anything to say to each other in those years of strong dark feelings between the Civil War and the beginning of Vatican 11. Quite apart from the church, the revolutionary generation could never have accepted O'Casey as a national dramatist or an accurate observer of their country – as we saw the 1916 Commemoration committee asked that he should not be performed during the Easter Week Commemorative ceremonies. O'Casey understood this perfectly, yet he could never resist going for their jugulars. But there is evidence that in happier times O'Casey at least could have shown a better spirit.

In 1964 he withdrew the ban on his plays, at first to allow them to be performed at the celebrations to mark the 400th anniversary of Shakespeare's birth, at the Aldwych Theatre, London, and later that year he gave permission to the Abbey to take 'Juno' over the Irish border into Derry, probably the most religion-torn city in the British Isles. The Abbey had been asked north by a priest. Hearing that the previous year a Protestant bishop had been among the audience in a Catholic hall, one of the very rare occasions that such a thing had ever happened in Derry, O'Casey gave his permission for the production, saying:

'. . . Glad to hear the Protestant Bishop came to see a play in a Catholic hall. Is this the beginning of the end of the stupid religious Apartheid in Ireland? I hope so.

'Derry is as Irish as Cork or Cahirciveen. Let the Orange and Green flags fly over the hall while the play is on, for we are flesh of each others' flesh, and bone of each others' bone, and there's no blottin' it out! . . .'

He died only a few weeks later, still separated in body but I like to think increasingly nearer in spirit to the more liberal Ireland in which this is written. An Ireland in which O'Casey might have stayed and is undoubtedly honoured in, but which even yet would have difficulty in restraining itself from violence at some of his more extreme statements. Whether the statements would have been so extreme if he had lived is of course a matter of conjecture.

But to sum up: O'Casey and Ireland were finished insofar as politics, art or religion were concerned when he left Dublin. He couldn't see it because a man's country is a monkey on his back which never leaves him. And the little, niggling, scribbling men who had decided to accept licensed posts as tame intellectuals in the new state resented not so much the One Who Got Away, as the one who wouldn't shut up, but continued to draw attention to their servitude. A free man can be a terrible bind sometimes. The result was heat without light. The heat also seared his relationship with men who might otherwise have been found ranged on his side; Frank O'Connor, Brinsley MacNamara, Liam O'Flaherty and Lennox Robinson come to mind in this category. But then his relationship with Irish artists was always unhappy. He was viewed with such hostility by the Abbey players that he was barred from the green-room. Furthermore his attitude of scepticism and derision towards the religious beliefs of 95 per cent of his countrymen would inevitably have forced him into silence or exile; his views on sex alone would have caused not just his works, but his person to be banned!

In silence he could not have survived as a writer without doing violence to his muse, so here too his muse would have forced him away. Dramatically the rhythm of the country had ceased to inspire him. Perhaps incidents like the shooting of Kevin O'Higgins, or the I.R.A. *v.* Blueshirt struggle would have provided a play if he had stayed, but it is highly improbable. Even before leaving Ireland he was turning towards experimentalism and to a preoccupation with form as much as with substance. 'The Silver Tassie', after all, was begun *before* he left Ireland. Even had Yeats accepted it, it is unlikely that O'Casey would have come back to Ireland for more than a few weeks, perhaps to attend the rehearsal and the opening night, but nothing more. In the event the rejection was only an act of arrogant folly on Yeats' part, a savage bite by one literary lion out of the reputation of a lesser one. It affected O'Casey in his pride and in his pocket, not in his domicile.

Undoubtedly as with Cassius Clay, whose tone occasionally recalls that of O'Casey, a psychiatrist would have tranquilised him, but if that had happened he would not have matched Clay by being, as both fighters claimed and both have proved themselves – the greatest.

8

THE BONFIRE

By Niall Carroll

WE hadn't heard much from Sean O'Casey for quite a few years before and so 'The Bishop's Bonfire' was regarded as a sort of belated letter home from the exile. And knowing what his feelings towards Ireland were like at the time we had a fairly shrewd idea that in his overdue Epistle to the Irish our embittered boy would have no presents enclosed for Mum and Dad, and that its pages would not exactly glow with prayerful greetings for the family.

But at least he had not finally shaken our dust from his feet and there was always the chance that there might be a tearful reunion some day and a spate of sentimental forgives and forgets.

Cyril Cusack put an end to any such wishful thinking in which we might have been indulging just then, when he put on the new play at the Gaiety in the spring of 1955. Dublin was shocked and resentful. That final curtain might have been of iron, clanking down between Ireland and O'Casey. And on his side it was clear beyond all doubt that Dublin's reception of the play had now put us all for ever beyond the bounds of O'Casey's forgiveness.

Sections of the first night audience hissed, the critics vied with one another as to who could denounce the new assessment of the present-day Ireland in the most scathing terms, and for the five weeks of its run the play was the subject of indignant outbursts in pub, club and coffee house. Naturally O'Casey spat venom back across the Channel in reply, and in return the boys with the typewriters gave as good as they got. Yes, we certainly had it out hot and heavy with him, and it was all very exhilarating while it lasted.

But at least on the surface the occasion demonstrated something of the mighty influence O'Casey still exerted on the Irish theatrical scene. Over the years of his exile as he sulked in his Torquay tent he had sent us no more than a few minor samples of his new work, in which only amateur and semi-professional companies showed any interest and the general public virtually none at all.

But when Cyril Cusack, home from foreign parts and laden down with laurels, billed his own name with a brand new, and obviously controversial, play by O'Casey, Dublin became at once wildly excited. There never was a first night like it in Irish theatrical history. Inside the Gaiety nearly two thousand people swayed and struggled to reach their booked seats, and another two thousand hopefuls jammed South King Street outside pleading for standing room. It really was a hectic night for the police, as squad cars from all over the city brought more and more of them to the theatre to prevent a riot.

In his notice next morning Seamus Kelly, of the *Irish Times*, wound up half a column of disparaging comment with the words: 'Positively the worst play I have ever had to sit through', a phrase which Cyril Cusack seized on and planted in his Gaiety advertisement in all the newspapers during the remainder of the run. It was that sort of zany occasion.

Box-office-wise it was all a bumper harvest for Cusack but artistically a pathetic and miserable flop. Had the play had any dramatic merit at all, what a rejuvenating effect it would have had on the Irish theatre which was dying a slow death from inanition at the time. It was not that 'The Bishop's Bonfire' lacked potential merit. There were the unmistakable O'Casey characters, the virile dialogue exchanges, the explosive humour, but all were stifled at origin by the deliberate intrusion of O'Casey's own personal feelings and his entirely undisciplined and uncontrolled anger. As often as the piece tried to rise to dramatic heights, so often O'Casey himself, blinded by his own fury of hatred, prevented it. As I wrote in the *Irish Press* next morning: 'Each brief new flight of the eagle ended in the swamp of bitterness and prejudice which have kept Mr O'Casey in the dramatic wilderness for so long'. In one unworthy sense O'Casey achieved his target in the 'Bonfire'. He obviously intended it to be a gross libel on the whole new Ireland and so it proved. It was his answer to a country which had earlier – and unfairly, be it admitted – rejected him, but it was the wrongest of wrong ways to go about it.

Actually he was far more unfair to himself than to Ireland when he deliberately jettisoned the most important of all the creative artist's qualities – Charity. And in all his intemperate rantings and ravings in the new play he did much less harm to Ireland than to his own integrity.

That O'Casey was the artist supreme no one pretends to doubt, and the mystery is why he should have put himself in a plainly impossible position in which, as a result of 'Bonfire', he became almost universally despised in this country. And not without some justification.

Could he be said, for instance, to be in a responsible state of mind when he had a middle-aged character in the play throwing himself on his knees and begging God to preserve the purity of Irishmen by helping them to keep their eyes permanently turned away from women? Quite obviously O'Casey was hopelessly and completely out of touch with the progress of life in this country. Equally obviously he was only anxious to pick on any isolated – and fictitious – incident on the Irish scene which would enable him to pour scorn on Ireland and its people, rather than provide him with material for genuine comment on our developing way of life.

In the overall picture of 'The Bishop's Bonfire' there was no denying that Dublin had totally rejected it and all its insulting sentiment. And, as it was the first serious play he had written for Irish consumption since he turned his last scowl on us from the deck of the mail boat, I have always held the theory that it was the gradual realisation that he had, artistically speaking, sinned against the Holy Ghost that really accounted for his later angry outbursts.

He vented his feelings almost immediately afterwards in the ominously named book, *The Green Crow*, called after a particularly destructive type of Russian vermin. It was a typical O'Casey title for what in fact was a diatribe directed against criticism of himself or his works. In it the Dublin reviewers who had denounced 'The Bishop's Bonfire' got it, raw-hide fashion. The chapter he devoted to them was really fascinating, but in a way not at all meant by him.

Some of us were singled out by name for special vituperative treatment, and needless to say we just gathered up all the mud and flung it back at him, concealing a stone or two in it here and there. I had never known such free-for-all abuse in a row in or out of the theatre.

'Rats piping from their Dublin peepholes', screamed O'Casey. 'Discredited artist, unpinnacled, senile-brained, gone to seed', screamed we.

I blessed him for the way he kept my weekly theatre commentary in the *Irish Press* bubbling with interest during the stormy controversy. Considering his status it was astonishing how he

131

allowed himself to be baited, but his own anger was his greatest weakness.

Where other big figures would have let the ball go unnoticed over the end line, he consistently played it back into the centre of the court. And I confess to being dismayed at one of his replies, it sounded so weak and so unlike the Lion of Devon. When I wrote in my column that when the fires of theatre history had burned themselves out there would be only three hot stones left among the residual ashes, representing his first three plays which he had written before he left us, he wrote back complaining that this was bad English and adding: 'Aren't ashes themselves residual on their own? Why say "residual ashes"?' But it was all a wonderful opportunity to keep interest high in theatre matters. And, of course, the rules were suspended as the exchanges went merrily on.

Once after a particularly bitter broadside from him I wrote that he reminded the Irish people of Owen Keegan in T. C. Murray's *Autumn Fire*, who tottered around in his nightshirt carrying a lighted candle in his shaking hand and protesting that he was as young and virile as ever he was. He completely ignored the reference when next he replied.

For all O'Casey's greatness it was easy to catch him out in numerous small matters. The obvious reason was that he poured out his denunciations with such anger that it was child's play to pick holes in them, but when he was his own temperate, calm self in attack, quick evasive action was the only tactic to adopt.

I remember my disappointment at an earlier stage when I made a contribution to a newspaper controversy which was conducted by one of the evening paper critics about the low standard of plays and production at the Abbey. There had been some demonstrations from the audience on the subject and O'Casey was one of a number of key figures who were asked for their views. He wrote that in all matters of theatre the audience and the audience alone must be the final arbiters. One phrase he used was: 'They don't seem to complain about plays of mine'. I thought surely that here was my chance to needle a devastating reply from him, so I asked him in print if he had always felt that way or if this was a brand new democratic slogan he had designed for himself? And would he, for instance, have proudly nailed his declaration to the Abbey's proscenium on the nights that the audiences were making a valiant effort to wreck the theatre during the first production of 'The Plough and the Stars'? I looked forward to a pulverising comment from him but had to be content with the insipid reply: 'With all due respects this young man doesn't know what he is talking about'.

After the 'Bonfire' flare-up it was inevitable that O'Casey's final estrangement from Ireland could not be long delayed. Undaunted – and unconverted – by its miserable failure he sat down and wrote another play for our special benefit, this time for production at the Dublin Theatre Festival. He called it 'The Drums of Father Ned', a title which gave us all a pretty good idea of what to expect from it.

But although Dublin was quite prepared to flock to see it, and we seemed to be in for another memorable first night, the play never saw the light of day, in this country at least. A first-class professional company secured the script and set about enthusiastically preparing for the production. They regarded it, indeed, as a big feather in their cap that they should have the honour of presenting a brand new Sean O'Casey work for the Dublin Festival.

But as rehearsals proceeded the snags began to show in the script and soon it was clear to the producer that 'Father Ned' was not going to transfer from page to stage in any smooth way. The company wrote to O'Casey explaining their difficulties and asking his permission to rearrange certain scenes and requesting him to do a little bit of rewriting.

'Censorship, the bishops and their croziers again', screamed O'Casey. The company tried to reason with him but not only would he not agree to alter a sentence in the play but he withdrew it entirely from production.

But that was not all. In a wild fit of anger he promptly banned the professional production of all his plays by the Abbey or anywhere else in Ireland. His only regret was that he could not also ban all amateur productions of the plays. He had sold his amateur rights years before when times were bad in the English theatre. Other authors had done likewise during the blitz period.

It was sensational news and theatre columnists were in clover again. I wrote on the following Monday morning that I had been reliably informed that there was no question of censorship but that the script of 'Father Ned' simply would not produce. Back came a venomous reply from Torquay: 'Carroll must publish the names of the people who gave him this information or else admit publicly that he invented it himself.'

It was more grist for the mill. I wrote: 'How naïve Mr Sean

133

O'Casey is, asking any newspaperman to divulge confidential sources of information, a principle on which the entire newspaper industry is founded.' He replied, reading the seven generations of critics, repeating that efforts were being made to suppress his views on Irish affairs and generally thundering his disgust at everything that belonged within our four shores.

Up to the early 'sixties all my dealings with O'Casey were in the published open-letter form of comment and reply. I had never met or spoken to him on the telephone. In all the circumstances I didn't particularly want to, but that day came when I had to face the music. As I have suggested here, it is an old trick of the newspaper world to telephone a big name – we did it many times with Shaw – and needle him into making a worthwhile comment.

One day *Sunday Press* News Editor, Gerry Fox, showed me the London Letter of the *Irish Times*, in which O'Casey was quoted as saying that the Abbey nowadays produced only rubbish and produced it in rubbishy fashion. He suggested I telephone O'Casey and remind him he had not been in Dublin for over thirty years – and was this just hearsay? It was too good an opportunity to let go, so I took several deep breaths and called his number in Torquay. I trembled a little as I heard his 'hello'. I told him I was speaking for the *Sunday Press* and before I could say any more he said gruffly: 'I don't know anything about the *Sunday Press*. What do they want with me?'

I said: 'They're interested in a statement attributed to you in the press about the poor standard of present-day Abbey plays and production. They know you haven't been in Ireland since the early 'thirties and are puzzled that you would express opinions founded on hearsay.'

He had been quietly belligerent up to this but the reaction to my query was instantaneous. I might say he erupted like a volcano.

'Hearsay?' he roared, as I instinctively held the receiver a few inches away from my ear. 'It's no hearsay. I know what's going on over there. I am in close touch. I know more about the Abbey and Dublin and Ireland than you and the *Sunday Press* that are on the spot.'

I felt myself disintegrating but the certainty that a magnificent half-column of copy would be the reward helped to bolster my courage.

'It's just that we find it strange to have someone like you talking at secondhand in such a direct way', I managed to say.

'Secondhand?' he roared again. Then he paused suddenly and said: 'I don't like to be talking to mysterious distant voices. Who are you?'

The images of 'The Bishop's Bonfire', *The Green Crow*, 'Father Ned' and Owen Keegan all floated wraithful past me in the terrible moment of truth. Brazenly as I thought, but I felt my voice dry and hoarse, I gave him my name.

I heard the slow, deliberate intake of breath over the line and then the long-drawn-out Ohhhhhh. . . . The silence which followed seemed never-ending. But when he spoke again his voice had undergone a complete transformation. It was soft, no anger in it at all but a slight note of paternal chiding:

'You said a great many foolish things in your time, didn't you, son?'

Considering the tone and the comment and recalling years of wordy battles between Dublin and Devon, what was one to say in answer? I tried to convey to him that my own generation were too young to have seen the rejection of his first great plays, that they felt they could not enthuse over his later works but had done their utmost to undo the wrongs of the 'twenties and early 'thirties in his own regard. He grudgingly admitted that Ireland now received his first plays with special warmth but would not concede that his later plays were any less meritorious.

His anger now completely gone, except when he mentioned the Abbey, he talked quietly about life in the newspapers and asked me if I was a full-time journalist. I told him I was and he said: 'Yes, I am a journalist too. We're all journalists, we writers. We interpret the world for others. That's our job.'

Then as if regretting his first outburst on the telephone, he told me: 'I read everything about Ireland in the newspapers and I'm always meeting people coming here from Dublin. There's nothing goes on across the Irish Sea that I don't know about. As a matter of fact I know all about your tide that wouldn't come in or wouldn't go out, down where you come from.'

To my horror he was referring to my Abbey comedy, 'The Wanton Tide', produced shortly before.

He was in great talking form and I knew I was meeting an entirely new Sean O'Casey.

Suddenly he said: 'You know, you ought to be ashamed of yourself to ring me up and talk in English.' He thereupon broke into fluent Irish and insisted that I use it also, so I struggled to keep up the conversation in the medium. I told him, in Irish, that

135

I had learned to speak the language in Galway but that when I came to Dublin I had no opportunity to speak it and had forgotten a great deal of it.

'No excuse at all', said O'Casey. 'Look at me. I make opportunities to speak Irish all the time with my family and with the people who call to see me from Ireland.'

There was more talk on minor everyday matters and then O'Casey sighed heavily and said: 'Ah yes, the Abbey . . . I wouldn't ever touch that crowd again'. I felt him sitting up straight in his chair as he said suddenly: 'Do you know the quotation – "Romantic Ireland's dead and gone, it's with O'Leary in his grave".'

'It's Yeats', I said.

'Well, I'll paraphrase it for you', said O'Casey. ' "The Abbey Theatre's dead and gone, it's with Yeats in his grave". So long, son.'

There was a click as the receiver was replaced.

It was over and I felt better than I had ever felt in my life. I had spoken to a Sean O'Casey who could at a moment's notice shed all the harsh qualities of character we had all been accustomed to debit him with and become a gentle human being exuding only humour, kindliness and goodwill.

It was a relief to know that there really were two Sean O'Caseys and a treat indeed to meet the second one.

9

TOWARDS THE END

By David Krause

'TELL them I'm only talking to God now', Sean said, prophetically as it turned out, for that was barely thirteen days before he died. I had answered the phone and called to him to say it was a reporter from London asking for permission to come down to Torquay to interview him, and he had sung out his reply in mock-solemnity, to the world and all its reporters: he was too busy talking to God. He hadn't sounded like a man who was dying, yet if he himself had sensed that the end was near he had chosen to hide his secret in a characteristic jest about a serious thing, his shriving time. We will never know the nature of that holy and probably merry dialogue between God and O'Casey, but there can be little doubt that when it was over, Sean was cleared and ready to pass on to the heaven in which he often said he did not believe. 'I'm an atheist, thank God', he liked to say, taking pleasure and comfort in this paradoxical phrase of Shaw's. Heretical humanist though he was, in his beginning and in his ending O'Casey was God's man and he was his own man. Since he believed that 'the best way to fit oneself for the next world was to fit oneself for this world', he must have died as he had lived, in a state of grace.

Few men had made themselves more fit for life in this world. If we were to venture a guess, perhaps that was what he was talking about with God, life not death. 'I will show you hope in a handful of life', he once said to me when we were discussing T. S. Eliot's *The Waste Land*. He was too full of life to brood about fear and dust. For his wife and children, for his friends, there was no thought of his dying that year, or indeed at any time. He had survived so many pains and ordeals throughout his eighty-four years, earning his grace in the traditional way, through suffering, that those of us who loved him seemed to sense some intimations of eternal life in him, and we were somehow unable to conceive of the world without Sean in it. It was only after he had suffered his fatal heart attack on 18 September that we sought to temper our sorrow with amazement: 'The wonder is, he hath endur'd so long.'

He still seemed far from the end of his endurance when I met him for that last time on a bright week-end early in September. I had already seen him twice before for several weeks during the summer in June and July, and now I had stopped at Torquay again on my way back from Dublin for the usual farewell visit before setting out on my homeward journey. He moved about more carefully now than he had earlier in the summer, for he was still recovering from an attack of his recurring bronchitis and other respiratory complications that had affected his heart, an illness which had laid him low in August and sent him, over his protests, to a nearby nursing home for several days. Apparently this attack had been more serious than anyone realised, but at the time we did not think it was cause for alarm, for he had come through greater dangers in the past. The worst was in 1956 when he had fought his way back from two major operations, kidney and prostate, only to have his heart broken at the end of the year when his twenty-one-year-old son Niall died suddenly of leukaemia. He was a long time recovering from that shock.

Sean had minimised his August illness, refusing to behave like an invalid. In fact, shortly after we met in September and had settled ourselves comfortably in his room, as if to convince me and himself that he was not about to perform his swan song, he leaped nimbly out of his chair and enacted an energetic mime-dance, pacing around the room in an exaggerated strut, raising himself on tip-toe with each swinging stride and flapping his arms so that he looked like a comical old bird trying to fly and not quite making it. 'It keeps me from forgetting that human beings are gay and funny fellas', he said with a broad grin as he sat down, rearranging the brightly-coloured beanie on the back of his head. 'And besides, it's good for the circulation.' I had begun by asking about his recent illness and he had demonstrated his reply, which was good for our mutual circulation. No, I thought, that dancing Sean was not a dying man.

But there was another shadow over his life now, in his mind more terrible than death, the increasing threat of total blindness. He had lived with this danger all his life, for his eyes had troubled him since childhood when he developed an ulcerated cornea in his left eye, which thereafter remained dim and filmy, and this placed a heavy strain on his already weakened 'good' eye, which periodically became ulcerated. Every day of his life he had to

138

sponge his eyes with water as hot as he could bear it in order to wash away the suppurating fluid that burned his eye-sockets and temporarily blotted out his vision. Over the many years that I had visited him, since 1954, I can hardly remember a day when he did not have to pause several times, in the afternoon and evening, remove his thick-lens glasses, press his thumb and fore-finger over his closed and burning eyes, and then go to the sink in his room for the ritualistic eyewashing.

As if this affliction were not enough, some of the hairs on his lower eyelids grew irregularly, pointing inward so that they jabbed at his eyeballs like needles, and this meant that often his wife or one of the children had to pull them out with a pair of tweezers. Sometimes the hairs were difficult to see, let alone pull, and meanwhile he would have to endure the pin-pricking pain, which grew worse with each flick of his eyelid. I was initiated into this ritual myself during my July visit, for when his wife Eileen, who said she had plucked thousands of such hairs from his eyelids throughout their marriage, had trouble locating a seemingly invisible hair that was torturing him, I was urged to have a go at it. As I held his magnificent bony head up to the light and probed with the tweezers, I trembled lest I should tear away some of his skin with the stubborn hair. Fortunately I was able to nip the hair and pull it out cleanly. It couldn't have been more than a 32nd of an inch in length, and he thanked me for delivering from him 'that bloody whoreson of a hair'.

He had been relieved of his pain by a stabbing 32nd of an inch, but nothing, neither science nor God, could save his fading eye-sight, which was apparently suspended now by little more than a hair's breadth. 'There is no pain he would not more willingly endure than blindness', his wife had said to me in an aside in the kitchen. He did not talk much about it, but it was obviously troubling him and was especially apparent in the way he strained and squinted at any written material, with the page of a letter or book held so close to his right eye that it pressed against his nose. So I discussed the matter with his wife when we were alone after I first arrived in June. Sean rested in bed for several hours every afternoon from around 2.30 to 4.30, a habit he had developed more to relieve his eyes than to sleep. He would slip a knotted handkerchief over his eyes and doze, or just lie there thinking; maybe he rehearsed some lines for a new play, or did what he called talking with God. While he rested, Eileen and I went for a stroll and had our talk. We walked from the crest of St Marychurch, the hilly suburb of Torquay where they lived, down the winding streets to the red cliffs of Babbacombe, overlooking a vast panorama of azure sea and sky. It was a familiar walk which Sean had taken with us in previous and better years, he with a cloth cap tipped low over his forehead to protect his eyes from the dazzling light and high wind, an ashplant swinging in one hand, the other linked snugly in Eileen's. Although he was about twenty-five years older than her, anyone who saw them would have known immediately that they were deeply in love with each other.

Eileen O'Casey is a strikingly handsome woman of auburn beauty and fine proportions, an open-faced woman with a gentle manner and a quick smile; and as if nature had not been generous enough to her, she also had the great good fortune to have lived with Sean O'Casey for thirty-seven years. Like her husband she was born and raised in Ireland, but later went to England to pursue a career in the theatre. She became an actress in London, met Sean when she played the role of Nora Clitheroe in his 'Plough and the Stars', and soon afterwards married him, in 1927. Since she was a Roman Catholic, they were married in church by a priest and their three children were properly baptized. But she no longer practises her faith, she practises Sean's faith.

We had moved away from the windy tor and settled under a tree on a grassy slope that led down to the sea-front. Then she began to talk about Sean's eyes. 'All the doctors say that in medical terms he should be blind now, and yet he can still see, just barely, because he wants to see, he needs to see in order to go on with his life and work. He couldn't bear to become a burden to us. So he sees through an act of will, an act of faith, and that's the way he has done everything all his life.' He could never be indifferent about anything, she said, no matter how minor it might be. He couldn't stand carelessness or untidiness, and always took great pains to be neat and clean in his personal habits. It worried him that he might one day become weak and helpless. He always had time for laughter and merriment, she said, but he had to keep his life and his mind in order.

They had gone up to London for several days early in the year to see a specialist when his already dim sight had suddenly begun to deteriorate at an alarming rate. After extensive examinations and X-rays, the specialist and his consultants had concluded that his left eye was stone blind, and there was little more than a faint

140

flicker remaining in the right eye, so that while he might make out some vague shapes, he couldn't really see any more. His eyes were simply worn out. 'It was a terrible shock', she continued. 'And yet, when we returned home he went back to his regular routine, writing letters every day, working on his new book of essays, and making plans for a new play. He couldn't read and I

Sean O'Casey – later years

helped him with that, as I had in the past, though he did manage somehow to make out an odd word here and there. The doctors said he was blind, but he went on scribbling notes and touch-typing day after day. And on top of that came the bad news that we might have to move, and the mere thought of it terrified me. He would never survive that.'

Their landlord had died and there was a strong chance that the house would be sold, which meant they would probably have to vacate their flat. They rented the second floor of an old villa that had been divided into three separate dwellings, located on the highest spot in St Marychurch, with green rolling valleys below them spreading out to the sea, which was visible on clear days. In good weather Sean sat in the sun on their small stone porch, wearing his broad-brimmed felt hat, or he went down to wander among the flowers and the birds in their garden – 'fifteen steps and then six steps, mind them carefully', as he often cautioned me. They were stony and steep.

'He knows the exact distance of everything in the house', Eileen continued, 'and when people see him moving about so freely and confidently they don't realise that like a blind person he does it all by memory and instinct. If we have to move to a new place he'll become confused and go crashing into furniture and walls and break an arm or leg, and he'll probably be demoralised or dead in a week. He'll be all right if we can stay here.' That was in June. The threat of having to move hung over them all summer. But in the end, in September, it was not his eyes but his heart that failed him. As his good friend Brooks Atkinson wrote in a moving tribute, 'In eighty-four years of unselfish living it was the first time that his heart had failed him.'

There was no sign of failure in him when we met early in September. He was tired from the boredom of his convalescence, but his mind was fully alert and his humour was characteristically sly.

'What does God say when you talk to Him?' I had asked after we had dispensed with the London reporter.

'He tells me the world is full of fools but he loves them anyway.'

'And what about you, do you love them anyway?'

'I only have trouble loving them when their folly grows out of stupidity instead of honest ignorance. Then I'm more inclined to hate them, or to hate the things that make them stupid. I love everyone and everything that's alive. I'm only indifferent to the dead. And now, for the love o' God, don't be asking so many foolish questions and let's get on with our work.'

'Our work' was the problem of trying to clear up countless questions and references in his letters, which I was collecting and editing. He had exchanged letters with some of the major literary

142

figures of his time, but he also corresponded with hundreds of unknown people from many countries, people who praised or criticised his works, asked him to explain or justify something he had written, carried on extended discussions about literature and life, politics and religion, told him their troubles, asked his advice, and even named their children after him. Throughout all the years that his plays were not being produced, these people became his intimate audience, and so the daily ceremony of writing and receiving letters kept him in constant touch with the world of ordinary people who apparently read and reacted to everything he wrote. He had written thousands of letters over the past fifty years, many of which I had been able to locate during a three-year search, and there were situations and controversies to straighten out, people and places to identify, and an involved network of events in his life to correlate. I had worked out a good deal of it, but a number of mysteries remained. Some of these matters taxed his memory, which was understandable, especially exact dates and time sequences, yet on many of them he seemed to possess an uncanny total recall. Often the point in question had happened forty or fifty years ago and, since I had been able to put together some of the pieces during my investigations in Dublin, I usually had enough details to know that his version was in all probability accurate, rounded out with shrewd and comic observations on why some people had spoken or acted as they did. He invariably told his stories in dialogue, giving what the others had said and what he had said, acting out all the parts in a well-flavoured style, and he was an excellent mimic. Listening to him one would have guessed that Sean himself was the original of the 'fluthered' Irishmen that Barry Fitzgerald had created in his plays. He spoke in a rasping tenor voice, drawing out the syllables of words with a consequential Dublin brogue that still retained the lilting cadences heard on the northside of the Liffey. He could smile like a Dublin charwoman and swear like a Dublin docker.

But there was much more in him than the randy comedian. There was a glint of steel in his bony face, power in his transfixed eyes, courage in the bite of his jaw. There was a craggy grandeur in his aquiline profile which sometimes invested him with the magisterial dignity of a Renaissance Cardinal painted by El Greco, especially when he complemented his perennial red beanie by wearing his blood-red robe on chilly days. His small eyes burned fiercely behind his thick glasses and he could lower his voice to a mighty whisper of rage when he reacted to some injustice in the world.

But there was much more in him than the courageous patriarch. By nature a shy and gentle man, he was uncommonly tender and solicitous with people he trusted, a gallant charmer with women and children, a sweet companion with friends. There was a gesture of ceremonial fun in the assortment of gaily designed and coloured beanies or skull-caps he always wore, some of them made by his daughter, others sent to him from friends all over the world. He smoked a pipe continuously, and he might drink an occasional glass of wine with guests, but he was a whiskey teetotaller, for he remembered too well his early life in Ireland when the labourers were paid in the pubs and often drank up their wages before they could bring them home to their wives and children. He loved all kinds of music. During his younger days in Dublin he had worn a saffron kilt and played the bagpipes, and he fancied himself something of a singer. At any moment he might burst into song with a lively ballad – perhaps one of his own, for he had written songs for all his plays – and whatever it may have lost in his croaking voice it gained in his delicate feeling. He was a man of deep impulses, and he could be moved so profoundly by the misfortune of a friend, or even a stranger, that he became ill with grief. For a man of his achievements, he had a tendency to doubt the merit of his work: 'Tell me what you thought was bad in it, not what was good', he said to me on a number of occasions after I had praised something he had written.

His moods were often mixed, and he could be an outraged comedian, a gentle genius, an insecure rebel. Perhaps he had lived too long in self-imposed exile from his native land, for his extended quarrel with Ireland was a lover's quarrel: he was impatient with his country's frailties but would leap to the defence if an outsider attacked them. He was capable of unwarranted extremes and could make rash judgements from reasonable assumptions; he could see slights where none were intended; he could be quick to anger and slow to forgive. Sometimes he rolled out his heavy weapons for minor skirmishes, and he could hurl rhetorical thunderbolts when he felt he had been unjustly used or abused.

When I mentioned some of these extremes to him he shook his head sadly, then rubbed his beanie so vigorously that wisps of silvery hair flared wildly around its edges: 'Put it down to my

144

tactlessness', he said, 'my inability to keep my big mouth shut, much to my sorrow and the sorrow of others. But what was the alternative?' He rubbed his beanie with another flourish and straightened his back. 'Tact? Polite submission, that's what tact really is, and it's something I never learned. Children are naturally tactless, but it's knocked out of them in school where they learn to be polite and submissive. I never had any formal education and maybe that's why I became the way I am.'

'Are you saying that formal education is a dangerous thing because it isn't dangerous enough?' I asked.

'I'm saying there should be a way of teaching young people without breaking their spirit and making them so damned submissive. When they learn right from wrong they shouldn't be afraid to say so if they see it around them, and they shouldn't be so refined that they're unable to do anything about it. The first thing a fella has to do if he wants to accomplish anything of value is to be tactless. The world is full of powerful people who want everyone else to bow down before them and be tactful, and if they're not running the schools they're running the churches. But formal religion is worse than formal education when it comes to filling people full of fear and submission. Did you ever see anyone as tactful as a bishop?

'But Christ wasn't very tactful, was He? Let's face up to it, He was a great public nuisance, always stirring things up, always telling people what they should and shouldn't do, and so few of them ever listening to Him and He had to shout it out again and again. Was He polite and submissive? Was He afraid to speak out? All for one and one for all, that's what He preached, and He was a great communist.'

'Christ, a communist?' I asked.

'Of course He was. Read Shaw's great Preface to 'Androcles and the Lion'. I wonder do they teach that in the schools, or in the churches? Christianity was communist from the beginning, it had to be if all men were to hold all things in common and be their brother's keepers. But you'd never know it from the way the clergy talk and act today, for they're all tactful capitalists now. Read what Christ said in the Bible: "Ask, and it shall be given you; seek and you shall find; knock, and it shall be opened unto you". The world needs more of them – Askers and Seekers and Knockers. Now take that word Knock, that's a fine word – Knock, Knock, Knock. There are many doors in the world that need a powerful Knock. Read what Shaw said about what Christ

145

said and did. "Gentle Jesus meek and mild is a snivelling modern invention, with no warrant in the gospels", that's what Shaw said. We can't get around it, you see, Christ was a tactless communist, God help Him, so don't be so damned sceptical about it.'

'It's just this, Sean', I said, 'every time I hear you talk about Christianity and communism, the Star of Bethlehem and the Red Star seem to become interchangeable, as they do in your play, "The Star Turns Red". And I have a strong feeling that the Russians, to say nothing of the Christians, would be even more sceptical than I am.'

'Ah, what is the stars?' he said with mischievous smile. 'They're all in the one blue sky that shelters every mother's son, Christian and communist, beggar and thief.'

That was a typical response. Whenever he got around to telling me what communism was and why he was a communist, he often began as if he were determined to drive the moneychangers out of the temple and ended by becoming gentle and dreamy. It wasn't that he was trying to be evasive, for he was wholly dedicated and even visionary on this subject. He was essentially a yea-sayer and loved to introduce hallelujah quotations from the Psalms in his conversation. How often I have heard him emphasise a point with one of the following phrases: 'Make a joyful noise unto God. . . . Blow up the trumpet in the new moon. . . . O let the nations be glad and sing for joy. . . . O sing unto the Lord a new song. . . .' He was tired of the old songs and pietistic slogans. He felt that the political jargon and cold-war clichés of the West and the East had obscured the basic goals of mankind, and he could set forth goals in a disarming if over-simplified manner when he said, 'Every man who puts his best effort into his life and work, be he a doctor or a bricklayer, is a communist whether he knows it or not, for he's helping to improve the common good, making the world a better place for himself and his family and his country, and all the countries of the world.' Thus, communism was his touchstone for the ideal society, and the fact that it was a scare-word to many people only increased his impulse to use it, tactlessly, as he would have said. It was his way of knocking on doors.

He seldom mentioned Marx or Lenin when he spoke about communism, for he was more likely to quote from Christ and Shaw, Shelley and Keats, Blake and Burns, Emerson and Whitman, Ruskin and Morris. On one occasion he called my attention to a little known passage in Keats's poem *Isabella* in order to show

146

me 'what communism was all about.' He asked me to take the book from his shelf and read the stanzas aloud to him, and he joined me from memory on the third stanza so that we must have sounded like a Greek chorus:

> With her two brothers this fair lady dwelt,
>   Enriched from ancestral merchandise,
> And for them many a weary hand did swelt
>   In torched mines and noisy factories,
> And many once proud-quiver'd loins did melt
>   In blood from stinging whip; – with hollow eyes
> Many all day in dazzling river stood,
>   To take the rich-ored driftings of the flood.

> For them the Ceylon diver held his breath,
>   And went all naked to the hungry shark;
> For them his ears gush'd blood; for them in death
>   The seal on the cold ice with piteous bark
> Lay full of darts; for them alone did seethe
>   A thousand men in troubles wide and dark:
> Half-ignorant, they turn'd an easy wheel,
>   That set sharp racks at work, to pinch and peel.

> Why were they proud? Because their marble founts
>   Gush'd with more pride than do a wretch's tears? –
> Why were they proud? Because fair orange-mounts
>   Were of more soft ascent than lazar stairs? –
> Why were they proud? Because red-lin'd accounts
>   Were richer than the songs of Grecian years? –
> Why were they proud? again we ask aloud,
>   Why in the name of Glory were they proud?

He took great delight in repeating the questions in the final stanza, and many times thereafter, when we happened to be talking about the oppressors and the oppressed of the world, he would roar out the last two lines a lusty chant:

> Why were they proud? Again we ask aloud,
>   Why in the name of Glory were they proud?

So he would usually turn to literature or the Bible when he wanted to underscore the nature of his communism, which was more deeply rooted in ethical values than in a political system. And it is not surprising that these values should have developed out of the doctrines of Christianity, for what little formal education he had received as a boy was obtained in the Church of Ireland. He had to leave the church school, St Mary's, at an early age because of his weak eyes, which were covered with ointments and bandages for several hours of every day. He recorded some of this information in his autobiography, but since he was vague about specific details I always tried to locate documented evidence during my visits to Dublin. On one occasion I found a copy of his Confirmation papers which indicated that he had been confirmed at Clontarf Church in 1898, at the age of eighteen, that he had received his First Communion on Easter Day of that same year at St Barnabas Church, and that he had been baptized in 1880 at St Mary's. For a long time he had been uncertain about the day and year of his birth, and a search through the files of the Registry Office, under his baptized name of John Casey, revealed the date as 30 March, 1880.

Two summers ago I brought back from Dublin a copy of another forgotten document out of his past to show him, this time the record of a prize he had won in Sunday School at the age of seven. It read as follows: 'Church of Ireland, United Dioceses of Dublin, Glendalough and Kildare. At a Diocesan Examination in Connexion with the Board held at St Mary's Schoolhouse on the (the day is blank) of 1887, II Class was awarded to John Casey of St Mary's Parish for Proficiency in Holy Scripture and Church Formularies. Signed, Plunkett – Dublin.' (the Archbishop).

'Are you sure it was only a second class prize?' he asked when I read it to him.

'No doubt about it, it says second class.'

'Ah, well', he said with a grin, 'that's not so bad for a half-blind little chiseller.'

'Then you do remember your childhood proficiency in Holy Scripture?'

'I remember it as through a glass lightly. It must have been the year after my father died. He was a great reader of books, and that was unusual then, for he was the only person in the neighbourhood who actually had bookcases filled with them. I wasn't able to read at the age of seven, because of my eyes, but like all children I could repeat anything if I heard it several times. The Bible was the important book in our house, and full of fine stories and mysterious words for a curious kid to imitate. I liked the sound of the words long before I knew what they meant, and it gave me a feeling of power to spout them in the house and in front of the other kids. And don't forget, my sister Isabella was a teacher at St Mary's so she stuffed me full of the right things to say to make certain I didn't disgrace her and the family name. Then there was my dear Mother, who never missed a Sunday at church, and later there was the Reverend Edward Griffin of St Barnabas. I was a stubborn kid with a mind of my own, but I wouldn't have done anything to let them down.'

Only last summer I had located one of the Reverend Griffin's daughters. She had gone to England with her clergyman husband, but now they were living in retirement in Ireland. She gave me some of her recollections of Sean – 'John not Sean, he was John Casey when we knew him' – as a young man of twenty-four at St Barnabas, the details of which I corroborated with him during my July visit. Sean, or John, and her father, the Rector, were as close as father and son in those days. At the particular time that she remembered, around 1904, prayer-meetings were often held on week-day evenings in the Church schoolhouse, and at the conclusion of the service the Rector would ask for a volunteer to lead the final prayer. 'It was then', she said, 'after an awkward pause while father waited for the volunteers, that my sister and I – we were girls of eight and ten – would nudge each other and whisper, "It'll be John again, he'll jump up again, and oh, he'll go on and on as he always does". He sat behind us and we were afraid to turn round and look, but soon we heard his voice ringing out loud and clear, in that drawling, lilting way he had of speaking. He didn't read from the prayer-book as the others did, he just made up his prayer as he went along, using some biblical passages but mostly his own words about the glory of God. As I said, at the time my sister and I joked about how he would go on and on with it, but we were silly little girls then, and when I think of it all now it comes back to me as something very moving and beautiful. He would have made a great preacher.'

Maybe he did become something of a lyrical preacher, especially in his later plays where he wrote humorously and heroically about the joy of life, in the fantasy of an enchanted Cock or in the ecstasy of a miracle on the banks of the Liffey. In the latter instance, in 'Red Roses for Me', when his autobiographical hero, Ayamonn Breydon, who attends a Church called St Burnupus and is a close friend of the Rector, joins the people of Dublin in a transformation dance and exhorts them to seek a new life, he may well have been making up another of his lilting prayers: 'Friend, we would that you should live a greater life; We will that all of us shall live a greater life. Our sthrike is yours. A step ahead for us today; another one for you tomorrow. We who have known, and know, the emptiness of life shall know its fullness. All men and women quick with life are fain to venture forward. The apple grows for you to eat. The violet grows for you to wear. Young maiden, another world is in your womb. . . . Our city's in th' grip o'God.'

The Rector's daughter also remembered that John was interested in other things besides prayer in those days, which explained why he soon changed his name to Sean. 'He was full of the Gaelic language and told us proudly that no Irishman was a true Irishman unless he could speak Irish. You see, on Sundays after church he often accompanied my sister and me on the long walk from St Barnabas to the Rectory, which was on Charles Street of Mountjoy Square. First we would walk his mother home, around the corner on Abercorn Road. We always called her Granny Casey. She was a neat little woman, she wore a pretty bonnet, and she gave us sweets. When we set out on our walk John was swinging a hurley stick, which he hid outside the Church. It was an ancient Irish game, he told us, and Irishmen should be proud to play it. After he left us at the Rectory, he went on to Jones's Road to play with his friends. Well, on those walks he would tell us stories about the Irish heroes, and sing songs in Irish. Once he taught us the chorus of "Cruiskeen Lawn", the part that's in Irish, and do you know, I still remember those lines:

> *Gramachree, mavourneen, slanta gal avourneen,*
> *Gramachree ma Cruiskeen Lawn, Lawn, Lawn.*

'He sang the song and we joined in on the chorus. We must have been a strange sight as we marched along singing merrily, two little girls in our Sunday dresses and John waving out the rhythm with his hurley stick.'

'Like the pied piper of Dublin', I said to him. 'You kept your faith in the Irish language through the years, but when did you lose your faith in the Church?'

'I never lost my faith, I found it, I found it when Jim Larkin came to Dublin a few years later and organised the unskilled labourers. I found it in Jim's great socialist motto: "An injury to one is the concern of all".'

'Socialist and Christian?'

'Socialist and Christian. They're both the one thing – communism – if only the people knew it. Jim knew it as well as he knew his penny-catechism, but the clergy condemned him for it during the 1913 strike, saying hell wasn't enough nor eternity long enough for the likes of him. Yet he was the Saviour of Dublin. He put his faith in the people and their need to live a better and fuller life. And that's where I put my faith.'

We must take him at his word and deed, for that is the faith to which he devoted his life as man and artist. He expressed it in his plays in comedy and tragedy, farce and fantasy. He expressed it in his autobiography and books of essays in narrative, argument and satire. He was a visionary humanist, a man of this worldly spirit. As an artist, the form as well as the substance of his plays is of such a magnitude that even in death he remains ahead of his time, for there is still no theatre able or daring enough to do justice to his pioneering achievements in dramatic technique, beginning with 'The Silver Tassie'. He spent the last thirty-six years of his life exploring new forms, rejecting all the orthodoxies and conventions of the theatre, even his own.

He was writing about that form and faith right to the end. When I saw him a fortnight before he died, he was finishing a satiric essay called *The Bold Primaqueera*. The joke in the title is aimed at the theatre of the absurd and alludes to Ionesco's play 'The Bald Prima Donna', known in America as 'The Bald Soprano'. Sean said he was fed up with what he called 'absurd plays by absurd playwrights who sing the same dreary song on the one weary note and then have the gall to make a bloody mystery of it'. He had in mind Ionesco and Pinter and their imitators. 'Not Beckett and Brecht', he insisted, 'they have the leap of the life force in them, even when they're pessimistic, because they're poets as well as playwrights, and I like what they do with words. Ionesco and Pinter belong in the cinema where pictures and pauses are more important than words. And speaking of words, exciting words in the theatre, look at the plays of John Arden, the best of the young playwrights today. I have an aggressive admiration for his 'Serjeant Musgrave's Dance'. But those absurd fellas, they'd put years on you. It's obvious they were never touched by the Holy Ghost.'

He was also fed up with what he called the 'primaqueera' element that he associated with the absurd ties in the theatre – 'the bona fide homosexuals and pseudo-intellectuals who infest the theatre'. By coincidence, while we were checking through some letters, I came across several that he had written twenty years ago to a friend in the London theatre. At that time he had expresssd similar views, and when the friend protested that Sean was prejudiced, he had replied: 'I shouldn't call dislike of "conceited amateurs, arrogant homosexuals, & impertinent dilettantes" a prejudice. I hate them – except when they're comic, like most of our Irish ones. We don't hate enough in England. The English don't know how. They think it a virtue. It isn't. It shows lack of life force.' To which he added 'amen' twenty years later.

But at eighty-four and approaching blindness he was not yet reary to say 'amen' to life. Somehow he managed to press on with his work, a new book of essays. Every day he sketched out some ideas or wrote letters, writing laboriously with a pen or tapping away at the typewriter, and his wife knew things were going well if she heard him humming tunes to himself. But since his failing sight prevented him from re-reading what he had written, he had to have his wife or a friend read it back to him so that he could think about where he had been and where he was going, make various changes, and move on again. The genial gardener came by once a week and he helped out with the reading and writing, also doing some of the re-typing. It was a slow and frustrating process, one which would have defeated anyone except a man like Sean, who was as patient as he was stubborn. So he went on with his words, asking and seeking and knocking. He was disturbed because his eyes were so bad that he could no longer read books. He regretted that he couldn't re-read Joyce, Shaw, Yeats, and George Moore, though he still retained a remarkable memory of their works. Joyce he loved the most. 'He tells us everything in *Finnegan's Wake*, that beautiful book of reality. I don't know what a lot of it means, but he created such magical patterns of words that I feel them long before I understand them; and often I simply feel them without understanding them. Only a true poet can do that to us.'

When we were together in June, talking about religion, he suddenly pointed his palms under his chin and chanted, 'In the name of Annah the Allmaziful, the Everliving, the Bringer of Plurabilities, haloed be her eve, her singtime sung, her rill be run, unhemmed as it is uneven.' He and his wife often talked about

152

Ulysses and *Dubliners*, especially their favourite story, *The Dead*. Eileen read to him every day, he listened to talks and plays on the radio, and to the recordings of classics sent down by the Society for the Blind.

I had read to him on our final evening together. We had taken a short walk before tea, up to the wall of St Mary's Church – in previous times we had regularly gone the whole distance around the wall and come back through the peaceful churchyard – and later we settled comfortably in his room. 'Don't call it my study', he corrected me, 'it's where I work'. There was signs of his work everywhere in the room. Crowded bookcases lined the walls and overflowed on the floor; piles of books and magazines were scattered over the large round table, at one end of which was an old Underwood typewriter with a half-typed sheet of paper in it; beside the machine a green eye-shade was hung over a goose-neck lamp; on the window ledge were two boxes stuffed with in-coming and outgoing letters; a red morocco folder on the bed was full of sheets of paper on which he had scrawled notes and random phrases. The electric fire glowed brightly, and there was a pungent smell of tobacco in the air. Sean sat on the bed puffing at his pipe, his legs stretched out and crossed at the ankles, a red and white Tashkent beanie on the back of his head.

'Are ye there, truepenny?' he called.

'I see you have the new edition of poetry by Austin Clarke and Patrick Kavanagh.'

I had been browsing through some of the books on the table.

'Eileen was reading them to me. Clarke's a better poet than any of us knew, a fine poet. Poor fella, he was overshadowed by Yeats. But Yeats's shadow fell over everyone.'

I read some of Clarke's poems aloud. Eileen had read *Forget Me Not* to him, so I began with the title poem of *Flight to Africa*, which drew some hearty laughter from him. Then I read from the *Later Poems* – *Inscription for a Headstone*, *Three Poems about Children*, *The Blackbird of Derrycairn*, and *Night and Morning*.

'Read the Headstone once again', he asked, 'the one about Larkin.'

> *What Larkin bawled to hungry crowds*
> *Is murmured now in dining-hall*
> *And study. Faith bestirs itself*
> *Lest infidels in their impatience*
> *Leave it behind. Who could have guessed*
> *Batons were blessings in disguise;*

153

> *When every ambulance was filled*
> *With half-killed men and Sunday trampled*
> *Upon unrest? Such fears can harden*
> *Or soften heart, knowing too clearly*
> *His name endures on our holiest page,*
> *Scrawled in a rage by Dublin's poor.*

He was deeply moved by this ironic poem, for he had lived through the 'Bloody Sunday' that it celebrated; he had served under Larkin at the time as secretary of the Irish Citizen Army; and he saw himself as one of the 'infidels' of 1913. His voice thickened with a Dubliner's rage at the mention of those times and Jim Larkin, the man he had called the Irish Prometheus. Then we talked about Jim Plunkett, who had written a play about Larkin and was now writing a novel about the events leading up to the 1913 strike. 'Are there any people over there besides Jim Plunkett who still care about Larkin's Dublin?' he asked. 'Really care in their Christian hearts?' He relit his pipe angrily and sent great clouds of smoke billowing through the room.

He was silent for a while, and I began to read some of Kavanagh's poems of which he seemed to like *Kerr's Ass* and passages from *The Great Hunger* the best. When I had finished reading the last lines of *The Great Hunger*,

> *The hungry fiend*
> *Screams the apocalypse of clay*
> *In every corner of this land.*

it was clear that he was still brooding about Larkin. 'There it is again, the hungry fiend, in Mucker or in Dublin, and it takes the rage of a poet to put it right. Larkin was the poet of the people. Why even Yeats, aristocrat though he was – in his own mind not in his class – spoke out for Larkin and the workers.'

So we came at last to Yeats, and the poems of Yeats. Contrary to what many people thought, Sean insisted, he did not feel bitter towards Yeats because of the Abbey Theatre's rejection of 'The Silver Tassie'. 'I was bloody mad at him, not bitter. That was in 1928 when I had a wife and a kid on the way, so the rejection meant hard times for the O'Caseys. But it wasn't only that, I was ripping mad because he was wrong about my play. And I still think he was wrong. Maybe one day there'll be a real production of that play – it's still one of my favourites, and I can see the whole thing, in my mind, glowing on a stage – then we'll find out who was right about it. After the rejection there were people in Dublin who did feel bitter towards Yeats – they always had, mainly because they were jealous and afraid of him – and they tried to get me to join them and go against him. Well, I told them what they could do with their dirty game, they could stuff it where the monkey put the nut. Yeats was wrong about my play, but he made the Abbey a great theatre, he and Lady Gregory. After he died it went downhill. There was no one left to fight for it and protect it from the political and clerical yahoos who torment the artist in Ireland. They're the fellas I feel bitter about.'

Then he began to praise Yeats as a poet. He didn't think much of him as a playwright. 'His poems are more dramatic than his plays, and his plays are really poems.' I began to read Yeats' poems to him, some of the *Last Poems*, which he especially wanted to hear. I read *The Circus Animals' Desertion*, *Parnell*, and *The Spur*. Then I mentioned that Liam Miller had set some of the poems to traditional Irish airs and had them sung by a group of young ballad singers in one of Dublin's pocket theatres during the previous summer. This interested him and I read several of them, *The Three Bushes* and *The Ghost of Roger Casement*. He enjoyed them and said they had a word-music of their own which revealed another side of Yeats, his close touch with the people, from whom he usually remained aloof. 'That was part of his greatness', Sean said, 'he hated the Irish crowd but he loved the Irish people.'

We closed out the evening with *Under Ben Bulben*, and Sean quoted the well-known fifth section from memory:

> *Irish poets, learn your trade,*
> *Sing whatever is well made,*
> *Scorn the sort now growing up*
> *All out of shape from toe to top,*
> *Their unremembering hearts and heads,*
> *Base-born products of base beds.*
> *Sing the peasantry, and then*
> *Hard-riding country gentlemen,*
> *The holiness of monks, and after*
> *Porter-drinkers' randy laughter;*
> *Sing the lords and ladies gay*
> *That were beaten into the clay*
> *Through seven heroic centuries;*

> *Cast your mind on other days*
> *That we in coming days may be*
> *Still the indomitable Irishry.*

'Good poetry', he said, 'but bad advice for Irish poets. Is it the Ireland of aristocratic parasites and enslaved peasants he's asking us to go back to? The Ireland of plaster saints and hedge scholars? The Ireland of the Big House and the little people? The Ireland of purple dust? Not bloody likely we'll go back to those corpses. But it's still a damn fine poem. And so like Yeats, to make good poetry of bad opinions. I wonder why he wasn't up to saying the same thing about "The Tassie", that I might be able to write a good play out of what he thought were bad opinions? Ah, that's a head without a tail.'

Yeats had tried to make some amends for his rejection of 'The Silver Tassie' when, in 1935, he finally had the play performed at the Abbey Theatre, in spite of virulent opposition. Thus, one of Yeats' last of many famous fights at the Abbey was for O'Casey; and when the two men met in Dublin for what turned out to be a final reunion in September of 1935 – it was O'Casey's last visit to Ireland, and Yeats died four years later – they settled their differences as men, though they remained in different worlds as artists, but both of them symbolic of 'the indomitable Irishry' in their different ways.

Eileen had come in with a pot of tea for the road, for it was late and soon I would be leaving for America. When I finally stood up to go, Sean said, 'My favourite lines of Yeats are not from the last poems but from his first play, "The Countess Kathleen". Do you remember what Oona says at the end, after the Countess has given up her soul to save Ireland?' And he intoned softly:

> *'Tell them who walk upon the floor of peace*
> *That I would die and go to her I love;*
> *The years like great black oxen tread the world,*
> *And God the Herdsman goads them on behind,*
> *And I am broken by their passing feet.'*

We walked out to the porch and he embraced me in a tender bear-hug.

'We've heard the chimes at midnight', he said.

'Bless you, Sean.'

'And you, too. Give my love to America.'

'See you next summer.'

'Right-o', he smiled, 'next summer, and all the summers that warm the green world.'

It was a clear night and the sky over St Marychurch was ablaze with stars. What are the stars? I didn't know, but I knew they were all up there, 'all of them in the one blue sky that shelters every mother's son'. As I reached the end of the garden, I turned for one last look and caught a glimpse of him through the trees, standing at the top of the steps. He was still there in the gentle night, gazing at the stars.

I feel now as I felt then, that he would always be there, as long as the summers warmed the green world.

10

NOTES ON A SERMON

THESE notes for a sermon in memory of Sean O'Casey were prepared by the Dean of Christ Church Cathedral, Dublin, the late Very Rev. N. D. Emerson. He preached the sermon on 15 November 1964.

Ecclus II, 12: 'There is one who is slow and needs help, who lacks strength and abounds in poverty; but the eyes of the Lord look upon him for his good; He lifts him up out of his low estate and raises up his head, so that many are amazed at him.'

1. Why commemorate him here?
    (a) He was a very distinguished citizen of Dublin
    (b) This is the Cathedral Church of Dublin
    (c) Sean O'Casey was born and reared in the Church of Ireland.
2. My personal interest is that:
    (a) I was rector of the Parish of St Mary in which he lived as a child, the Church of his baptism.
    (b) In the same year as he, and in the same parish, was baptised Sara Allgood, who gave unforgettable interpretations of some of O'Casey's most significant women characters.
    (c) I spent many years around the scenes and among the people immortalised in O'Casey's plays, and know that the plays are photographic – a stranger to the life of the Dublin tenements might think O'Casey's characters are all caricatures or are merely comical. Ignorant audiences have laughed at tragedy on the stage but tragedy is not the less tragic for being narrated in the accents of a Dublin slum. The sentimentalist walking through the same streets under the influence of Georgian Dublin may dream of rich interiors, of carriages and crinolines and romance by candlelight; but as O'Casey knew them they were the overcrowded and insanitary haunts of poverty. As we know them they are likely to collapse, as two did recently with the loss of human life – their days, thank God, are numbered.
    (d) In the first volume of O'Casey's autobiography the parish clergyman who insisted, he tells us, on his attending school

while suffering from a severe disease of the eyes, is named the Rev. T. R. S. Hunter – T.R.S. were the initials of the curate of St Mary's, and Hunter came from the Rector's name which was Dr James Hunter Monahan. The description of the clergyman's appearance fits the curate, not the Rector, of nearly eighty years ago. Children of that day got little sympathy or understanding.

3. Naturally, Sean O'Casey has his detractors – he has been called a Communist and an Atheist. In Ireland the term Communist is often no more than a convenient word to describe those who think the current social order could be improved. It would be asking too much to expect a man whose early years were spent in the tenements of nineteenth-century Dublin and whose early manhood experienced the Dublin strike of 1913, and who used the intelligence God gave him in good measure, to say that he saw no need for a radical change in the human situation. He called himself a Rationalist in later life but I don't think he ever disparaged the ethical teaching of our Lord Jesus Christ. Anyhow, Christianity is not irrational. What if he called himself a Communist? It is not a word of precise definition, and I think the dramatist was of too individual a character to want any totalitarian system.

So, too, with the word Atheist; it defies definition, and commonly means someone who does not conform to the conventional practices of the Traditional Churches. Perhaps he railed a little against religious practices, but it looks as though he rebelled against the ways in which religion was practised rather than against the deepest truths of that religion which is the religion of eternity. 'Atheist' may mean a rejection of the customary forms of religion, a rejection in part due to the contrast between creed and conduct which may be discerned in most of us.

Further, O'Casey's writings show a quite remarkable familiarity with the language and thought of Holy Scriptures, and with the Book of Common Prayer. Those who know the Bible and the Book of Common Prayer will perceive this noteworthy fact. Had he rejected these things with scorn they would not have sunk their imprint upon his mind as they did. Some say he was a blasphemer, and profane things occur in plenty in his writings, but are not unwitting profanities and blasphemies almost our native idiom? O'Casey characters on the stage speak as real people speak – in this as in many other ways he holds a mirror up to nature, and that may not add to his popularity.

4. Some who disliked O'Casey's politics have further disliked the fact of his Protestantism – to some the Protestantism of the republican O'Casey is an indigestible fact; to others the republicanism of the Protestant O'Casey is equally indigestible. You may recall that in the volume *I Knock at the Door* the little boy Johnny is puzzled over the discovery that Wolfe Tone, and Henry Grattan and Parnell etc., were Protestants – possibly that discovery moulded his thoughts and his future in a decisive way.

O'Casey was a Protestant, and the child of Protestant parents.

*St Barnabas Church, where he worshipped. It figured in
'Red Roses for Me'*

In the account he gives of his invalid father he dwells upon his father's studies and the books he treasured – he tells us the names of some of them and they show his zealous interest in Protestant principles and religious controversy – he does not disclose that his father had been for years associated with the Irish Church Missions, and his collection of books was what one would expect to find in those circumstances.

It may be noted, too, that O'Casey was no anti-clerical; whatever he may have felt about the curate of St Mary's, he had immense and affectionate regard for the Rev. Edward Griffin, Rector of St Barnabas's parish, East Wall. You will remember how Mr Griffin figures in 'Red Roses for Me', where the background is St Barnabas's Parish and its colony of Ulster railway workers who were members of the Orange Order.

Not many years ago a research student from an American university asked me for some information about the O'Casey background in St Mary's parish, and then went on to inquire if there had been a church of ours in the city called 'The Church of the Twelve Apostles'. I said there was no such church of that dedication and asked him what made him think there was. He replied that he had asked Sean O'Casey if he had been a Roman Catholic, and O'Casey had answered, 'No, I belong to the Church of the Twelve Apostles'. I was too stupid at the time not to see that he meant that Rome was the Church of St Peter but we were the church of all the Apostles. My American friend was no wiser, so we missed a typical O'Casey *jeu d'esprit*. He had already called the Parish Church of Clontarf, St John Baptist's, where he was confirmed, because our Lord's Apostles were figures in the East window – so we read in volume two of his autobiography *Pictures in the Hallway*.

5. Secular students of O'Casey may investigate the ways by which the Protestant child, while remaining firmly Protestant, developed into the ardent Nationalist and republican – essential as that is to an understanding of O'Casey, it must not be discussed here. For us the man we commemorate is the man of letters, no insignificant figure in the distinguished line of Dublin dramatists – we think of Sheridan, Wilde, Shaw and O'Casey, all of them Dublin men – but O'Casey alone has immortalised the hopes and fears, the loves and hates of the plain people of this city. He dramatised without exaggeration, for exaggeration was not needed; and he has put real people on the stage. He can portray patriotic bluster as faithfully as National idealism – but far more significant, he had revealed in those plays which took us by storm forty years ago the faith and the charity which shine like a halo upon the squalors and trials of tenement life – no one could bring out better than he the virtues which blossom in the dust, and the failings which are our common inheritance.
6. Further, let it be said that O'Casey, in his famous plays and in his remarkable autobiographies, has given us most important and historical and sociological material: the Dublin of the late

161

nineteenth and early twentieth centuries has no more adept social historian – for that, too, he has earned an immortality.

7. Today, therefore, we honour the memory of a son of our city, and a son of the Church of Ireland: we assign to him no moral or spiritual perfections – he and we are alike sinful – but he was one of us, and he brought, and will go on bringing, literary renown to Ireland. We take a decent pride in that long life which rose to fame over many obstacles.

No verdict on O'Casey is called for here – let us be content to remember his own words from *Sunset and Evening Star*: 'It is difficult enough for us to judge the things of time; it is beyond us to judge the things of eternity.'

PART TWO

THE O'CASEY I KNEW . . .

Anecdotes collected
by Colm Cronin

THE O'CASEY I KNEW

Collected by Colm Cronin

THIS chapter contains the memories, anecdotes, reminiscences, and opinions of several people who at some stage of their lives came into contact with Sean O'Casey.

Although there are only ten contributors they all have something to add, some little piece of information which throws that extra bit of light on O'Casey himself or on some particular event or occurrence.

Most of these have been connected with the Abbey Theatre in its early days and these give us a fresh picture of the playwright, fresh in so far as they remember the man at the beginning of his career. The others met him out of interest or business and, perhaps, they present a more objective view. All were deeply impressed and found that the man himself was very different (on most occasions) from the conception of him which they had derived from his writings.

Time tints the memory and brings about a certain amount of imagination when some of these people try to bring to mind their connections and conversations with the man. One must allow for this and yet be thankful for the portrait that is etched by all.

* * *

Kit Casey (John Christopher) is a nephew of O'Casey's who lives in Caledon Road. A stevedore, he is one of the few O'Caseys living in Dublin.

To me his name is Jack, although we know who you're talking about when you refer to Sean O'Casey, although really there's no such name.

He didn't come from Limerick as has been said. His grandfather came from Cahirciveen in Kerry and when he came to Dublin he turned from Catholic to a Protestant.

He started writing first when he was in 25 Hawthorne Terrace, where they had a little stage of their own, with footlights and all; oil lamps they used to use.

They weren't as poverty-stricken as the books say. He wasn't a poor boy as depicted by some writers. While he was with the O'Caseys he never knew what want was.

Uncle Mick was the brains of the family. He was responsible for all the wit in the first three plays. They were all Mick's original wit, who was a very intelligent man. He got first place in a civil service examination you know. There are pen sketches of him in the Central Model School you know, and I believe they say that he is the brother of Sean O'Casey. He was a success at anything he went at. You know that Fluther is Mick and that all those phrases are Mick's. I was with him when he went to see 'Juno' and he turned to me and said, 'Kit, that's me'. Give us a mug or a jug, derogatory, Johnny get your gun boy; all those are Mick's words.

He never referred to Mick, only when he went away. I suppose it's because Mick was living and he was the only one who'd contradict him about anything he said. *Inishfallen* was only published after he was dead. The remarks about Mick weren't truthful. Mick himself wrote songs and poems, spontaneously and he'd sing them himself too. The brothers never had much time for Jack. He was a square peg in a round hole. The way he pictured the family as poverty-stricken was very wrong. There are several mistakes in his autobiographies, he said he buried my father but I have the bill here from Kerrigan in the North Strand, who traded under the name O'Neill.

And he didn't bury his mother either. Mick buried his mother. He never worked. Only fifteen months with the Great Northern Railway and a few months with a builder that he knew but if his mother hadn't some hot scones ready for him when he came in in the evening she'd get a scolding from that terrible tongue of his. You know he borrowed twenty sovereigns from my mother and he hadn't the decency to pay it back.

He wrote plays at the expense of the ingenuity of his brothers and when he fell out with Mick and when he went away he couldn't write a good Dublin play.

He was a curious type of youngster. If you asked him for a match you wouldn't get it unless you asked him in Irish. It was the same way with clothes. All the clothes he wore had to be made in Ireland, he was very Irish and nationalistic. But of course he had to change all that when he went to England.

I never cared for him or got on with him. One day I was in his room with a friend of mine, where he had some shift bookshelves and this fellow was at one of the books. I told him to

165

leave them alone and then I heard Uncle Jack's footsteps coming up the stairs. Well he caught my friend with the book, *The Imitations of Christ* it was, and took it off him, looked at it and then he blamed me for it. Then he threw another book at me and told me to read it but when I looked at it I wasn't interested in it and I told him so. 'You know as much about Charlie Chaplin and Tom Mix as Peter and Paul', he said.

At the time we lived at 6 Oxford Terrace. My father seemed to be the most popular of the O'Caseys and every Sunday evening they'd all meet in our house. A family within a family, very proud and they kept together. They all met for a social evening and they used to sing and recite and so on. Mick always asked Johnny to sing. I remember he sang *The West's Awake* one evening. Sometimes he'd sing in Irish but that was a foreign language to us at the time. One evening he brought the pipes along and when he was asked to do something he played them. Well, you know yourself that the sound of bagpipes in a house is disgusting. The following week when he tried to fill them with wind he couldn't do it. Mick had got a gimlet and bored a hole in them, so that, as he said, he'd never play the blasted things again.

He was christened in St Mary's church. When they had the pipe band going they used to parade around the city from Seville Place. Well, one day they turned into Mary Street with Jack leading the band. A member of the Dublin Metropolitan Police came up to him and told him that he couldn't have a band playing within the church limits while a service was going on. But the band wasn't playing at the time, only marching past. Jack would only converse in Irish and he was brought to the Bridewell and brought before a judge. He would only give his name in Irish and he told the judge that he was going to address the court in a language that he didn't know. Anyhow he told him that the band wasn't playing within the limits of the church as forbidden by law. 'You have the Minister here to testify against me but I know the man well for he baptised me in that very church', he said. And the result was that he was let go.

I knew a lot of those characters that are in the plays. Rosie was a girl in Church Street. She was well known and I knew Mrs Tancred. Young Tancred was found dead in Jamestown Road. A sister of his was married to a cousin of mine. Big Tom had a pub in the North Strand. Uncle Peter was quite a character. I won't tell you his name. He was a great man, quite different from

166

the man in the play, quite the opposite in fact. He belonged to all the movements. He was a very small man who never got the top boots to fit him. He was very patriotic and in no way cowardly. I often thought that the young Covey was married to another cousin of mine. Anyway I think that he got the idea for him from this fellow who was always a Red, always preaching that kind of stuff.

There's a lot said about him going away and it's not true. They have it all wrong. Fallon (Gabriel) didn't even know that he was going away. He went over for the transfer of a play from the Royalty Theatre to the Fortune. The producers wanted him over you see. And he met his wife to be and he fell in love. He never had any intention of stopping but it just was destiny, though he was sour with the Abbey. And he had to collect the Hawthornden Prize too. So he decided to stay and that was that.

*   *   *

Miss Ria Mooney acted, and later directed in the Abbey Theatre for several years. She is one of the twenty-five new Abbey shareholders recently appointed by the Irish Government.

I was in the Rathmines and Rathgar Musical Society in 1924 but I had never heard a word about him until after 'Juno'. I never saw it until I joined the Abbey. Of course I had seen him many times, I mean I must have but I have no clear memory of him. The first time I recollect was the opening of the 'Plough'. I remember him before it, his face was very animated and his eyes were all screwed up. Afterwards I met him. I was going home and you had to cross over the stage in those days to get out. Well the stage was empty and Sean was coming over from the other side and for the only time I saw that his face was white, expressionless, without any animation whatsoever. He stopped me and thanked me for the way I played Rosie. He said I saved his play. If the people had disliked Rosie the other two acts would have failed. He said I made them like her and I wondered how, and what he meant when he said that I saved his play.

During breaks we used to go into a lane at the back of the Abbey and I used to see country girls out there, about fifteen years of age or so and they used always to be with soldiers. They had glittering eyes and white faces with red rings of crimson paint on their cheeks. I commented on them to someone and I was told that they were prostitutes. And I felt so sorry for them that

167

when the Covey called me a prostitute I was hurt, hurt on their behalf. I must have conveyed this feeling to the audience and I got sympathy from them. That I suppose is what he meant when he said that I saved his play.

Thursday night was the night the riots started. I can remember well a young man with black hair in the stalls (I often wonder who he was), and he was waving his fist at me and telling me to get off the stage, that I was a disgrace to my sex, my religion and my country.

You know that they tried to kidnap Barry Fitzgerald, Shelagh Richards and myself. Someone came knocking at our door but I wouldn't let my father open the door and let them in. We had to go to the Theatre every other night by car. During my act the lights would be put on in the auditorium and the walls were lined with detectives. They threw pieces of coal, pennies, anything they had. Some nights later they used stink bombs.

My school friends cut me for playing in it. Some people, friends of mine, came to me and asked me if I was going to play that horrible character. They said that I should tell my father confessor. Of course I had no intention of telling my father confessor, but before the first night I mentioned it to a priest, but he only laughed and said 'Aren't you an actress?'

When the curtain came down the riots began. Some woman tried to set fire to the curtain and it was raised. Several climbed up on the stage and I still can see Barry Fitzgerald in fisticuffs with a man who had climbed up.

One distinguished actor dissociated himself from O'Casey's plays and I think that Sean never forgave him.

One day there was a matinee, so instead of going home we all stayed on for tea. During the interval we had tea in the green-room and Gort cake. Rummel, the well-known pianist, came along with Lady Gregory and he played for us. That was the only time I ever spoke to Lady Gregory. She put her hand on my shoulder and said 'You've done well, very well, little girl'.

At that time there was a meeting of Cumann na mBan and Sean was asked to defend his play. Shelagh Richards, Gabriel Fallon, Barry Fitzgerald, Frank Hugh O'Donnell, Lyle Donaghy (the poet in whom Yeats was very interested) and myself all went along with Sean to support him. It was the first time I heard Maude Gomme speak. She attacked his plays and mentioned Mary Bentham and her child.

Well when Sean went up to defend himself he could hardly speak as his eyes were very sore from the lights, and he asked if he could wear his cap to protect his eyes from the glare. He put it on but it didn't do any good for he still couldn't continue. One felt very sorry for him. The whole thing turned out to be a fiasco. He couldn't defend himself.

I met him in London at the time he was writing 'Tassie' and he told me that he had spent three weeks trying to write the Corporal's speech. He liked to go amongst the workers at the time and talk to them but he had to give it up because they tipped their caps to him and called him Sir. He didn't like that and I often wonder if that was why he dressed rather shabbily afterwards.

I asked him why he didn't live in Dublin and he told me that he never would because the people were so horrid to him.

I never knew a Sean O'Casey who wasn't kind, gentle and sensitive. But he wasn't shy. He'd come into the green-room after a performance and if he thought so he'd say that we were bloody awful, which, of course, didn't endear him to a lot of people.

At the time I was going to direct 'Red Roses for Me' he was living in England. I wrote to him about production and he'd write back, sometimes contradicting what he had written in a previous letter. We had a vitriolic correspondence and you know it wasn't too safe at the time to be getting letters from Totnes with a stamp on the back which said 'Friends of the Soviet Union'.

Well we seemed to be getting nowhere and Sir Bronson Albery suggested that I go over and stay with him for a while, for five minutes' conversation would be a lot better than all the correspondence.

When I arrived, Eileen and that lovely son of theirs, Niall, who died later, met me and they were so friendly. There was an intangible middle-class Dublin atmosphere about the house. When we were going in to have high tea Sean joined us, I think he had been writing in the study. I was very glad to see him and I think that he felt so and everything was forgotten.

I was after reading *Drums Under the Window* and I mentioned it to him and how I found that the tempo increased as it went on. Towards the end the writing becomes so rapid that I found it hard to read it, it was so fast. Well we talked about it and his writing and he said to me, and it was only then that he mentioned those vitriolic letters, 'When I take a pen into my hand something comes over me and I can't help being bitter, even when I write letters.'

*   *   *

Mr Paddy McDonnell is a former Dublin County Gaelic footballer who was connected with nationalistic activities towards the beginning of the century.

Sean O'Casey

I got to know him through the O'Toole Pipers Band. He was the first secretary in 1916. We had meetings then and we used to discuss various things, books and plays and such. George Bernard Shaw was his favourite. I think that he aped Shaw to perfection. He always quoted him.

The two of us started a dramatic class. He took part in the first play we produced, 'Nabocklish'. He played the Englishman, he was a peculiar Englishman with the big boots on stage. That was put on at 41 Parnell Square and later at the back of the houses in Leinster Avenue. At these classes he cottoned on to a girl called Maura.

Later he became friendly with Frank Cahill, a teacher. They started the band. The first play he put on paper was about Cahill, called 'The Flower and the Frost'. We wouldn't touch it at all, it was too personal. Cahill and himself went for walks along the canal banks. It was from Cahill that he got all his stuff for his plays.

Fluther Good was a parishioner of ours. All those people in his early plays were entities at the time. Frank took an action against some of the theatres at the time and he got a ha'penny damages. It was the Countess Markievicz who urged him on because O'Casey had left the Citizen Army because of the Countess and this was a throwback at him, although he did a lot for the Cahill family.

He had an old friend, Canon Brady. The canon was very fond of Sean. He thought that he'd convert him but he hadn't a ghost of a chance. O'Casey would quote the Koran to him.

He showed me several poems of his which were read at the club. We had meetings when we used to read like that in the club once a month and afterwards the listeners would criticise it. I remember advising him to submit them to a magazine and to send his plays to someone to read and his answer was 'nobody would prostitute his brains'.

There's one little incident that shows how fanatical he was to do things. At the club we used to have mock battles at times, just for training you know. Well one Sunday night we started a mock attack, boarded the room, barred the doors, and the lot and Sean was to try and gain entry. We beat him back with sticks and brushes and when he tried to get in the window but he actually kept at it until he finally got in. The language was terrible he lost his temper and cursed us all. He was 'brought up' for using bad language but eventually the thing was forgotten about.

171

He was always Labour and Larkin was his little God. He idolised Larkin. He was always talking about him as were the people who left the I.R.B. with him. They just had a row with us, there was nothing dirty about it but a few left with him.

I think that when he left the country he forgot all about us, he lost himself. He got more bigoted than he was previously. I only went to see the 'Plough'. If there had been no riot he wouldn't have got that far. He lost caste with our boys for being anti-national and anti-religious. That's what really happened with myself. I used to visit him at 422 North Circular Road, then I lost touch with him.

I went to visit him when he returned in 1936. He was staying at the Standard Hotel. He was his natural self, still friendly. He always made the point of trying to get his Irish over and he used it on every possible occasion. I never saw him after that visit.

* * *

Mr Paddy Sheils lives in Spencer Avenue, off Seville Place, in the area in which O'Casey lived as a youngster.

I remember him as a young fellow, I was only ten or eleven at the time. The family used to live in the room down below us and I remember seeing him going in and out with books and papers under his arm. He used to sit in a back room, a very small room, at night studying with a candle, a small one that only cost a farthing then or with an oil lamp.

I never remember him doing any work although they say that he used to work on the docks. But I don't think so. Now and again he worked for the G.N.R. (Great Northern Railway) but that was only casual work at the time.

Our families never bothered much with one another. He didn't talk that much. Now Mick was different, not like Johnny. His mother was bitter in her own way about religion you know. So maybe that's why we never bothered much.

There was a shop belonging to Mrs Brady at the corner, where the butcher's is now. She took a liking to Johnny and she used to have him in there singing songs and he used to sing some of them in Irish, he was learning it at the time.

They used to go to St Barnabas's Church on a Sunday evening and you know after the service they'd sing 'God Save the King (or Queen)'. Well Johnny used to be silent for that, he'd never join in and didn't some of the women complain to the minister

172

about this, saying that he should like the rest of them. When the minister got on to him over it Johnny said that he wouldn't sing it and he never would. And he never went back any Sunday evening after that.

*   *   *

Harry Brogan at sixty-one is the oldest member of the Abbey Players. He joined the company in 1926, later left and rejoined some eleven years afterwards. Since then he has played in almost every major production and is regarded by the critics as one of the finest actors to have trod the Dublin stage. Some have even stated that he has, on occasions, surpassed F. J. McCormick at his best.

I first met him in 1917 in a pub across from the old Abbey. From the first time I saw him I took him to be a man who, in my estimation, wanted to go places before his time. He wanted to get there by hook or by crook. He was doing nothing at the time, only trying to get his plays in and he had this humble playing-down attitude of 'poor me'.

He was secretary of the Citizen Army and he left it because he saw that it was going to become militant. He didn't like my face, said the Countess (Markievicz). The face he didn't like was the face of Ireland. He got on the mail boat because he was a worn bitter old man and if he remained he'd still be with us.

He owed more as an Irishman to the Abbey and the Abbey Players than anyone. It made him. Only they did his first plays; he'd never have got anywhere.

Ireland let me down, he said. Ireland never let him down. He didn't stand and fight and he's never given a reason except 'Ireland let me down'. If he didn't get his plays on then he'd never be heard of today. I just hold that he wasn't a good Irishman. Now Shaw was. He stood out for the men of 1916. O'Casey was a jumped up cod of an Irishman and if he loved his country he'd have stayed. In none of his works has he given proper reason and he wasn't at all like he appeared in that silly film.

Another thing, he was the great social revolutionary yet he went down to Coole under the wing of Lady G. (Gregory) as they called her. He mentioned in one of his books how the gracious lady used to go down every morning and give apples to the kids, as if that was the biggest thing in life.

You heard the great story about when F. J. McCormick played Seamus Shields in the first production of the 'Shadow of a Gunman'. Afterwards O'Casey came up the stairs and said to him 'You're after making a hames of my play, Mr Mac'. 'How did I make a hames of your play'? asked F. J. 'You made a hames of it at that particular line when Donal says "I remember a time when you yourself believed in nothing but the gun" and Shields says, "Aye when there wasn't a bloody gun in the country".' Anyway F. J. asked him, 'how would you say the line?' and O'Casey replied 'Oh, but I'm not an actor'.

I always abhor him for condemning his brother over drink. He slated Mick. I think that he could have left him out altogether. I think that he's written all those things to build himself up as the great O'Casey. 'I had a brother a drunkard.' 'I looked after me mother.' Millions of people at that time did the same. You got the impression in the film that he hadn't a penny, and that he hadn't the money to bury his mother. Well there was a saying, if they don't bury me for pride they'll have to bury me for stink. In the film they said that the undertaker wouldn't bury her because he hadn't any money but any undertaker at the time in Dublin did so and you paid him later when you had it. The way he went on you'd think that he was the only man who ever had a mother.

I played in the 'Tassie', in the 'Plough', in the 'Gunman', in 'Juno'. I think that I played in everything. All the critics have praised me as being the great exponent of O'Casey yet I abhor him as an Irishman. All those books were an attack against Ireland. When playing at the Aldwych in London I met his wife, he was too sick to attend, and she said 'Joxer, you made his play'. They wrote especially to Dublin saying that I was to be brought to Paris for the Festival. That they weren't to go without me, but I couldn't.

I knew George Lawlor, the man who started the 'Plough' riots, very well. He used to come out to visit me very often. He had every reason to. The Church Street Boys' Brigade wouldn't bring their flag into a pub. I think that it was a disgrace.

A friend of mine, Hugh Masterson, who was over the Father Matthew Players, wrote a letter to O'Casey one time: 'Dear Mr O'Casey, would you mind reducing the royalties on the "Plough and the Stars" which we are putting on to raise money for a church rebuilding fund.' And he wrote back: 'As those crowd of publishers never gave me a crust when I was in Dublin the royalties are now doubled.'

*   *   *

Christine Hayden is a retired Abbey actress who joined the company in 1917. She played Mrs Anderson in the first production of the 'The Shadow of a Gunman' and two years later she played the part of Mrs Tancred in 'Juno and the Paycock'. She is married to Eric Gorman, secretary at the Abbey.

I started with the Abbey in 1917. I knew him to see him although it was really only when the 'Shadow' was done that I came to know him at all. I found him very quiet, nice, downright, shy in the beginning almost as if you'd think that he had an inferiority complex. But he became more sure of himself with success.

I played Mrs Anderson in the 'Shadow'. It was a lovely show. In 'Juno' I was Mrs Tancred and there's one thing about him that I remember when doing 'Juno'. Well when rehearsing there was no reaction at all, of course, with no audience. But on the first night it was different. You know in the second act there's terrific jollity and Maureen Delaney was singing 'If I were a blackbird' and everything was going great. Sean was very anxious about the whole thing, he never went out in front at all.

I was in the wings ready to go on and I said to him 'I hope they won't laugh at me when I go on'. He turned round to me and said, 'They wouldn't dare'. Well everything went fine and when I came off he looked at me and said, 'What did I tell you?'

Of the man I remember him coming into the green-room telling yarns to F. J. McCormick. Barry Fitzgerald and himself were very friendly, and also Arthur Shields. He used to dress very shoddy, an Ulster and a cap and of course his eyes were bad. He sort of squinted. And he looked older and rather haggard-looking for his age.

I was there the night of the row, at the side of the stage when Yeats made his wonderful speech. Oh, it was really terrible. It was ridiculous to my mind. You'd think that we were an island of saints and scholars and that there wasn't a prostitute amongst us. Rosie was done in a very inoffensive way.

He attended rehearsals, sitting in the stalls. But he never interfered except to whisper a word of a suggestion in Lennox's (Robinson) ear.

I remember at the 'Shadow' I said to him 'Sean, you must be very proud of the success of it'. 'Indeed I'm not', he said. 'I've been knocking at the door of the Abbey for many years. 'Twould

175

have been better when the money would have been very useful to my mother.' He was very devoted to his mother.

He felt very deeply about things. Any man who could write as he did must have.

He was very fond of Lady Gregory and she admired him very much. She took him under her wing more or less.

I had a letter from him once, he wrote a wonderful hand, and he ended it with a quote from the 'Shadow', 'Am I right or wrong Mr Gallagher?' Oh he was a great letter writer. In England he used always write what milk he wanted in longhand when you'd think that his wife would do it.

One thing I am certain of, the moment he left this country he lost something. Around the city he could tell you, there's so-and-so, people in his plays that he had based characters on. But he didn't know the English people.

There's a story I heard recently about a certain man, whose name I won't tell you for various reasons, who when he was in England went to Torquay to see O'Casey. He had never met the man before but anyway he went to the house and knocked at the door and Sean came out. 'I've come to see Sean O'Casey', he said. 'Well you've seen him', says Sean and shut the door.

*　　　*　　　*

Dr John Larchet, now with the Royal Irish Academy, conducted the orchestra in the early days of the Abbey.

I was with the Abbey from 1908 until 1935, conducting the orchestra. Well you wouldn't call it an orchestra but an ensemble. 'The Plough and the Stars' opened on a Monday night. All we heard were murmurs of dissent and it wasn't until the Thursday night that the real trouble began.

You know how you can sense an atmosphere without anything actually happening, or seeing anything. In the theatre we sensed the feeling of coming and going. Everything went well until the second act and the scene in the pub. It was really Rosie we thought they objected to and not the speech which was in Pearse's words.

Before the act began someone came up to me and praised me and the playing and sound of the orchestra. Then he said to me 'I suppose that some of those instruments are valuable'. I said that they were. Then he said, 'If I were you I'd have them moved'. He addressed me as professor which suggested that he was a student.

176

Well, of course, I mentioned this to the members of the orchestra. Then I locked the piano and they took their instruments out of the way.

After the speech, the one that takes place outside, there was a rush on the stage and they climbed up onto it over the piano. Before the curtain could be lowered two men and a girl got up. One man at all events tried to get through but he was struck through the curtain. I went onto the stage from behind and I saw a young lady being pinned to the floor, one man was sitting on her, two others held her arms. They let her go free later on. She was the niece of a well-known person, since dead, and I won't mention her name.

As regards O'Casey himself, I knew him very well. He was a quiet gentle-spoken man. The thing that surprised me was that he wrote such tremendously strong plays. You'd be astonished.

When afterwards I read his letters I felt that he was very unhappy and that he seemed to have changed. I felt that he wasn't the same man and that he suffered from nostalgia. When he left he was cut off from the source of his inspiration.

He was very interested in music and I found that he had very good taste. He seemed to have read a good deal of the great masters. I know that for certain plays of his we used to select pieces that would be in keeping and which would help the atmosphere. I remember himself and Lady Gregory sitting in the stalls, listening to the selections of the orchestra, choosing the most appropriate ones.

Summing up I would say that he was unfair to those three, Yeats, Lady Gregory, and Robinson, to have forgotten what the Abbey did for him.

*   *   *

Mr John Keohane, a Sligo businessman, is well known for his activities with the Yeats International Summer School. A great deal of the more informed activities of the school revolve around his newsagency. Well known by many writers and scholars, here he outlines his first and only meeting with O'Casey.

It all began when I told a friend I intended going to Cornwall for a holiday. He thought I might be near Torquay and gave me Sean O'Casey's address. In my luggage I included O'Casey's autobiographies and a copy of the *Irish Times* of a few days previous containing a report of the criticism levelled by Micheal Mac-

Liammoir at the Abbey Theatre during his one-man show in Sligo.

On the return journey it was necessary to change trains at Newton Abbot, with a delay of one-and-a-half hours. The first taxi-driver I saw had never heard of either Sean O'Casey or Trumlands Road in Torquay, however to her credit she found the place quickly.

I mounted the steps and rang the bell. A tall woman, whom I judged too young to be O'Casey's wife, came to the door. When I asked if it would be possible to see Mr O'Casey understandably I was refused.

He had been home but a week from a nursing home, and doctor's orders were 'No visitors'. Perhaps my disappointment was very marked for as I looked down at the books in my hand I heard, 'Do you want to have those signed?' At this point I was invited in and shown to a comfortable room where I found myself seated facing the portrait of O'Casey as a young man, painted by Augustus John. When Mrs O'Casey, as the woman proved to be, learned I was from Ireland she went off returning a few moments later to say, 'he will see you'. Thus it came about that I had the pleasure of spending half an hour with Sean O'Casey just two weeks before his death.

Except for the wine-coloured embroidered cap his dress was such as any ordinary man wears. His handshake was very firm for a man of his years, his accent unmistakably Dublin.

He accepted the *Irish Times* and when I mentioned about MacLiammoir his comment was, 'Someone is always attacking the Abbey'. He assured me he did not receive any Irish papers regularly. His wife told me that he was unable to read as little as a line in a newspaper, everything had to be read to him.

Most of the time he talked of the Abbey. He was critical certainly, but not bitter, 'I never see a balance-sheet', and again, 'In the old days when one of my plays was being performed, they always sent particulars of numbers of people attending each performance, they don't do that nowadays.'

When he learned I lived in Sligo he had another talking point. Seamus McGowan, a Sligoman, he said was one of his best friends during the 'troubled times', but 'I suppose the poor fellow is dead and gone'. Unfortunately I did not then know and when I learned two weeks later O'Casey was dead. Seamus McGowan was a native of Sligo as O'Casey said; he too was interested in the Gaelic League and the Labour movement. At the time of the split he took the Free State side and was the first court clerk in Sligo under native government. He died at a comparatively early age.

My time was running out and thinking of what had transpired so many years before between Yeats and O'Casey over the 'The Silver Tassie' prompted me to mention that I hoped to see Mrs Yeats on my way back – did he have any message for her? 'Please give her my warm wishes, and also to her son and daughter, it is many years since I have seen either of them.' The message was conveyed as he wished.

As I got up to leave such had been his kindness it was hardly surprising when he asked 'could we arrange to have you driven to the station'.

I had watched this man autograph my book clearly and precisely in spite of his disability and now that firm handshake again. I felt he still had a few years left.

When I reached the gate I stopped, and looking back could not help feeling that Sean O'Casey must have been a lonely man in self-imposed exile, lonely because his surroundings were so out of context with the man himself, so different from the city that inspired him. How often he might have struggled with a temptation to return home is perhaps something that we shall never learn.

* * *

Aidan Hennigan is London editor of the *Irish Press* and was a frequent caller on the O'Caseys.

Although I had visited his home at Torquay, the close friendship I had with Sean O'Casey was really developed over the phone.

It started more or less when he roundly abused me for ringing him early one morning. After my stammered apologies he asked me, 'Are you courting?' and when I said I was he replied, 'God help the poor girl. It will be another Irish romance, twenty years I suppose.'

Often when I rang him afterwards he would answer the phone and say, 'This is the gardener speaking – what do you want O'Casey for?' or 'O'Casey does not want to speak to anyone'.

After this outburst all I had to do was to wait a little while and he came back again. 'O'Casey cannot be bothered talking to any of the Irish papers or for that matter to anyone in Ireland.'

179

Invariably this was the introduction to a long conversation and once started O'Casey would talk non-stop for as long as twenty minutes on subjects ranging from the Abbey Theatre to Communism, from writing to television.

In later years many had thought of O'Casey as an irascible, rather bitter old man. This was far from the truth, at least as far as my own personal experience went. Often, at the height of a tirade directed at the Abbey Theatre, I would say to him, 'You are being a bit hard, aren't you?' and he would laugh with infectious good humour and reply: 'I love to have a go and shake them up.'

And for all his criticisms of Irish institutions he was remarkably keen to find out what was happening at home. I never had a conversation with him in which he did not ask many, many questions about every facet of Irish life.

A point he often made to me was that work was the only answer to anyone's problems. 'Of course', he would add, 'I have to work – O'Casey is not a rich man you know.'

There are many things I remember about O'Casey. He was not overfond of newspapermen, and I believe he heartily disliked critics. But once you gained his confidence he would talk without hesitation.

When 'Juno and the Paycock' and 'The Plough and the Stars' were being produced in the Aldwych Theatre for the World Theatre series he asked me to go along and to tell him what they were like.

I made the mistake of replying that the critics would give a more objective view. It was the first time I heard O'Casey really mad on the phone. I managed to catch words like 'phonies', 'hell', 'damnation' and a few other unprintable adjectives.

When Brendan Behan died O'Casey was very moved. He spoke about the tragedy of Behan's drinking and the great talent that had been killed.

My impression of the later O'Casey was that despite his crusty exterior he was a kindly man bearing as best he could the infirmities of his years. I think too he had tremendous humanity.

*   *   *

Seamus Scully works for a Dublin firm of electrical suppliers. Here he relates the beginning of a relationship which lasted until the playwright's death.

One day in 1949 while on holidays in England I phoned Sean O'Casey. I had never met him but knowing the Dublin he knew I felt he might like to talk about it. The reply was that of a man with a real Dublin voice. It was O'Casey himself. It was a robust voice and in this case somewhat frightening but it was not the bellowing sound that I had expected. In confused words I mentioned my reason for ringing him, who I was, emphasising my Dublin background and home and why I thought that he might like to have a little chat with me about his Dublin of the past and mine of the present. His reply included such remarks as being an old man who was trying to forget Dublin, so many wanted to see him when he wished for restfulness and not to be an object of curiosity. However he finally said that if I was really keen on meeting him I could call on him the following evening after four, as he had to rest his eyes each day after dinner and was limited in his reading and writing.

So the next day I went to Totnes seeking Station Road and the house called 'Tingrith'. I nervously rang the bell and in reply the door was gently opened by Sean himself.

He could have been a Dublin working man who had just been disturbed from his evening meal after a day's heavy toil; dressed in crumpled flannel trousers, a suede jacket, underneath a dark jersey with a rolled collar; on his head was a tweed cap, high magnified spectacles spanned his long pointed nose, half surrounded by thick grey bushy eyebrows.

He looked me over, suspiciously, with blinking eyes. He welcomed me in Irish which startled me further, and which I had difficulty in replying to in the same tongue. In a brief conversation our suspicions vanished – perhaps it was the common language which had bridged the personalities, but I believe it was the gentleness of his voice: it was not that husky tone which we so often associate with the aged, his had a sweet and mellow ring. This was not the bitter raging man that I had visualised. In all I visited him four or five times during my Torquay stay and later I took snaps of him and the family in the garden beside the chestnut and laburnum trees. The following week I stopped with him for the weekend after holidaying in the Lorna Doone country. On the Sunday morning after Mass and breakfast with his wife I went to his bedroom where he was shaving and there with his face surrounded in lather we chatted of the recent events in Dublin and he hummed old ballads of our city. He talked of his last visit to Bernard Shaw a few weeks before Shaw's death.

Later when I visited Ayot St Laurence, the home of Shaw, on the mantelpiece of his sitting room was a large photograph of O'Casey.

Later in the summer of 1951 his younger son Niall came on his first visit to Dublin and called to see me as his father had wished it. He joined with me and my friends in our hikes over the mountains and we visited the Abbey and the Art Galleries. He was a good companion but quiet and shy and wished for no publicity. On his return home his father wrote me again showing his courtesy and appreciation for my kindness to Niall and how he had enjoyed his holiday and my friends. And then when the great tragedy occured in the death of this son at twenty-one I found it so difficult writing him as I realised how such a death must have affected such a devoted family man.

I wrote him as I felt a Catholic should and I fear that I am one of the 'Job's comforters' singled out in the most pathetic chapter of his writings, *Under a Greenwood Tree*, and part of his reply to me was: 'Yes, we sadly miss Niall, he often spoke of you. By the way Seamus a mhic O, why do you think that God's ways are understandable? It wasn't God who killed Niall, it was leukaemia – unless God created the bug or the virus, or whatever causes it, and if a God exists, I'd hardly say that he had any hand in it. As Shaw says "It isn't we who are in God's hands, it is God who is in ours" and if we don't deal with the things that plague and destroy us, then we damn well have to suffer.'

Later when I was obliged to go to London he contacted many of his friends with a view to getting me a better position there, and was also anxious about my health and advised me to try to get out of the city and its smoky atmosphere. 'I am very sorry you had to come to London – wish you had come years ago. You see it is particularly hard to get clerical work here or anything else. I have written to a friend of mine to have a chat with you. He is not one that can plant you in a job – just an ordinary worker of very high intelligence brought up a Protestant and none the better for that, thank God. He knows the common ropes of London (and Dublin) well and his knowledge may be of great use to you and can advise you on many common things. You won't be able to save much in London – things are so dear, but be satisfied with covering costs. Leave the rest to God. It is a tougher place than Dublin.' He suggested several places for 'digs'. 'Not to grudge a few pounds for comfort, that health was worth more than a quid or two.'

When I returned to Dublin he too was happy and said: 'I am glad that you are safe in Dublin. I guessed from the first that you wouldn't find rest in London – the dove has returned to the Ark. Good thing that you did not go to New York. Do not worry if things do not fit at first, and don't let them rush you. Don't worry as to the kind of your boss, so long as he pays you he is your friend. I think that you would never have been happy in London, and Dublin is the surest way to heaven for you. It's not an easy way, but it is the way you know, and the way you like. You are better there. Now the London fog begins to pack the sky and that would not be good for you. I don't think an English city would be good for your health, for the air of Dublin is a far, far better, so don't leave Dublin unless you have to.'

In reply to my omission in sending him 80th birthday greetings he expressed gladness at such default (it would be different if he was getting a year younger, but at this stage he preferred to ignore calendar and clock).

After a long illness he wrote to me: 'Of course there was a long spell – one of five months or more when I didn't bother about hearing from anyone and the whispers of the world were faint ones. Eileen was the only one I wanted to see – the one voice I wanted to hear. I can walk at a good speed now, but haven't yet swung back into work. I am here amongst the flowers. Mind your health, old son, you'd lose a lot if you lost that.'

Later: 'I am very busy now at work, have many letters to answer, and I have to find time for Eileen, for eating and for sleep. I am writing this at one in the morning.'

Later: 'Someone poured a shower of the "Catholic" paper *Hibernia* over my head the other day. Why I do not know. Wasn't the *Standard* sufficient? This must be a brief note as my good eye is troublesome and it is too painful to use for long.'

I still continued to write to him and send him paper cuttings of Irish interest on the understanding that he was not to reply, but he still continued to reply in brief handwritten letters expressing his thanks for my trouble. He was now in his eighty-third year – suffering from the irritating complaints of the aged – one eye completely blind, the other almost completely dimmed, only able to read and type by holding his head at the most awkward angle, everything having to be read back to him by someone else to avoid further strain. To within a fortnight of his death by sheer will-power he continued reading and writing and

183

making preparations for a new play, in spite of the eye specialist's verdict that his eyes were worn out and that he really could not see. In a Dublin slum as a child his mother had fought to save his sight, in far-away Devon the frail old writer, with the aid of his devoted wife, was still undefeated. The fight is over – Eternal Peace. Ar dheis De go raibh a anam.

PART THREE

THE MAKINGS
OF GENIUS

1

THE BIG THREE

By John O' Donovan

'THE Shadow of a Gunman', 'Juno and the Paycock', 'The Plough and the Stars' are known to Dubliners as the Big Three. The label is affectionate, thoughtless, inaccurate and perhaps a little malicious, for your Dubliner believes that these were O'Casey's first three plays, written under the inspiration of living in Dublin, an inspiration he deprived himself of by going to England in a huff, where he caught Communism, wrote a lot of non-plays, and passed his latter years writing querulous letters to the Irish papers attacking the clergy.

Two O'Caseys, in other words, as distinct and separate as an Eskimo and a Hottentot. Exile O'Casey was beyond the Pale metaphorically as well as literally, but the beloved Early O'Casey saved him from total excommunication and there were no really venomous attacks on him except, of course, by old friends and religious journals. Early O'Casey had gained his grip on Dubliners by holding up to them a mirror in which they saw themselves reflected with a fidelity they felt to be perfect, yet there was no ruthless sting about it. His characters were comical enough to satisfy the Irish lust for laughter, and although the tragic actions in the plays were perpetrated by men there was a vague but reassuring feeling that they had been contrived by a just God bent on punishing human wickedness. There was no repulsively evil character in the Big Three, no morality was challenged, and the text of any sermonizing was the unexceptionable and familiar 'Love Ye One Another'. Between Early O'Casey and Dublin there was no impediment to a marriage of true minds, and it was delightfully flattering for the citizens to be assured by foreign critics that the plays they relished so much were world masterpieces into the bargain. Local critics hadn't been so enthusiastic. A Dublin Hanslick of the 1920s had shaken his head primly over 'The Plough and the Stars' as a series of music hall sketches. But then, as Dr Johnson had noted, the Irish are a fair people: they never speak well of one another. The Dublin critics, almost without exception, continued their venal attacks until the end, and you have to go back to the London critics' reception of Ibsen to find the equal of the buffleheaded nonsense spouted about O'Casey on the production of his 'Bishop's Bonfire' in Dublin in 1955. What was published at the time might suggest to the outsider that it would have cost O'Casey his life to set foot in his native city. The truth is, had he come he would have been hailed like Voltaire in Paris in 1778, and, like Voltaire, might have been killed by kindness.

'The Shadow of a Gunman' was the first of the Big Three but not O'Casey's first play. It was preceded by half a dozen short pieces, some of which have been lost. The published surviving texts, viewed in the light of the later plays, have passages that foreshadow the great things to come, although without that light it isn't so easy to see in them the hand of genius, except perhaps in the last few pages of 'The Hall of Healing' where the true O'Casey power makes itself felt.

The leap forward between a piece like 'The Hall of Healing' and 'The Shadow of a Gunman' is gigantic, technically and thematically, but still doesn't put 'The Shadow' anywhere near enough to 'Juno' or 'The Plough' to qualify for real membership of a Big Three. 'The Shadow', like the St Anthony Chorale Variations, appears in retrospect like a try-out for the major work which followed. What the Big Three have in common is their theme of the effect of Irish civil strife on the innocent.

'The Shadow' tells of an oddly assorted pair, Seamus Shields and Donal Davoren, who share a lodging in a tenement house in Mountjoy Square, a decayed square of one-time Georgian splendour, which O'Casey renames Hilljoy Square. The time of the play is May 1920, a period of strife which the British describe as the Irish Civil War and the Irish describe officially as the War of Independence, and colloquially as the Troubles. Shields, when he musters the energy to get out of bed, peddles laces and braces for a living. Davoren regards himself as a poet. A friend of Shields leaves his pedlar's bag in the lodging at the beginning of the play, explaining that he cannot go peddling that day. We later learn that he has been shot dead by the British, and when the bag is opened it is found to contain not braces and buttons but Mills bombs. A girl, Minnie Powell, who lives in the tenement, has taken a shine to Davoren, being as much attracted by his mistaken tenement reputation as a gunman on the run as by his person. (It is he who is 'only the shadow of a gunman'.) Minnie takes the bag of bombs up to her room just before a raid is made on the house, in the hope that the Auxiliaries will not ransack a girl's room. But they do, and they take away Minnie, who is shot dead when the Auxiliaries are themselves attacked on leaving the house. The poet, having let Minnie take the risk and the rap without lifting a finger to save her, beats his breast to a Shelleyan chime of 'Pain, pain, pain ever, forever', and cries out that shame is his portion now till the silver chord is loosened and the golden bowl is broken. 'Oh Davoren, Donal Davoren, poet and poltroon, poltroon and poet.'

It is easy enough to accept Davoren's estimate of himself as a poltroon, but not so easy to swallow him as the poet O'Casey tries to make of him. Donal Davoren doesn't convince the spectator that he is much more than poetic. Admittedly it is hard to present artistic talent on the stage so that it will convince those who won't accept a mere statement of claim or the convention of flowing hair and flowing tie. Louis Dubedat can be swallowed as an artist of genius, but Marchbanks the poet sticks in many a throat, as Davoren sticks in mine. Davoren is given to quoting Shelley in moments of emotion, which your true poet would be too egotistical to do – he would quote himself. Davoren is not only the shadow of a gunman, he is the shadow of a character. He lacks the energy and vitality which are the secret of the greatness of all O'Casey's major creations. He is weakened and made irresolute by greater self-awareness than most O'Casey characters exhibit, and O'Casey hadn't the skill that can make a similarly weakened Hamlet or Ivanov memorable for ever. We are, I think, intended to believe that Minnie's death will cause Davoren to live the rest of his life a broken reed, ashamed and remorseful, seeing the haggard face of a shabby coward every morning in his shaving mirror. The truth more likely is that Davoren revelled in the luxury of sentimental woe, and told and re-told his sins with increasing refinement of style, each slim volume being most favourably reviewed in the *Irish Times*.*

Seamus Shields, being more definite and energetic in himself and in his utterance, is the more successful creation. He belongs to the great family of Joxer and Fluther. I have sometimes wondered whether Seamus and Donal are not a deliberate

*O'Casey's verse must have been as agonising to Yeats as *Finlandia* to a Mozartean. The unwritten counterpoint to the noble melody Yeats sung in his letter to O'Casey rejecting 'The Silver Tassie', is 'Hey (HEY), you, (YOU), get offa my cloud.'

portrayal by O'Casey of two sides of his character that he was conscious of: the poetic side, with its corollary of inactivity and cowardice in the face of physical danger; and the cynical, disillusioned soldier of the Citizen Army who believed in the argument of the gun as long as there wasn't a gun in the country. If so, it is significant that Shields should be the more energetically conceived of the two.

The chink in O'Casey's armour as a playwright was his lack of complete mastery of form. He is not one of the great dramatic symphonists who can develop their theme through three long acts, varying, enlarging, and never really digressing even in the episodes introduced to relieve tension. In 'The Shadow' he brings on the other lodgers for no reason except that he cannot keep going without such irrelevant episodes as Tommy Owens, the Grigsons, Mrs Henderson and Mr Gallogher. These characters, though very entertaining in themselves, are not really worked into the fabric of the play. They are patches, brilliant patches which could only come from a master hand, but still patches.

The love scene between Minnie and Donal Davoren is not convincing, as Minnie is not a flesh-and-blood girl. Indeed none of the girls in the Big Three, with the glorious exception of Rosie Redmond, is a successful creation. (Mollser is successful because sexless.) Good respectable girls never fired O'Casey's imagination, perhaps because good respectable girls do not exist; and when, for plot purposes, O'Casey found it necessary to invent them it's hardly surprising that he didn't attain even the modest success that man achieved with God.

'The Plough and the Stars' is O'Casey's biggest canvas, with his most richly worked set of characters. But it is a masterpiece flawed by the O'Casey weakness of form and by a last act in which there is an all-out assault on our emotions, with tragedy teetering more perilously than ever on the brink of melodrama. 'Juno and the Paycock', less monumental and with less masterfully wrought characters, is a more moving play. O'Casey's strength is as evident here as in the bigger play, but his weakness is less apparent.

There is no fumbling about the opening as there is in 'The Shadow' and 'The Plough'. The first line, Mary's reading from the paper the news about the killing of young Tancred, 'On a little bye-road out beyant Finglas, he was found', plunges us straight into things with Shakespearian directness, and from that line until the last the movement does not falter.

Juno Boyle and her husband, the Paycock, are a tenement pair, and the play is the story of them and their two children. The son, wounded in the Rising, has now (1922) apparently betrayed an old comrade. Why he should have done this is not made clear from his character or from his lines: it has to be accepted as a mere plot device like Othello's handkerchief. The daughter is going out with an uppish schoolmaster who has drawn up the will of the family's rich relation, under which they stand to inherit a couple of thousand pounds. The family has a brief

A Dublin tram in O'Casey's day

taste of luxury (on credit), but the will has been badly drafted, the prospect of money vanishes, the son is carried off by the I.R.A. and shot for his treachery, the daughter is made pregnant and deserted by the schoolmaster, and the end of all is that Juno leaves her worthless husband and his butty Joxer Daly in the stripped lodging, going off with a protective arm around her daughter.

Juno is the play's great character – O'Casey's great character – an Irish Mother Courage without the German's overriding commercial passion. All who surround her are her inferiors in strength, good-heartedness, self-awareness, even in common humanity. Although O'Casey treats young Mary and Johnny Boyle with sympathy (he couldn't be kinder to Johnny) one feels that they are more their father's children than their mother's, and it is part of Juno's greatness of heart that she does not throw this in their faces as she might well be pardoned for doing. She doesn't abandon herself to grief, she wastes no pity on herself, and while her husband falls drunk on the floor, projecting his own state of chassis on to the world, with his satellite Joxer still hovering around him, it is Juno who gathers together the few threads which still hold her to life and hope, and sets off with her daughter Mary to help into the world a child which shall have no father but 'what's far better – it'll have two mothers'.

O'Casey's success in drawing Juno is the more wonderful by contrast with his failure with young Mary Boyle. Mary expresses herself in impossible dialogue:

> MRS BOYLE: An' has Bentham never even written to you since – not one line for the last month?
>
> MARY: (tonelessly) Not even a line, mother.
>
> MRS BOYLE: That's very curious. . . . What came between the two of yous at all? To leave you so sudden, an' yous so great together. . . . To go away t'England, an' not to even leave you his address. . . . The way he was always bringin' you to dances, I thought he was mad afther you. Are you sure you said nothin' to him?
>
> MARY: No mother – at least nothing that could possibly explain his givin' me up.
>
> MRS BOYLE: You know you're a bit hasty at times, Mary, an' say things you shouldn't say.
>
> MARY: I never said to him what I shouldn't say, I'm sure of that.
>
> MRS BOYLE: How are you sure of it?
>
> MARY: Because I love him with all my heart and soul, mother. Why I don't know; I often thought to myself that he wasn't the man poor Jerry was, but I couldn't help loving him, all the same.

It is not sufficient defence to say that Mary was literary enough to fancy such 'plays for childher' as 'A Doll's House' and 'The Wild Duck'. She is just another symptom of her creator's unease in the company of bourgeois respectability, an unease born of his knowledge of slum conditions in which tuppence-ha'penny not only looked down on tuppence but positively refused to exchange a civil word with it. The situation was worsened by O'Casey's being a poor Protestant and thereby excommunicated by the rich Protestant minority, living among the poor Catholic majority who, no matter how warm their hearts, could not bring themselves to pull down the barrier erected by a religion which preached the brotherhood of man.

In 'The Plough and the Stars' O'Casey goes back from the Troubles to the Easter Rising of 1916, but there is no marked change in the atmosphere of the play from 'Juno', nor in the kind of character in it. Perhaps we should not expect that there should be, because only six years separate the period of the two plays. Indeed, some small adjustments could convincingly lift 'The Plough and the Stars' from 1916 to 1920. O'Casey's viewpoint has not changed. It is still 'you lost your best principle, me boy, when you lost your arm'; still 'it's nearly time we had a little less respect for the dead, an' a little more regard for the livin''; still 'take away this murdherin' hate'. But the tragedy of 'The Plough' is not so much the personal tragedy of a Dublin family as the tragedy of Ireland, and one of the effects of this is that its last act hasn't the overwhelming emotion of the last act of 'Juno'. Clitheroe's death affects us as little as a mortality statistic: he is just a war casualty. Mollser's death from tuberculosis merely raises a sigh of relief, since the poor child is better off dead than alive with such a mother in such a house in such a city and with such an affliction. Bessie Burgess's death from a British soldier's bullet aimed in error is so contrived that there is a suspicious smell of onions from the handkerchief that O'Casey thrusts to our eyes. Yet when all this has been said, 'The Plough' remains the greatest Irish play of its era and it is likely to tower majestically in the Irish theatre for a long time to come. The second act, set in a pub outside which a speaker (unnamed by O'Casey but it's Patrick Pearse, the 1916 leader) is addressing a patriot meeting, can be ranked near the Eastcheap scenes in 'King Henry IV' as a masterpiece of low life comedy. It is rumbustious, bawdy, farcical, exuberant and strangely touching. It is one of those acts which can never quite fail in the theatre, no matter how bad the production or inept the performers. Yet it is the hardest of all O'Casey's acts to perform properly, for the audience must be touched by the underlying sadness and futility of life as lived by these people as well as tickled by their comicality.

The story of 'The Plough and the Stars' is the story of how the Rising affects the inhabitants of one Dublin tenement. The Clitheroes are an apparently happy young married couple, but Nora Clitheroe does not want her husband to risk his life in the fighting, and there are suggestions that he might well stay at home if it weren't for fear of what his comrades might say. He is killed. Nora's baby is born dead, and between that and her husband's killing, she goes out of her mind in a Lady Macbeth-like way. A little consumptive girl dies, an Irish soldier is mortally wounded, and finally the pro-British Bessie Burgess is killed by a British bullet while trying to drag Nora away from a dangerous window. In lesser hands a play with this kind of last-act slaughter becomes a theatrical risk, and all would have been lost if O'Casey had littered the stage with his corpses instead of killing most of them 'off'. It is its magnificence as a portrait gallery that makes 'The Plough' great. Fluther Good, Uncle Peter, Mrs Gogan, the Young Covey, Bessie Burgess, and the delectable Rosie Redmond are all portraits of Rembrandt-like power and pathos; and even Nora Clitheroe, though still a lay figure, stirs with true life.

It is misleading to think of the Big Three as plays about slum life in Dublin. They are that different thing, three plays about people who happen to live in a Dublin slum, who would be essentially the same, if born and bred in a palace. Joxer and Captain Boyle are not just two bowsies or gurriers. They are two universal human types, the imposter and the satellite who can at will see through him and not see through him. In other times, in other circumstances, Joxer and the Captain present themselves to us as Caesar and Mark Antony, or Napoleon and Marshal Ney. The power and the artistic economy with which O'Casey shows us their relationship, and his insight into the two characters, are probably more penetrating than he himself realised. Juno herself is universal as Juliet's Nurse, and Fluther is to be found as often in the Washington Senate or the Moscow Praesidium as in Hilljoy Square.

Joxer and Fluther loom so large on the Irish stage that they have had a paralysing effect on many young Irish playwrights and actors, an effect like that of Beethoven on his immediate successors. It is hard for somebody whose first introduction to this Gog and Magog was by the performances of the late F. J. McCormick to say whether their theatrical magnitude resides completely in themselves or partly in McCormick's impersona-

tion of them. Dubliners who saw McCormick tend to think of
'Juno' as the play Joxer is in and 'The Plough' as the one Fluther
is in. Yet McCormick's performances were not two distinct
studies but one vivid, brilliant, searingly memorable picture of a
predominant Dublin slum type. In age Joxer and Fluther were
O'Casey's contemporaries, born in the Dublin of the 1880s, and
although they were plentiful in my youth they are few and far
between today. Yet Dublin actors, even those in their early
twenties, who are unlikely to have studied joxers at first hand,
or seen McCormick's performance, seem to be imitating
McCormick, so deeply has his impersonation impressed itself
on the race memory of Dublin. Even Dubliners who never have
been on a stage in their lives but who have the Irish facility for
humorous mimicry, instinctively fall into the McCormick style
when imitating a male Dublin slumster.

The young women in the Big Three are, as I have already said,
dull. Not in a thousand years could O'Casey add to the sister-
hood of Juliet or Rosalind or Ann Whitefield, because he is
Irish enough to feel that good girls do not run after men, and
he has no occasion in these plays to exhibit young women in
pursuit of their prey. The chief effect produced by his girls is
the one he probably wanted least – that if you could muster
enough interest to open Nora Clitheroe's blouse, or Minnie
Powell's, or Mary Boyle's, you would find the collection of
scapulars and holy medals which such girls award themselves for
what they are pleased to call good conduct. But let a girl be a
daughter of joy and O'Casey falls in love with her and lavishes
all his skill and energy and humour upon her. Who can resist
Rosie Redmond? What healthy man, no matter how respectable
in his morals and prudent in his sexual affairs, would prefer
Minnie to her?

O'Casey stood in his own light to some extent by writing his
dialogue phonetically. The pronunciations are so familiar to
Dubliners that they aren't much inconvenienced by the phonetic
spelling. I am not so sure that others will not find the attempt to
pedantically reproduce Dublin slum pronunciation off-putting,
and will fail to see the universality of the characters because of
the parochiality of their speech. It might be no bad thing to
publish an edition of O'Casey in conventional spelling so that
non-Irish readers could be relieved of preoccupation with trees and
enabled to see the wood in its full splendour. One other thing. If
the editor of this version were to root out the intrusive adjectives

which pop up like mushrooms in the dialogue of 'The Plough', the first really ominous sign of O'Casey's growing intoxication with words, then he would be rendering as good service to O'Casey as Mahler did to Schumann when he thinned out the orchestration of the symphonies.

2

THE MAN IN THE PLAYS

*By Gabriel Fallon**

THE history of any national drama is a vast landscape with
occasional mountain peaks, ranges of small hills, and large tracts
of seemingly endless desert. At all events this is the picture
presented in any clearsighted backward glance at the Irish scene.
It is generally acknowledged, except by the myopic few, that the
mountain peaks, two in number, are those of Synge and O'Casey,
the latter by virtue of his first three plays.

Sometimes, of course, one hears a solitary voice (in this
instance a poet) declaring that the genius of Synge was an invention of Yeats; and O'Casey in the hour of his success was beset
by literary men who variously described his work as photography,
an exploitation of Dublin's poor, and utterly worthless in form
and content.

Such accusations die hard. As recently as 14 January 1966, in
the course of an interview in the R.T.V. Guide, Dr Micheal
MacLiammóir, himself a great and sensitive artist, publicly
expressed his inability to agree with those who hail O'Casey as a
genius. Expressing the view that there is at the moment no
indication of a literary upsurge, 'no manifestation of what
seemed to be showing its head at the beginning of the century',
he went on to say:

'Under the leadership of Yeats, Ireland seemed to be dis-
covering a manner, a mode. There was a great moment then in
Ireland's history, especially in her theatre. To me, O'Casey was
the end of it. I am not as great an admirer of O'Casey as many
other people – I don't think he was as great a dramatist as is
believed now – but he was a first-rate man in his own way, an
unique figure.' Coming from a man of Dr MacLiammóir's stature
this is in itself a great tribute. Much in O'Casey realism must
have been alien to Dr MacLiammóir's view of the theatre. However, it is when Dr MacLiammóir goes on to say this that I take

* Author of *Sean O'Casey, the Man I Knew*. Routledge & Kegan
Paul, Ltd., London. Little Brown, Boston. 1965.

issue with him: 'He (O'Casey) arrived on the scene of this great accident, this disaster between the Irish and the English, and there he was, a smart cameraman, taking all those wonderful pictures of it.'

I doubt if Dr MacLiammóir consciously intended to be denigrating in using the phrase 'a smart cameraman'. As much might be said of Maxim Gorki on the head of *The Lower Depths*, but, somehow or other, I cannot imagine Dr MacLiammóir saying it. Indeed, as Dr MacLiammóir must well know, the whole naturalistic movement triggered off by Emile Zola could be compelled to abide questioning on this 'camera' charge. To take from life is part of the dramatist's creative process. His genius as a dramatist depends largely on his possessing an alchemy of his own with which he transmutes what he takes. O'Casey in his first three successful plays shows much evidence of this alchemy.

Literature – particularly dramatic literature – is in its own way a criticism of life; it is part of man's unceasing effort to understand life, to probe its meaning. It is an attempt to hold experience at arm's length and examine it, to reach that unity which man feels must underlie the multiplicity disclosed by his experience. But, whatever it is, it is not photography.

Much comfort has been given to supporters of the 'cameraman' theory by Saros Cowasjee's futile attempt in *Sean O'Casey, the Man Behind the Plays*, to track down the 'originals' of the O'Casey characters. He draws an intriguing picture based on second-hand evidence of O'Casey sitting in a Dublin tenement scribbling down the remarks of 'Captain' Boyle and 'Joxer' Daly. Boyle and Daly are – as they would be with any worthwhile dramatist – composite characters born from long and deep brooding on dozens of 'originals'. As one who was closely associated with the dramatist when 'the story of Johnny Boyle' was forcing its way up through the dramatist's unconsciousness I can assure the holders of the 'camera' theory that they don't know what they are talking about.

Anyone who knows their Dublin and who is familiar with the Irish temperament will realise how easily – particularly after O'Casey's rise to fame – one could meet literally hundreds of people who would tell you that, 'Sure, I knew O'Casey well'. The result is that apocryphal descriptions of the dramatist and his work still abound. Not so long after the dramatist's death I bumped into a character who said to me: 'Ah, yes, poor Sean;

197

many's the half-dollar I lent him!' This concerning a man who was so proudly independent of monetary assistance that when a royalty cheque had been delayed he pawned a new pair of trousers rather than ask a friend for a loan of a few shillings!

There may be something in the theory that men of taste always hate and mistrust men of genius and that this feeling is returned with compound interest. Taste is an avoidance of extremes, whereas genius is rich, seminal, copious, offensive in its vitality. This could account for the dislike of the early O'Casey by poets like Austin Clarke and F. R. Higgins, who when the Abbey was crowded to the doors and beyond them declared that the Theatre had been 'given over to the mob'. Most of Dublin's literary group reacted in the same manner. This, too, could account for O'Casey's savagely expressed dislike of Coward, of such a play as 'Journey's End', of his contempt for his fellow Irish dramatists, of his almost insensate hatred of George Russell.

Richard Findlater in his book *The Unholy Trade* makes a distinction, in his chapter on 'Playmaking', between the 'playwright' and the 'dramatist'. The former, according to Findlater, uses his technique to flatter the playgoer's prejudices in the most accommodating way that he can devise. 'He makes it his business to know what the public wants, and to supply it. He appeals to the L.C.M. of its emotions, avoiding the irritants of poetry, tragedy or polemic, ringing the changes on a set of stock responses and situations. He writes down to the audience: the dramatist writes across it.'

'The dramatist' on the other hand 'is an artist who uses the stage as the channel of his personal vision. He is writing primarily not to tell a good story, to meet a consumer's demand or to make money – though he may incidentally accomplish all these things – but to express something he wants to say through the medium of actors, to embody his experience in a work of theatrical art.' At first sight Findlater's distinction may seem to be a little too naïve. On reflection, however, one sees that since a distinction must be made this is the only way to make it.

Indeed the truth of the Findlater distinction is strangely supported by Dr MacLiammóir who, in the interview already referred to, discusses his own role as a playwright. He does so with a humility which is unfortunately all too rare in the theatrical profession. 'My best play', he tells us, 'was probably "Ill Met by Moonlight". I say probably; I don't know really. I think all my plays are good entertainment: and not necessarily marvellous

198

plays. To be quite frank, I think I could have written a much better play, strangely enough, had I not been an actor and had one eye on the public. But there is that actor, that theatre demon, in me, so that every time I want to go all out and be completely and sincerely myself, as every work of art has come from a completion in oneself, an uncompromising thing as Joyce did in his way and Yeats in his – I find myself thinking 'Oh, that won't get over, I don't think they'll like that', so I have really written my plays with one eye on the public.'

That brilliant and incontrovertibly honest piece of self-criticism could only come from a man of genius, a genius so many-sided that it fits uncomfortably into the one person; actor, painter, dramatist, writer in two languages, speaker of five, a wit so matched against his hero Wilde, that in 'The Importance of Being Oscar' it was impossible to distinguish one from the other. All his plays without exception are good entertainment. But in my opinion the one in which he almost reached that 'uncompromising thing' was 'The Mountains Look Different', almost Greek in its tragic intensity.

However the whole point in drawing attention to Findlater's distinction between the 'playwright' and the 'dramatist' is to assert that in his three great plays Sean O'Casey was the latter. He used the stage as the channel of his personal vision. He was not writing merely to tell a story, to meet a consumer's demand, or to make money, though he did incidentally accomplish these things. He was certainly not writing in the spirit of 'art for art's sake'. As Findlater says of him: 'In his early plays . . . it was not dramatic form but human content with which he was concerned. He was busy with the urgency of what he had to say, not with the problems of how to say it.' In short, he was writing because he had to.

'Do you believe for a moment', wrote Paul Claudel to Jacques Rivière, 'that Shakespeare, Dostoievsky or Rubens, or Titian, or Wagner did their work for art's sake? No! They did it to free themselves of a great incubus of living matter *Opus non factum*. And certainly not to colour a cold artificial design with borrowings from reality.' It was exactly the same with O'Casey. He had to rid himself of this incubus of living matter that came forth in 'The Shadow of a Gunman', 'Juno and the Paycock', 'The Plough and the Stars'. Had he preoccupied himself with form as he did in most of his later work, these great plays would not have been written.

E. M. Forster tells us that man in the creative state is, so to speak, taken out of himself. 'He lets down, as it were, a bucket into his subconciousness and draws up something which is normally beyond his reach. He mixes this thing with his normal experiences, and out of the mixture he makes a work of art. It may be a good work of art or a bad one . . . but whether it is good or bad it will have been compounded in this unusual way, and he will wonder afterwards how he did it. It may employ much technical ingenuity and worldly knowledge, it may profit by critical standards, but mixed up with it is this stuff from the bucket, this subconscious stuff, which is not procurable on demand. And when the process is over, when the picture or symphony or lyric or novel (or whatever it is) is complete, the artist, looking back on it, will wonder how on earth he did it.'

Letting down a bucket into the subconscious is perhaps not the happiest way of describing what happens; but 'twill serve. As often as not no conscious effort is required from the bucket-owner. Something from the subconscious suddenly and surprisingly emerges. The element of surprise is always present. In those days and nights after 'The Gunman' (interrupted only by his one-act 'Phantasy' 'Cathleen Listens In') Sean O'Casey brooded over 'the tragic story of Johnny Boyle'. Never a word about Juno, or the Captain or Joxer Daly; always Johnny. And the 'big scene' was to be the shooting of Johnny, in the dark by the roadside (a scene which was ultimately, and very rightly, cut by the Abbey Theatre directors).

When the play finally emerged on the opening night and I discussed it with him I was amazed that he should seemingly know so little about the work he had created. His reaction to each detail of characterisation, to development of plot, to every tragic or comic situation, was one of genuine surprise. He had written a play; he had done so under the lash of disappointment and shame which curled from the cool reception with which an Abbey audience had greeted his 'Phantasy'. He had written a play about Johnny Boyle, a tragic victim of two wars, the war of liberation and the more bitter war of brothers; and that was that. Of course, he was prepared to accept all that I said to him about this play he had written. But he was genuinely surprised by it. E. M. Forster mentions Jane Austen's attitude on looking back upon *Emma:* 'Dear me, how came I to write that? It is not ill-conceived'. It was even so with Sean O'Casey.

It had been a very different story with the 'Phantasy', 'Cathleen

Listens In', which a critic described as 'not a play at all but a safety valve for some funny opinions he (Mr O'Casey) holds on present day Ireland'. In this satire on the political situation of the time a very conscious Sean O'Casey was at work. He knew what he was about even while he was about it. The fact that the audience received it in silence cut him to the quick. Its value in the O'Casey canon is negligible. Indeed, it is questionable if the Abbey Theatre would have accepted it had it come from anyone but the author of the successful 'Gunman'. It is important only in so far as it marks the beginning of the dramatist's attempt to escape, as Findlater puts it, 'from a world of people to a world of puppets, from raw experience to angry opinions'.

Between 'Juno' and 'The Plough' he was to make another 'conscious' effort, this time in a one-acter called 'Nannie's Night Out'. Incidentally, a young man named Ron Ayling writing in the autumn-winter 1965 issue of *The Dublin Magazine* indicts me for saying that Nannie in this play died from gunshot wounds and not, as he, Mr Ayling, at the top of his voice assures us, from a heart attack. Mr Ayling, who has pledged himself to accept the O'Casey Autobiographies as if they were Holy Writ, attacks me with all the woolly insistence of an infuriated ewe defending her favourite lamb. Well, I played in the first production of the darned thing and my faulty memory must be attributed to my low rating of the piece. O'Casey himself didn't think much of it and even in his hind-sighted view rated it lower than 'Cathleen Listens In'.

Lady Gregory obviously suffered from my memory defect for she refers to it in her Journal as 'Lizzie's Night Out'. Lizzie or Nannie, it hardly matters in the light of the author's major work – and whether she died of a heart attack, a gunshot wound, or simply of a Tuesday hardly matters either. It is inevitable, of course, that American 'scholarship' in the person of one Robert Hogan should describe 'Nannie's Night Out' as 'one of the superb one-act plays of the modern stage, and it must take place next to the great one-acts of O'Casey's colleagues – Strindberg, Synge, Shaw'. Well, it is welcome to do so; though, thankfully for American scholarship, I know a number of American professors who would unrepentedly bar its way.

'Nannie' got a better reception from the audience than 'Cathleen' had got. After all, Sean was now the author of 'Juno'; and that they had not forgotten. But he was far from satisfied; he knew he could do better than that. So the old brooding spirit took hold of him again and within a fortnight he told me he was thinking of another play. We didn't discuss it for the simple reason that he showed no inclination to do so. It was obvious to me, however, that something worth-while was on the way. The bucket was dipping into the subconscious again.

Evening after evening we talked about other things. To be sure he would occasionally refer to the fact that he had 'done damn all today' or that he had actually written 'four bloody lines of dialogue'. Once he mentioned that he thought the play would have 'something to do with 1916'. A few weeks after that he said he would probably have to do some cutting on it. Then the evening came when he asked me if I would care to listen to a scene from it. I said I would. Taking three and a half pages of closely-typed dialogue and bringing them close to his eyes in his customary manner, he read me a scene which took place between a character called The Covey and a priest, a Catholic missioner. It was a very funny scene but it never appeared in the play.

A few weeks later he told me that he thought he would call one of his characters 'Fluther Good'. Now both of us knew by appearance a well-known Dublin north-sider named Fluther Good. This real Fluther bore not the slightest resemblance to what ultimately transpired to be the character in 'The Plough'. But Sean liked the name and was determined to use it. Indeed the name has a symbolic quality though Sean did not specifically say it had. I have no doubt whatever, though, that he felt it. For if 'The Plough and the Stars' may be said to have a hero (its heroine being Bessie Burgess) that hero is Fluther who risks his life in an effort to trace Nora Clitheroe. The next time Sean mentioned the play it was to ask my opinion of the title, explaining that it was George Russell the poet who had suggested the symbolism of the earthly and starry ploughs as a banner for the Irish Citizen Army. A fortnight after that he told me the play had been accepted.

I have told in my own book how some of the Abbey Theatre players (particularly F. J. McCormick and myself) entertained high hopes for the success of 'The Shadow of a Gunman' and how astonished we were that the directors were presenting it for three nights only, a fact without precedence in the history of the Abbey. About the author himself we knew little or nothing. We heard that he was a labourer, that he wore a cap and hob-nailed boots, and that the directors were putting on his play in order 'to let him see how bad it was'.

As our acquaintance with the author ripened we learned by degrees that he had been a member of the secret revolutionary organisation, the Irish Republican Brotherhood, that he had taught classes in the Irish language, had acted as secretary to the Irish Citizen Army, had written reams of ultra-patriotic verse; and that, for reasons best known to himself, he had forsworn everything national and Gaelic.

Armed with this knowledge we began to see his plays (beginning with 'The Gunman') in a new and possibly a clearer light. We assumed, of course, that Donal Davoren, poet, was the author himself. To a great extent he is intended to be. But then there is not a little of the author in Davoren's companion Seumas Shields.

'I don't want to boast about myself – I don't want to boast about myself, and I suppose I could call myself as good a Gael as some of those that are knocking about now – as good a Gael as some that are knocking about now – but I remember the time when I taught Irish six nights a week, when in the Irish Republican Brotherhood I paid me rifle levy like a man. . . .'

The voice is the voice of the pedlar Seumas Shields but the facts are part of the history of Sean O'Casey. Again, Davoren's poetry is typically Sean's:

> Or when sweet summer's ardent arms outspread
> Entwined with flowers,
> Enfold me, like two lovers newly wed,
> Thro' ravish'd hours –
> Then sorrow, woe and pain lose all their powers,
> For each is dead, and life is only ours.

The time was to come when he would read me pages of verse of this nature, all of it dedicated to a girl with whom he was passionately in love. Shelley and Burns were his favourite poets, though for such a fervent admirer of the latter there is a strange error in 'The Gunman' where he attributes the authorship of *Annie Laurie* to the bould Robbie. That popular ditty was written not by Burns but by one William Douglas.

Much of Sean, the didactic pacifist, is to be found in Seumas Shield's speeches in the second act of 'The Gunman'.

'The country is gone mad. Instead of counting their beads now they're countin' bullets; their Hail Marys and paternosters are burstin' bombs – burstin' bombs, and the rattle of machine guns; petrol is their holy water; their Mass is a burnin'

203

buildin'; their De Profundis is "The Soldier's Song", an' their creed is, I believe in the gun almighty, maker of heaven an' earth – an' it's all for the glory o' God and the honour o' Ireland.'

What a change this is from the man who after a visit to Wolfe Tone's grave at Bodenstown could find it in his soul to cry out, 'Talk of peace is nonsense, and deep down they know that this talk of peace is nonsense'; the man who hoped that a living people would 'write with a sword, an epitaph to Emmet on the hearts of their foe'; the man who expressed himself in verse as follows:

> Beneath thy flag fresh hopes we feel,
> Ireland, dear Ireland
> We'll gild its fold with glint of steel
> And rifle's flame, dear Ireland.
> In garish day, 'neath night's damp dew,
> Its green and white and orange hue
> Shall signal death to England's crew
> And hope to thee, dear Ireland.

That the author of 'The Gunman' was acutely conscious of this volte-face is evident in lines which immediately follow 'The country is gone mad' speech; for when Davoren says: 'I remember the time when you yourself believed in nothing but the gun', Shields with a saving sense of humour replies: 'Ay, when there wasn't a gun in the country. I've a different opinion now when there's nothin' but guns in the country. . . .'

Two speeches later Sean is unconsciously hinting at the theme which will to a great extent animate 'The Plough and the Stars': 'It's the civilians that suffer . . . I draw the line when I hear the gunmen blowin' about dyin' for the people, when it's the people that are dyin' for the gunmen! With all due respect to the gunmen, I don't want them to die for me!'

When 'The Shadow of a Gunman' was produced in Hebrew in Israel the critic of the *Jerusalem Post*, writing about this 'strange and bitter drama depicting the cowardice of a poet and most of the Irishmen on view', pointed out that 'presumably the interest of Israelis in the Ireland of the 'twenties springs from a comparison with memories of Mandatory days. But I do not think that Israel produced weak-willed hypocrites such as those whom O'Casey etched so savagely. The great Irish dramatists of the Abbey Theatre did not think highly of their countrymen, however much they valued liberty for their country.' Perhaps it is that we Irish have a greater sense of humour than the Israelis for all of us, including our freedom-fighters, laughed heartily at 'The Shadow of a Gunman'.

When Sean O'Casey came to write 'Juno and the Paycock' – the first of what James Agate called the two 'blazing master-pieces; the greatest since the Elizabethans' – it looked as if he had forsworn the evil of didacticism. He had said what he wanted to say far too directly in 'Cathleen' and it had been received in cold silence by the very audience that had given a warm welcome to 'The Gunman'. He was finished with all that; or was he?

Lady Gregory in her Journal of 8 March, 1924, wrote as follows: 'In the evening to the Abbey with W. B. Yeats, "Juno and the Paycock" (Sean O'Casey's) – a long queue at the door, the theatre crowded, many turned away, so it will be run on next week. A wonderful and terrible play of futility, of irony, humour, tragedy. When I went round to the green-room I saw Casey and had a little talk with him. He is very happy. . . . And he said, "I owe a great deal to you and to Mr Yeats and Mr Robinson, but to you above all. You gave me encouragement. And it was you who said to me upstairs in the office – I could show you the very spot where you stood – 'Mr Casey, your gift is characterisation' and so I threw over my theories and worked at characters and this is the result".'

That he had worked hard was very evident in 'Juno'. Boyle, Joxer, Johnny, Mary and Juno herself are characters very much 'in the round'. They are what they are, and absolutely. Shields and Davoren in 'The Gunman' are to a great extent mouth-pieces for their author. The 'characters' of 'Cathleen' are all mouthpieces. But the characters in 'Juno' are characters in their own right; objectively drawn, in every sense 'creations', no longer attached by umbilical cords to their author, possessing souls which can be saved or damned.

There is a sense in which they could be described as tailor-made, so well did they fit the players for whom they were in-tended – Sara Allgood, Barry Fitzgerald, F. J. McCormick and the rest. Sean had benefited considerably by his sojourn in the Abbey's 'theatre workshop'. He had come to know the players, to be familiar with their acting techniques, and this unconsciously influenced him in the creation of these characters. This, of course, is the common experience of any dramatist in close touch with a repertory theatre.

'Juno and the Paycock' lays bare the futile tragedy of civil war; and it is an indication of how much it expressed the feelings of the Irish people that not one word of protest was heard despite the fact that the play was presented at a time when the noise of battle had barely died away. Had the play ended on Juno's final exit in Act Three – 'Sacred Heart o' Jesus take away our hearts o' stone and give us hearts o' flesh! (An echo from Ezekiel) Take away

Dublin's Amiens Street railway station, where O'Casey once worked

this murdherin' hate, an' give us Thine own eternal love!' – it would still be a great tragedy. What makes it a masterpiece is the scene of blistering irony that follows in which the flannel-mouthed wasters – Boyle and Joxer – mix maudlin sentimentality and patriotic jingo till it produces the drunken conclusion that the whole world is in 'a terrible state o' chassis'.

What gives 'Juno' its universality, and has made it acceptable, despite its Irish Civil War theme, to the minds of many nationalities (not excluding the Japanese) is to be found in its message –

if it can be said to have a message – which expresses itself in two lines in Act Three when Mary Boyle, broken under the full impact of the family's tragedy, cries out:

'Oh, it's thrue, it's thrue what Jerry Devine says – there isn't a God, there isn't a God; if there was He wouldn't let these things happen!'

And Juno, that valiant woman, replies:

'Mary, you mustn't say them things. We'll want all the help we can get from God and His Blessed Mother now! These things have nothin' to do with the Will o' God. Ah, what can God do agin the stupidity o' men!'

In that last sentence lies the message of 'Juno and the Paycock' – what can God do against the stupidity of men, those men to whom He has given the gift of free will. Hardly the message of an 'irreligious' playwright.

It should be noted that the representative of labour in 'Juno', Jerry Devine, fares rather badly at his author's hands. In 'Cathleen' Sean had already lampooned labour in his 'Jimmy, a workman' and his 'Tomaus Thornton, a neighbour'. In 'Juno' when Devine fully grasps the situation in which his loved one finds herself his remark is:

'My God, Mary, have you fallen as low as that?'

compelling Mary to reply: 'Let us say no more, Jerry: I don't blame you for thinkin' it's terrible. . . . I suppose it is. . . . Everybody'll think the same . . . it's only as I expected – your humanity is just as narrow as the humanity of the others.'

So much for Jerry Devine, socialist, poet, trade unionist, whose verses on 'Humanity's Strife with Nature' Mary begins to quote, verses that in form and content bear the unmistakable hall-mark of Sean O'Casey. So, too, does the form of the dialogue given to Jerry. Actors complain – and not without reason – that it is stilted, 'unnatural'. Yet those who knew Sean O'Casey will agree that it is very much his own personal style. There was to be a further sample of it in 'The Plough and the Stars' in scenes between the Clitheroes in Act One.

That Sean O'Casey was dissatisfied with 'Nannie's Night Out' there was not the slightest doubt. There is a sense in which it might be said that he had written it merely 'to keep his hand in'. He was beginning to be persuaded (by me particularly) that he had written not only a great play, but a masterpiece, in 'Juno and the Paycock', and so he eventually came to bring forth 'The

207

Plough and the Stars', a work in which he enshrined his personal vision of the insurrection of Easter 1916.

In 'Juno' he had poured out his sympathy on the victims of the Civil War; in 'The Plough' he was to do the same with Easter 1916 as a background. In this play the universal is the plight of ordinary folk – particularly women – when caught between warring combatants. Its point is as applicable today in any war-torn place as it was in Dublin in 1916. 'The Plough' is the work of a pacifist; this fact is crystal clear.

Though he had been at one time the secretary of the Citizen Army whose members gave a good account of themselves, though faced with desperate odds, that memorable Easter, Sean had made it obvious in his booklet *The Story of the Irish Citizen Army* that we would never see him with a rifle in his hand. Although he kept company with men preparing for battle he was not willing to go forth with them to the ultimate issue. Some of his comrades of that time still hold this against him, but the Irish people as a whole have never charged him with a dereliction of duty.

When the Abbey Theatre presented his play to packed audiences at the Aldwych Theatre, London, a few years ago, the English drama critic Harold Hobson, disturbed by the rapturous reception which the play received, particularly from Irish exiles, was at some pains to point out that the work was directed against the ideals of 1916 and the sacrifice made by the men who fought and died in the Rising. But Mr Hobson seemingly overlooked a passage in the play which redeems it of much of its pacificism and brings to the fore again the blazing Irish patriotism which informed all of O'Casey's early prose and verse. It is that passage in Act Four in which Sergeant Tinley describes the rebels as a 'gang of hassassins potting at us from behind roofs'. And he goes on: 'That's not playing the goime: why down't they come into the owpen and fight fair!' And Fluther (unable to stand the slight) replies: 'Fight fair! A few hundred scrawls o' chaps with a couple o' guns an' Rosary beads, again' a hundred thousand thrained men with horse, fut, an' artillery . . . and he wants us to fight fair! D'ye want us to come out in our skins an' throw stones?' In the light of that near-factual description of the events of 1916, and O'Casey's reaction to them, Mr Hobson was merely wasting his words.

Another feature of 'The Plough' is its author's treatment of the play's avowed communist, The Covey. Not content with making

208

him a figure of fun he robs him of any human feeling in the scene with Rosie Redmond in Act Two:

> THE COVEY (savagely to Rosie): Nobody's askin' you to be buttin' in with your prate. . . . I have you well taped, me lassie. . . . Just you keep your opinions for your own place. . . . It'll be a long time before th' Covey takes any insthructions or reprimandin' from a prostitute!
> ROSIE (wild with humiliation): You louse, you louse, you! . . . You're no man . . . you're no man . . . I'm a woman, anyhow, an' if I'm a prostitute aself, I have me feelin's. . . .

Added to his treatment of Jerry Devine in 'Juno' and the two labour representatives in 'Cathleen' it is obvious that Sean O'Casey found no heroes in the movement with which he was associated for so many years. In 'Juno' the heroine is the suffering mother, most strikingly seen in Juno herself. In 'The Plough' heroism is divided equally between Bessie Burgess and Fluther Good.

I have told elsewhere how jealousy, quarrels, misunderstanding and rumour led to an inept first production of 'The Plough' and sparked off a 'riot' which was responsible for considerable misunderstanding of the play. When the play, shortly after its Dublin production, was played under James Bernard Fagan's management in London (with Sara Allgood as Bessie Burgess – the part had been specifically written for her) it became for James Agate Sean O'Casey's second 'blazing masterpiece'. To those who have any knowledge of the theatre in depth a 'blazing masterpiece' it still remains.

When the shock of Yeats' rejection of 'The Silver Tassie' (an unwise judgement if ever there was one) doomed O'Casey to permanent exile and robbed him of that 'theatre workshop' which the Abbey Theatre had provided, the dramatist found himself writing *in vacuo*. As Richard Findlater puts it, he became 'a victim of his own dogmas'. Yeats had told him in the correspondence which followed the rejection of 'The Silver Tassie' that an author's opinions should burn themselves up in the dramatic flame. O'Casey retorted by instancing Shaw and declaring that the only way to burn opinions was to burn the holder along with them. He was determined to go his own way from now on; and to forget Lady Gregory's 'Mr Casey, your gift is characterisation', possibly because the characters which deeply interested him were no longer a part of the life around him.

Probably no critic of standing cried up the later work of Sean O'Casey so much as the late George Jean Nathan. I have always believed that had Nathan even once turned his thumbs down Sean might have paused to consider the direction in which he was going. It is therefore ironic to find Robert Brustein, Professor of Dramatic Literature at Columbia University, and winner of the 1962 George Jean Nathan Award as the outstanding drama critic in the United States, writing about Sean O'Casey in the foreword to his recent work *The Theatre of Revolt* as follows: 'There are those who may regret the omission of Sean O'Casey; but he has always struck me as an extremely over-rated writer with two or three competent Naturalist plays to his credit, followed by a lot of ideological bloat and embarrassing bombast.'

Even those who are prepared to admit the bloat and the bombast will challenge the mere 'competence' of O'Casey's earlier plays. Let the last word be with Richard Findlater, no lover of the dramatist's later work. In these earlier plays, writes Findlater, 'O'Casey was concerned to prove nothing but the reality of poverty and pain, showing, with a kind of savage love, the complexity of life behind creeds and slogans, ironically observing the confusion of the ideal and the actual, the glory and the squalor, the tragic and the trivial. . . .' Findlater finds that what is distinctive about these early plays is their Elizabethan mixture of tragedy and comedy. 'This', he writes, 'is not a deliberate contrivance of variety in theatrical effect, but the bitter-sweet confusion of life itself, in art, translated with a passionate coherence and unity of effect that makes these tragic-comedies minor masterpieces.' 'Minor' no doubt – Mr Findlater is not as impulsively enthusiastic as James Agate – but 'masterpieces' yes; masterpieces, and as such they have nothing whatever to do with either mere competence or smart photography.

3

THE EXCITEMENTS AND THE DISAPPOINTMENTS

By Kevin Casey

THE Theatrical 'Twenties were bright and gay, tinsel bright and terribly gay and the bright young things were brighter and younger than ever before. The Tiller girls were saucy and daring and Mr Cochrane's Young Ladies, boa-feathered and beaded, smiled and smirked and pranced about, showing permissable amounts of theatrical thigh. If you happened to be passing the Ivy Restaurant, you might have seen Felix or Gordon, Noel or even Gertie, suavely enthusiastic, teeth flashing like neon, congratulating each other on their latest success. And if your interest in the theatre had grown to the extent that you sometimes actually went to plays, you could have seen 'Battling Butler', 'Bluebeard's Eighth Wife', 'The Gentleman from Dartmoor', 'Her Cardboard Lover', 'Kitty's Kisses', 'Mayfair and Montmartre', 'Mrs. Dot', 'That's a Good Girl', and a host of other theatrical classics. The well-bred laugh was almost everything; sex was soporific (such a bore really); life wasn't very complex (Come Charles, tell me about that woman. I can steel myself to hear it); and for strong emotion there was 'The Chinese Bungalow' with Mr Matheson Lang's memorable, soul-searing, heart-wrenching line: 'If Sadie be guilty then the Chinese husband, Yuan Sing, may find consolation with her pure sister Charlotte.'

In 1928, R. C. Sheriff's play, 'Journey's End' was produced in the West End and was an immediate success. Ostensibly about the First World War, it is really a cleverly disguised piece of public school waffle. It deals with a Captain Dennis Stanhope who has spent three years on the British front and who fortifies his nerves by making frequent excursions to a bottle of whisky. His second-in-command is an elderly ex-schoolmaster called Lieut. Osborne who, in the intervals between the off-stage shrieking of shells, edifies the company by describing the beauty of New Forest scenery and the romance of the Roman excavations in Sussex. All is more or less well until young Raleigh arrives and complicates the issues of a perfectly simple, chequer-board war. He has been at the same school as Stanhope – we sense the neatly striped tie, the rolled-gold cuff links, the smell of well-oiled cricket bats, the jocosity of annual reunions – and regards him as a faultless hero. Stanhope, however, is less than pleased at the arrival, for he is afraid that details of his drinking habits will filter back to Raleigh's sister with whom, we are encouraged to believe, he has that kind of platonic understanding which only British playwrights and some British audiences seem to comprehend. We are not at war but in a strange land whose inhabitants have discovered the grotesque secret of perpetual youth.

Osborne gets killed in a raid and Stanhope's upper lip is pliable enough to find its way round the rim of a consoling glass of rationed champagne. Then Raleigh is wounded and Stanhope receives orders to return to the trenches from which he may never emerge. Misty-eyed, the audiences of the 'twenties learned that a well-educated Englishman will never shirk his duty. In the glow of her elderly maturity, Terence Rattigan's Aunt Edna may be a silly old bore; it is some consolation to realise that she was worse, far worse, in her youth.

It was to this suffocating theatrical climate and to audiences like these that Sean O'Casey came with his raw and ugly, powerful and uncompromisingly honest war play, 'The Silver Tassie'. It ran for eight weeks and was a financial failure. For O'Casey's battlefield had nothing at all to do with the playing-fields of Eton; his war was a gigantic futile tragedy, not an emotional game.

Its second act marked O'Casey's first important break from the naturalistic techniques which he had used so well in his early Abbey Theatre plays. Had he wished to do so he could certainly have continued writing in the old vein, but he always believed that experiment was an essential part of a writer's development and when he saw Ernst Toller's expressionistic play 'Masse Mensch' he was immediately impressed by the powerful effectiveness of this form. Toller, who might be described as a pessimistic Socialist, believed that great art was never really timeless. 'Whether we consider', he wrote, 'Sophocles, Aristophanes, Dante, Shakespeare, Kleist, Buchner, Schiller, they all use "topical problems" and try to give them an "eternal" interpretation. They were the mouthpieces of an era, inspired by the era, of a community struggling in the era.'[1]

This 'eternal' interpretation of 'topical problems' is an adequate summary of what Expressionism seeks to achieve. It is concerned, not with photographic representation, but with human destiny and the essential significance of each situation. By the use of allegorical and symbolic characters, it tears off masks and exposes the gap that so often lies between appearance and reality. An extremely difficult form, it is used with great effectiveness in the second act of 'The Silver Tassie' to depict the essence of all wars.

O'Casey's next two plays, 'Within the Gates' and 'The Star turns Red' are totally expressionistic and contain many of the complex linguistic patterns which, in an attempt to create a new language of the theatre, he was to develop in all his succeeding work. The later plays delve into the possibilities of new structures and new forms; they have scenes of naturalism, expressionism, farce, lyricism, symbolism and melodrama. They are like theatrical kaleidoscopes in which life is coaxed and shaken, beaten and bullied, into highly coloured, highly ornate, highly unusual shapes and patterns. By 1934, O'Casey had arrived at one of his many unalterable conclusions on the theatre. 'Gay, farcical, comic or tragical, it must be, not the commonplace portrayal of the trivial events in the life of this man or that woman, but a commentary on life itself. This is the main thing to be done if drama of today is to be in the main stream of the great drama of the past. To achieve this the veneration of real-ism, or, as Archer called it, pure imitation, must cease and imagination be crowned queen of the drama again.'[2] And this is what his plays are – a commentary on life as he saw it and imagined it to be; life with a capital L, life as an almost tangible thing to be exulted in and glorified. The dramatic clashes in his plays are between forces of life and anti-life; youth, wildness, freedom, romantic love on one side; age, bitterness, hypocrisy, piosity and fear on the other.

This short essay cannot claim to be a detailed critical assess-ment of Sean O'Casey's plays. It is, rather, an attempt to com-municate some personal reactions, the excitement and dis-appointment which they have caused me. The theatre may be a social art but it must be entertaining, in the way that the plays of Shaw and Brecht are entertaining, before it can be successfully didactic. I must confess that I am a great deal more interested in the energy and urgency of O'Casey's plays, in their shape, their language and theatrical effectiveness, than in their power to con-vince me of some intellectual or ideological argument. To me, his plays are lyric, not merely because they make use of song and dance but because their overriding preoccupation is feeling.

The first act of 'The Silver Tassie' takes place in 'the eating, sitting and part sleeping room of the Heegan family'. This setting is most carefully described in the printed text[3] and, significantly there is a strong emphasis on colour. '. . . a white light . . . a stand, the legs gilded silver, the top gilded gold . . . purple velvet shield . . . silver medals . . . a few gold ones . . . red and yellow ribbons . . . a bedspread of black striped with vivid green . . . a red coloured stand . . . silvered gilt framed picture . . . crimson jersey with yellow collar and cuffs and a broad yellow belt, black stockings, and yellow football boots.' Colours play an important part in all O'Casey's plays; they keep on cropping up in the dialogue and it is sometimes possible to assess a character by the colour of the clothes which the text demands he should wear. While it is true that a man's clothes, like a man's wife, can often be a superficial indication of his personality, it is also true that as O'Casey continued to broaden his spectrum, at one end vivid, at the other drab, his characters, with the notable exception of Father Boheroe in 'The Bishop's Bonfire', tend to fit a little too conveniently into slots marked black and white. Few good dramatists have loaded the dice so blatantly. This kind of character analysis is, of course, strangely pre-Freudian, but outside the limits of the strictly naturalistic theatre is not a matter for easy condemnation and is defended with spirit and conviction in a number of the essays collected in *Under a Coloured Cap*.[4]

Harry Heegan, 'a typical young worker, enthusiastic, very often boisterous, sensible by instinct rather than reason' is the hero of 'The Silver Tassie'. At the beginning of the first act he is playing in a football match and his almost legendary feats of skill and athletic daring are being discussed by his father, Sylvester, and a Joxer-type buttie called Simon Norton. Conflict is introduced by Susie Monican who shields her unrequited love for Harry with a bitter religious fanaticism. She insists on listing the things which she considers to be completely opposed to a young man's joy in life. Predominant amongst these are the Last Judgement and the fires of Hell. 'It's persecutin', Sylvester says, 'that tambourine theology of Susie's. I always get a curious, sickenin' feelin', Simon, when I hear the name of the Supreme Bein' tossed into the quietness of sensible conversation.' Harry has to return to the war later in the evening ('He has gone to the trenches', O'Casey tells us, 'as unthinkingly as he would go to the polling booth'), a predicament shared by Teddy Foran who, in a richly comic scene, becomes enraged at his wife's obvious pleasure in his impending departure – she admits to being in a 'doxological mood' – smashes all the cutlery in their flat and chases her into the Heegan room where she is joined under the bed by her defending hero Sylvester.

This comic material is used so that Harry's triumphant entrance will be forceful and vivid in contrast. Accompanied by his girl, Jessie Tate, and a friend, Barney Bagnal, he is jubilant at having kicked the winning goal and won, for his team, the Silver Tassie. He refers to this cup as 'the sign of youth, sign of strength, sign of victory'; in the last act it becomes a symbol of all he has lost. Jessie and he drink wine from the cup but the troop-ship's siren can be heard and the women, who can understand the domestic importance of a soldier's allowance but not the universal tragedy of a soldier's job, bundle their men back to war.

This, O'Casey insinuates, is the waiting world, a natural composite of farce and melodrama, going along as usual, unprepared and unknowing. There are no false heroics, no misty-eyed departures, yet the unthinking indifference of those who are staying at home underlines the separateness of the soldiers. Like puppets, for they seem naïvely uninvolved, they are going blindly and alone towards their own tragedies.

The second and expressionistic act takes place 'In the war zone; a scene of jagged lacerated ruin of what was once a monastery'. This setting is surrealistic; the sky is red, the dark bulk of a howitzer gun can be seen through an archway; an arm of the life-sized figure on a broken crucifix stretches towards a stained glass window of the Virgin; on a pedestal beneath the crucifix are the red-lettered words PRINCEPS PACIS.

The monastery is being used as a Red Cross centre and soldiers stand around or lie on stretchers in careless, aimless groups. Above them is 'The Croucher', a shell-shocked soldier whose head and hands look like those of a skeleton. As an organ is heard playing in the distance, the Croucher leads the soldiers in intoning a parody of the Book of Ezekiel. A short extract should give some indication of the scene's immense power.

CROUCHER (resuming): And I prophesised, and the breath came out of them, and the sinews came away from them, and behold a shaking and their bones fell asunder, bone from his bone, and they died, and the exceeding great army became a valley of dry bones. (The voice from the monastery is heard, clearly for the first half of the sentence, then dying away towards the end): Accendat in nobis Dominus ignem sui amoris, et flammam aeternae caritatis. (A group of soldiers come in from fatigue, bunched together as if for comfort and warmth. They are wet and cold, and they are sullen faced. They form a circle around the brazier and stretch their hands toward the blaze.)

1ST SOLDIER: Cold and wet and tir'd.

2ND SOLDIER: Wet and tir'd and cold.

3RD SOLDIER: Tir'd and cold and wet.

4TH SOLDIER (very like Teddy): Twelve blasted hours of ammunition transport fatigue!

1ST SOLDIER: Twelve weary hours.

2ND SOLDIER: And wasting hours.

3RD SOLDIER: And hot and heavy hours.

1ST SOLDIER: Toiling and thinking to build the wall of force that blocks the way from here to home.

2ND SOLDIER: Lifting shells.

3RD SOLDIER: Carrying shells.

4TH SOLDIER: Piling shells.

1ST SOLDIER: In the falling, pissing rine and whistling wind.

2ND SOLDIER: The whistling wind and falling, drenching rain.

3RD SOLDIER: The God-dam rain and blasted whistling wind.

1ST SOLDIER: And the shirkers sife at home coil'd up at ease.

2ND SOLDIER: Shells for us and pianos for them.

3RD SOLDIER: Fur coats for them and winding-sheets for us.

4TH SOLDIER: Warm.

2ND SOLDIER: And dry.

1ST SOLDIER: An' 'appy.

(A slight pause)

BARNEY: An' they call it re-cu-per-at-ing!

The gun and the crucifix, the organ music and this parody, opposing forces, the sacred and the profane. O'Casey chose the ritual of chanting as a universally recognised method of worship and reshaped it into powerful dramatic despair. The sharp irony of opposing forces becomes even more obvious later in the act when the corporal leads a chant of worship to the howitzer.

216

CORPORAL: Hail, cool-hardened tower of steel emboss'd,
With the fever'd, figment thoughts of man;
Guardian of our love and hate and fear,
Speak for us to the inner ear of God!
SOLDIERS: We believe in God and we believe in thee.

These are men pressed into corporate anonymity by the ritual of war, dreamily responding to what is required of them and yet unable to sever completely the nostalgic cord that joins them to what was once their world: thoughts of opulence and the inevitable missus. And the only contacts which they now have with this world, a Visitor and a Staff-Wallah, two farcical figures who stand out in sharp relief against the expressionistic background, reinforce this isolated loneliness by their bumbling, ineffectuality.

Some critics have argued that this act could be left out of 'The Silver Tassie' without making any appreciable difference to the play's overall impact. I disagree. Although Harry Heegan is not identified by name, we know that he is one of this anonymous group. We have seen his triumphant departure and will see his defeated return. This act shows, in the most powerful possible way, the forces that worked on him between these two events. And it ensures that there is no false heroic glamour attached to his wounds. War, it tells us, is utterly meaningless; it maims, dehumanises and corrupts. If it were omitted, the play would be about the very real, but rather insular, personal tragedy of Harry Heegan, and not a striking indictment of constituted authority.

The third act is set in a hospital ward. Sylvester and Simon are patients in this hospital, enjoying a rest, reluctant to take a bath, indignant that everyone doesn't sympathise with the burden of their imaginary pains. They provide rich comic relief – though we keep on remembering the very different hospital in the previous act. Susie Monican has now become an alert, efficient and thoroughly unrepressed nurse, but her transformation is not at all as startling as that of Teddy Foran, who is now blind and helpless, or Harry Heegan who has to wheel himself around in an invalid chair. Bitter, moody and inconsolable, he has been deserted by Jessie and betrayed by Barney with whom she is now in love. 'Oh Susannah, Susannah, how are the mighty fallen and the weapons of war perished', says Sylvester when he sees Susie Monican being kissed by the dandy surgeon Maxwell. The quotation might be aptly applied to Harry; nobody is interested in his past but everybody seems embarrassed at his presence.

Act Four takes place in a 'room off the dance hall of the Avon-
dale Football Club'. Sylvester and Simon again provide the comic
contrast but the essential mood of the act is tragic. Harry, consumed with bitterness, follows Jessie and Barney like an ominous
shadow. 'Here he comes', Jessie says, 'prowling after us again!
His watching of us is pulling all the enjoyment out of the night.
It makes me shiver to feel him wheeling after us'. 'We'll watch',
Barney replies, 'for a chance to shake him off, an' if he starts
again we'll make him take his tangled body somewhere else.'

As in the first act, Harry drinks from the Tassie but the 'sign
of youth, sign of strength, sign of victory' has now become a
bitter cup. '. . . red wine', he toasts, 'red like the blood that was
shed for you and for many for the commission of sin.' He is
persuaded to play his ukulele – the only thing he can now do
well – and we are again haunted by the second act for the exhorta-
tions are written in a manner that re-echoes the chanting of the
soldiers. He sings a negro spiritual, fights with Barney and
leaves, but not entirely without hope. 'What's in front we'll face
like men', he says to Teddy. 'The Lord hath given and man hath
taken away.' Mrs Foran is given the brilliantly ordinary and
very memorable curtain line: 'It's a terrible pity Harry was too
weak to stay an' sing his song for there's nothing I love more
than the ukulele's tinkle, tinkle in the night time.'

The ukulele's tinkle, tinkle – thing small enough to be understood and enjoyed. But war remains incomprehensible and
tragedy can build a barrier against both understanding and
compassion. I admire 'The Silver Tassie' because it is an ex-
ceedingly modern play, a passionate and deeply-felt outcry
against several levels of injustice. Technically, it is a fine achievement; very few writers could or can juxtapose so many elements
to form such a convincing and cohesive theatrical whole.
Language is used expertly, not only in the day-to-day communi-
cative sense but also to create environment, a rich, textural back-
drop against which the characters can be seen in ironic or
pathetic contrast. As in the plays of John Arden, a writer whose
theatrical genius is strangely similar to that of O'Casey, it is
impossible to identify oneself conveniently or consistently with
any one of the characters. The play changes our attitudes and
viewpoints: we struggle, we give in; the essential magic is at
work.

'Within the Gates'[3] and 'The Star turns Red'[3] are stylish and
difficult plays, picturesque, formal and often irritating. The first

is set in Hyde Park. In his interesting, though sad, book, *Sean O'Casey, the Man I Knew*[5], Gabriel Fallon describes how fascinated O'Casey was when he discovered that bizarre cross-section of life which, every week, praises, abuses, heckles and weeps for humanity at Speaker's Corner. 'It was not so much on the formal platforms as in the small knots of off-stage disputants', Mr Fallon wrote, 'that Sean found those characters in action that lifted up the dramatist's heart in him.' And although many of the speakers whom I have heard there seem to be intent on imitating vintage O'Casey characters, the dramatist, in an effort to get back to the poetic significance of the theatre, chose to treat his material in an entirely expressionistic manner. The play is divided into four scenes – a morning in spring, a noon in summer, an evening in autumn and a winter's night. It starts with a symbolic chorus of nature's rebirth and ends with the symbolic death of Jannice, a young prostitute who is searching for a cause, a purpose, an identity in life.

She believes that a character known as the Atheist is her father, but from him we learn that she is really the illegitimate daughter of a student of theology – a fine example of dice-loading at its most blatant. The Atheist had her released from a Church Institution by pretending that he was her father and since then has done his best to take away 'a supernatural 'eaven from over 'er 'ead an' an unnatural 'ell from under 'er feet', but without success. Jannice is tormented by her vision of hell fire: 'Green-eyed, barrel-bellied men glare and grin at me; huge-headed, yellow-eyed women beckon to me out of the glow from the fire that can never be quenched. Black feathered owls with eyes like great white moons, peck at me as they fly through the glow from the fire that can never be quenched.' 'You led her from one darkness into another, man', the Dreamer tells the Atheist when he admits that he hasn't taught Jannice song. 'Will none of you ever guess that man can study man or worship God, in dance and song and story!' The Dreamer speaks with O'Casey's voice but he is surrounded by the forces of anti-life; futile argument, cowardice, cunning and hypocrisy. The play is about the battle between conscience and instinct, the spirit represented by religion and the flesh symbolised by the Dreamer, who stands in some uneasy yet secure place between Christianity and Atheism. In the first scene, a Bishop visits the Park with his impossible sister, to see the other half living. He has no idea who Jannice is but we realise that he is the one-time student of theology. He feels drawn to her but when she goes to him for help in the second scene he is emotionally sterile and unable to offer anything but platitudes. The Dreamer offers her love; afraid of his philosophy she flirts with him, but chooses religion in the form of a Salvation Army officer who claims that he can give her peace everlasting. But she soon discovers that a fear of God can often be the expression of a fear of life, and in the third scene she finally goes to the Dreamer and discovers love.

As these semi-symbolic figures are going about their way, there are some splendid moments of broad, naturalistic comedy. These are provided by minor characters, hecklers, chair attendants and passers-by. This short extract is typical of the humour which O'Casey injects into his sub-plot. The man with the umbrella is attempting to explain the theory of relativity.

MAN WITH UMBRELLA: (pompously) Now try to remember that all th' old idears of the cosmos – Greek for all things th' 'uman mind knows of – are buried with Copernicus, Kepler, Newton, en' all that crew.

GUARDSMAN: (emphatically) 'Course they is, en' deep too.

MAN WITH UMBRELLA: Now we all know that the clock created time, en' the measuring-rod created spice, so that there is really neither spice nor time; but there is such a thing as spice-time. See? Get that?

MAN WEARING TRILBY: (with confidence) Quite; that much is perfectly clear.

MAN WITH UMBRELLA: Right. Now suppose that one night, when we all slept, th' universe we know sank down to the size of a football, an' all the clocks began to move a thousand times quicker – no, slower – it wouldn't make the slightest difference to us, for we wouldn't realise that any difference 'ad tyken plice, though each of us would live a thousand times longer, an' man couldn't be seen, even under a microscope.

GUARDSMAN: (jocularly) Could a woman be seen under a microscope?

MAN WEARING CAP: (to Guardsman) Levity's outa plice, friend, when men are trying to think out th' truth of things.

GUARDSMAN: But 'ow could th' world sink dahn to th' size of a football? Doesn't seem a sife thing to me.

MAN WITH UMBRELLA: (with cold dignity) I said *if* it did, friend.

GUARDSMAN: (trying to find a way out) Yes; but if a man couldn't be seen under a microscope, wot abaht 'is kids?

MAN WITH UMBRELLA: I simply stated a hypothenuse, friend.

MAN WEARING CAP: (to Guardsman) It's only en hypothenuse, you understand. (To Man with Umbrella) But it's en impossible one, I think. D'ye mean that under your hypothenuse, en hour of the clock would stretch aht into ten years of time?

MAN WITH UMBRELLA: Exactly that in spice-time; en 'undred years if you like.

MAN WEARING CAP: Wot? Then in your spice-time, a man doin' eight hours would be workin' for eight 'undred years!

GUARDSMAN: (to Man with Umbrella) You're barmy, man! Wot abaht the bloke doin' penal servitude fer life? When is 'e agoin' to get aht? You're barmy, man!

NURSEMAID: (to Guardsman – chucking his arm) Are you comin', Harry? If you don't 'urry, I'll 'ave to go, 'en you'll 'ave to go withaht even a firewell squeeze.

MAN WITH UMBRELLA: (annoyed – to Guardsman) Look, friend, if I was you, I'd go with the girl; for it's pline your mind 'asn't been educyted yet to grasp the complicyted functions of wot we know as spice-time problems.

Now this exchange may not be very important to Sean O'Casey's overall purpose but it is an admirable piece of characterisation. Even on the printed page it conjures up a vivid picture; the intense little man with the umbrella growing steadily more annoyed, the man with the cap who isn't really sure where he stands but is determined to make contribution, the solid, practical Guardsman who wants to find a flaw and impress the nursemaid who really couldn't care less. In contrast, the principle characters are regrettably remote and it is difficult to feel very strongly about Jannice's predicament. Her discovery of love has come too late – 'Death has touched me', she says – the forces of anti-life have drained away her vitality and a chorus of Down-and-Outs, a dark, desperate, fearful band who beat their breasts and lament over life, symbolise her approaching death. The Bishop refuses her his blessing, but without having fully accepted the Dreamer's philosophy she now knows that religion and joy are not incompatible. 'I'll go the last few steps of the way rejoicing', she says. 'I'll go, go game and I'll die dancing.' She joins the Dreamer in a hysterical dance and, before dying, has her hand guided in making the sign of the Cross by the Bishop

221

who has found new compassion. 'Go home, go home, for Christ's sake, woman', he says to his sister who is shocked to see him so changed, 'and ask God's mercy on us all.' In outline, this plot is dangerously like the many old melodramas of the whore with the heart of gold who seeks love and doesn't live to enjoy it. It is only fair to say that many critics – notably David Krause – have found the play to be a devastating criticism of both religion and life. I can follow Mr Krause a little way along this road but must stop abruptly at the first corner. If Sean O'Casey wished to say that Christianity would be an excellent way of life if Christians would only practise it, the point seems valid but the manner of expressing it quite inordinately complex. An argument based on a clash of ultimates can hardly leave us with any real conviction; the mind demands some of those instantly recognisable moments of shared experience which strike responsive chords. This is not a criticism of the Expressionistic manner but of the way in which O'Casey allowed it blur his purpose. His characters are thrown too far out of focus and the predominant note is one of sentimental confusion.

Ultimates clash again in 'The Star Turns Red'; apparent personality struggles are really battles of totally opposed ideologies. It is Sean O'Casey's least successful play and even when the political problems which it examines were a great deal more relevant than they are now, it is difficult to believe that it was anything more than mildly interesting. Dedicated to the men and women who fought through the Dublin lockout of 1913, it has two kinds of characters – some completely symbolic and others suggesting a sense of reality. On one level it is the story of a young man, Jack, his love for a girl called Julia and his conflict with his brother, Kian. On another, it is the story of the struggle of Red Jim, who symbolises Communism, with the Purple Priest, who symbolises the Church, and the Lord Mayor, a symbol for the State. The action is operatic; a shooting, a whipping, a battle fought to the music of Glazounov's Preamble to his *Scenes de Ballet*. It means very little to me. I prefer to pass on to a gloriously funny and completely successful farce called 'Purple Dust'.

Basil Stoke and Cyril Poges are British financiers who, having made their money on the stock-markets, are attempting to live the life of dashing, romantic, bottom-pinching, bucolic squires. They have bought a Tudor-Elizabethan mansion in Ireland and it is being renovated by a number of marvellously inactive and incompetent workmen who touch their forelocks in mockery and do everything possible to shatter their masters' dreams. Basil and Cyril have Irish mistresses, Avril and Souhaun, whom the workmen can remember as little girls running around in tattered petticoats; the first appearance of this entourage sets a tone of high farce from which the play never wavers. They dance around wearing smocks over their morning clothes and carrying miniature rakes, hoes and spades:

BASIL: (singing) Our music, now, is the cow's sweet moo,
The pigeon's coo,
The lark's song too,
And the cock's shrill cock-a-doodle-doo,
ALL: In the bosky countrie!
(Chorus)
Hey, hey, the country's here,
The country's there,
It's everywhere!
We'll have it, now, last thing at night,
And the very first thing in the morning!
(The workmen are unimpressed)

1ST WORKMAN: Well, God help the poor omadhauns! It's a bad sign to see people actin' like that, an' they sober.

3RD WORKMAN: A sthrange crowd, they are, to come gallivantin' outa the city to a lonely an' inconsidered place like this.

1ST WORKMAN: At home, now, they'd be sinkin' into their first sleep; but because they're in the counthry they think the thing to do is get up at the crack o' dawn.

3RD WORKMAN: An' they killin' themselves thryin' to look as if the counthry loved them all their life.

1ST WORKMAN: With the young heifer gaddin' round with next to nothin' on, goadin' the decency an' circumspection of the place.

3RD WORKMAN: An' her eyes wiltin' when she sees what she calls her husband an' widenin' wondherfully whenever they happen to light on O'Killigain.

O'Killigain is a local hero and he is aided in placing obstacles before the Englishmen's progress by one of the workmen, a richly romantic, almost mythological chacter called O'Dempsey. 'I believe in efficiency', Cyril says, 'I demand efficiency from

223

myself, from everyone. Do the thing thoroughly and do it well; that's English. The word given and the word kept; that's English': but the most efficient thing in sight is the skilful way in which O'Killigain and O'Dempsey make love to Avril and Souhaun. All else is chaos. The two financiers quickly lose their enthusiasm for nature when they come face to face with cows, 'irresponsible' horses, 'entherprisin' hins' and 'cocks that'll do you credit'. In a wonderfully farcical episode, 'plaster falls and a hole appears in the ceiling, almost directly over the fireplace; then a thin rope, with a bulb attached to its end, comes dangling down, followed by the face of a heavily yellow-bearded man, who thrusts his head as far as it can go through the hole.

YELLOW-BEARDED MAN: (to those below) Hay, hay, there; is this where yous want the light to go?

POGES: (with a vexatious yell when he sees where the rope hangs) No it isn't, no it isn't, you fool! (indicating a place near the centre and towards the back) There, there's where it's wanted! Where my desk will be! Oh they're knocking down more than they're building up!

YELLOW-BEARDED MAN: (soothingly) Don't worry; just a little mistake in measurements, sir. Never fear, we'll hit the right spot one o' these days! The one thing to do, sir, is to keep cool.

At the end of the first act Avril goes away with O'Killigain. '. . . they cantered away together', Basil says, 'Naked and unashamed the vixen went . . .' and the workmen, unaware that he is speaking figuratively, discuss the scene with relish until they believe that they have actually witnessed it. 'The sight near left me eyes when I seen her go prancin' out without as much as a garther on her to keep her modesty from catchin' cold', says the first workman, and his companion agrees: 'This'll denude the disthrict of all its self-denyin' decency'. The yellow-bearded man, who has again stuck his head through the hole, is disgusted. 'Oh, isn't it like me to be up here outa sight o' th' world', he says, with aggravated anguish in his voice, 'an' great things happenin'!'

The misfortunes continue to pile up. The First Workman lets slip the information that the house is 'tottherin' down', gigantic rats are seen, Cyril's Annamese vase and Cambodian bowl are broken, though O'Killigain has thrown some doubts on their authenticity – '. . . . they went from Derby in thousands to Singapore and Saigon for suckers to buy them' – and Cyril demolishes a wall with a garden roller. 'Didn't I think it was an earthquake!' the yellow-bearded man says. 'An' don't be tellin' me these things while I'm up here. Can't you wait till I'm down in th' world o' men, and can enjoy these things happenin'!' And to complete the confusion that ends the second act, Basil shoots a cow. 'Oh what a terrible country to have anything to do with!' says the bewildered Cyril. '. . . . A no-man's land; a waste land; a wilderness!'

In the last act, furniture is manhandled, the local Canon pays a call and collects a subscription, Cyril's pleas for old fashioned dignity are ignored, the girls go away, and the two financiers are left alone as waters from a flooded river tumble in through the hall. 'Would to God I were in England', Cyril laments, 'now that winter's here!'

'Purple Dust' is a magnificently funny, skilfully constructed, buoyant, youthful farce, in which O'Casey lampoons both the English and the Irish character. Stokes and Poges try to live in the past but the present defeats them again and again. Their fussy authority and dreams of grandeur clash with the casual ineptness of the Irish who, ironically, are themselves rooted in the past and who remember their ancestry with the same degree of nostalgia that prompts Cyril to recall 'the les grand dames and the les grander monsieurs' who once lived in the house. O'Dempsey is a dreamer and is possibly more dignified than the Englishmen, but O'Casey laughs at a flaw in the Irish character when he makes him say: 'Me name's O'Dempsey, of the Clan that were lords of Offaly, ere his ancient highness here was a thousand years from bein' born; a clan that stretched back as far as the time before an Englishman thought of buildin' a weedy shelter; an farther back to a day or two afther the one when the sun herself was called upon to shine'. And he laughs at a weakness in the English character when he has Cyril reply contemptuously: 'You don't look it, my poor man'. And this devastating exchange is capped beautifully by O'Dempsey's: 'I feel it'.

'Purple Dust' is neither O'Casey's best nor most ambitious play but within its own well defined and accepted limitations, it is, I believe, his most successful.

'Red Roses for Me'[3] is, to some extent, a play of propaganda but the characterisation does not suffer as a result and Expressionism is used only when it is the most dramatically effective method of illuminating the action. It is a romantic play and its central character, a young poet and artist called Ayamonn Breydon, is an idealised creation. A man of passionate, almost fanatical, sincerity, he is one of the leaders of a union and is attempting to obtain a wage increase of a shilling for his fellow workers in a railway yard. As in the case of all O'Casey's spokesmen, his vision of life is strong and colourful. 'I tell you life is not one thing, but many things', he says to Sheila, his girl friend, 'a wide branching flame, grand and good to see and feel, dazzling to the eye of no one loving it. I am not one to carry fear about with me as a priest carries the Host. Let the timid tiptoe through the way where the paler blossoms grow; my feet shall be where the redder roses grow, though they bear long thorns, sharp and piercing, thick among them!'

The play's theme is concerned with Ayamonn's struggle to preserve this vision from constant forces of opposition. Sheila is a Catholic; her meetings with Ayamonn are against her parent's wishes and she pleads with him not to go ahead with his plans for the strike. Opposition also comes from 'a zealous Irish-Irelander' and strong believer in Fenianism, Roory O'Balacaun, and from Mulcanny, a cynical freethinker who believes that all the answers to man's salvation are to be found in science. Brennan o'the Moor, the 'owner of a few aul houses', a charitable, argumentative, likeable, strong-headed old Ulsterman, is the only one who can sympathise with Ayamonn's ideals.

The first act is mainly argument and exposition. In the second act the argument becomes less intellectual, less theoretical and a good deal less subtle; Sheila tells Ayamonn that he will be given a job as foreman if he agrees to leave the union but he believes so strongly that the liberation of the worker is his purpose in life that he can say: '. . . . Go to hell, girl. I have a soul to save as well as you'.

The third act is symbolic; the people of Dublin experience a dream vision of the way that life could be. Three neighbours of Ayamonn, Eeada, Dympna and Finnoola, black-shawled street dealers, symbolise the sorrowful Ireland. 'That's Dublin, Finnoola', Eeada says, 'an' the sky over it. Sorrow's a slush under our feet, up to our ankles, an' th' deep drip of it constant overhead.' 'A graveyard where the dead are all above th' ground', Dympna agrees. They remember Ireland's past – 'A gold-speckled candle, white as snow, was Dublin once' – but jeer at Brennan when he sings a romantic song. Ayamonn defends the song and exhorts the women and some men who lounge against house gables and the parapets of a bridge, to rouse themselves and see that the 'graveyard' could become a field of life and the slush of sorrow melt into contentment. And as they respond to his passionate belief, the scene does begin to change. The setting sun burnishes the sky and the 'houses on the far side of the river now bow to the visible world, decked in mauve and burnished bronze; and the men that have been lounging against them now stand stalwart, looking like fine bronze statues, slashed with scarlet'. Elevated, the people sing to the city and Finnoola, who has become brightly dressed and youthful, joins Ayamonn in a dance of celebration. But the sound of marching feet is heard and the scene darkens slightly. Ayamonn realises that the police are preparing to break the strike. He leaves and the colours fade, the people shrink back into lounging positions and, without Ayamonn's voice to sustain their belief, accuse each other of dreaming.

The final act takes place in an atmosphere of harsh reality. Mounted police baton-charge the strikers and Ayamonn is killed. But his death is not useless; the people now begin to experience some of the change that had transformed the city in their vision. 'It was a noble and a mighty death', one man says and Sheila realises that the shilling a week increase was not a purpose in itself but a symbol of a better and brighter future. Life is accepted; something new has been born.

'Red Roses for Me' is an excellent play and the one in which O'Casey's vision is most clearly and successfully presented. Theatrically it cannot but hold interest; its characters are defined and vital, its experimental third act dramatic and beautiful. Ayamonn is the natural development of Harry Heegan in 'The Silver Tassie' and The Dreamer in 'Within the Gates'. His attractiveness lies, not in his ability to produce rational argument or calculated invective, but in his power to stir the imagination. And the same thing may be said of O'Casey. When he partially forgot his political and social theories and threw no propaganda or sermonising in the way of his dramatic vision, he produced work of unequalled attractiveness.

Unfortunately, he returned, in 'Oak Leaves and Lavender'[3] to his preoccupation with the struggle between Communism and Fascism. It is an ingeniously constructed, semi-realistic and not very interesting play. It is set in a manorial house in Cornwall during the Second World War and in a Prelude, the ghosts of the people who once occupied these rooms mourn the passing of the good old days. The house is being used as a first-aid centre and as a headquarters for the Home Guard. An eccentric English housekeeper, a group of local workmen and Feelim O'Morrigun, an Irish butler, provide some moments of comedy that are reminiscent of scenes from 'Purple Dust' but O'Morrigun's son, Drishogue, ensures that these moments are few and far between by an almost ceaseless flow of Communist propaganda and anti-Fascist abuse. He very quickly becomes a bore and when, in the second act, we hear that he has been killed, it is difficult not to feel some considerable relief. O'Morrigun, however, is inspired to increase his contribution to the war, as is the house's owner, Dame Hatherleigh, and in the last act the house has been transformed into a factory in which the future is being symbolically forged. In an Epilogue, Dame Hatherleigh joins the dancing ghosts, convinced that the future will be a rebirth of all that was most glorious in the past.

This short synopsis does the play an injustice but not, I believe, a very great one. O'Casey's vision, which shines so clearly through 'Red Roses for Me', is dim and clouded here. 'Oak Leaves and Lavender' is full of accidental 'alienation' effects; most of the characters seem intent on irritating us and it is the brief and unimportant moments of comedy that remain most clearly in the mind.

'Cock-a-Doodle Dandy'[3] is a satiric fantasy, an imaginative extravaganza, bitter, pointed and very, very funny. The Cock is a symbol of fertility and when he takes an interest in a most infertile, crabbed and joyless Irish village, he has a magical effect. The village has rejected life and embraced a misery imposed on it by Father Domineer and a hypocritical old crawthumper called Shanaar; when the Cock, or Life, is first seen, the people are quite prepared to believe that he is the devil incarnate. Life has become a negative affair in which the shadow of Original Sin looms large and constant.

At the beginning of the play the Cock, a large bird, 'of a deep black plumage fitted to his agile and slender body like a glove on a lady's hand' dances before the house of Michael Marthraun, weaving a joyful, life-filled spell. Marthraun, a superb example of the Irish gombeen man, and his friend Sailor Mahon, a small businessman, discuss recent inexplicable happenings in the neighbourhood. Mahon isn't unduly worried but Marthraun is afraid that his daughter, Loreleen, his second wife, Lorna, and Marion, the maid, are attracting or have been possessed by some evil spirits. An old man, Shanaar, agrees that this could be so. He is dubious about everything that isn't sober and sorrowful and his talk is full of a wild mixture of half-digested Pagan mythology and almost totally misunderstood Christianity. When the 'crek-crek, crek-crek' of a corncrake is heard, Shanaar, who is suspicious of birds and who believes that he can exorcise evil, advises Marthraun and Mahon to ignore things with which they don't know how to deal. 'But suppose a hen goes wrong?' Marthraun asks, 'what are we to do.' 'It isn't aysey to say, an' you have to go cautious', Shanaar says thoughtfully. 'The one thing to do, if yous have the knowledge, is to parley with th' hens in a Latin dissertation. If among th' fowl there's an illusion of a hen from Gehenna, it won't endure th' Latin. She can't face th' Latin. Th' Latin downs her. She tangles herself in a helluva disordher. She busts asundher an' disappears in a quick column of black an' blue smoke, a thrue ear ketchin' a screech of agony from its centre!'

But he is less sure of himself when he hears a rumpus from Marthraun's house and is told that something is flying through the rooms, destroying holy pictures and causing what Captain Boyle would describe as a hillaboloo. From the safety of a distance he tries his Latin but without any conspicuous success. It is Robin Adair, a post office worker, who quietens the Cock and brings him out for Marion to admire. Life, Robin believes, can be very beautiful if joyfully accepted; rejected, it becomes sour and bitter.

And the villagers, with the exception of the three women and Robin Adair, reject life. Led by Father Domineer they hunt the Cock and try to destroy it so that they can settle back once again into the normal pattern of grey misery. But the Cock's magic begins to work; a kind of joyful frivolity begins to flow; chairs collapse, a whiskey bottle is bewitched and Marthraun's new top hat, a proud symbol of his political gombeenism, disappears. The women are transformed by their acceptance of this new vision of life and they are able to influence the men into a temporary gaiety. Father Domineer, however, denounces them with fanatical rage. Dancing and joy are, for him, symbols of a paganism which he sees growing steadily around him. With bell, book and candle he attempts to exorcise the Cock. The house is filled with a wild commotion; bruised and tattered, he limps out, believing that he has succeeded, but the stage grows dark, the Cock appears and amidst great noise and confusion, carries the priest away. The play's action then speeds up into Keystone Cop-like absurdity. Eventually, the priest is rescued and the Cock has disappeared. But all who have seen what life can be decide to leave the village and experience the joys of living in some other place.

Into his main pattern, O'Casey weaves two sub-themes; a girl's search for a miracle in Lourdes and a labour dispute which erupts into violence. The whole is a delightful and powerful exposition of the vision which runs so consistently through his best plays. Throbbing with exhuberant gusto, 'Cock-a-Doodle Dandy' glorifies life and consigns the forces that conspire against it to a particularly bleak and bottomless hell where they are devoured by the flames of fear, hypocrisy and reluctant chastity. And it shows that these forces can be destructive in many ways, for Father Domineer kills a man in anger and Loreleen is mobbed by a misguided crowd who tear her clothes and leave her bruised and bleeding. The play is a hymn to life – Life! Life! Life! – a colourful, vital and quite irresistible dramatic spectacle. It's dialogue is amongst the most polished and perfect that O'Casey ever wrote; of all his plays it is the one which I would most like to see getting the imaginative production which it deserves.

'The Bishop's Bonfire' is a restatement of O'Casey's arguments, a remarkable work to come from a man in his seventies but not a good play by his own standards. It is a satiric comedy with scenes of fantasy and melodrama. It contains many echoes of previous plays; slapstick comedy is provided by workmen; Canon Burren could be an artfully disguised or newly promoted Father Domineer; love is suppressed and gombeenism is having a bank holiday. The dramatic clashes are, once again, between life and anti-life, joy and misery, sex and chastity. O'Casey himself described it as being about 'the ferocious chastity of the Irish, a lament for the condition of Ireland, which is an apathetic country now, losing all her energy, enthusiasm and resolution'.

Its plot is extremely simple. The inhabitants of the village of Ballyoonagh are preparing to welcome home Bill Mullarky, a local lad who has made good and who is now a Bishop. Reiligan, a Councillor and Canon Burren, the Parish Priest, plan to greet Mullarky with a bonfire made from 'piles of bad books an' evil pictures'. The workmen whom Reiligan has employed to re-decorate his house are less interested and a good deal less enthusiastic about the return. It is their arguments, brawls, theories and general indifference that carry the play along and provide a rich and humourous contrast to the official enthusiasm. The most notable of the workmen is Codger Sleehaun, an old man who seems to embody all the characteristics of the men in the heckling scene which I quoted from 'Within the Gates'. He is argumentative, determined, dogmatic and cautious and provides all the play's better moments. The sub-plot concerns Reiligan's two daughters. Keelin is loved by one of the workmen but her father's strong sense of class distinction and the workman's inherited inferiority complex make any satisfactory relationship impossible. Fooraun is bound by a vow of chastity and is unable to marry Manus Moanroe whom she loves. When he breaks into the house to steal some money so that he can escape to a new life, she attempts to stop him and he shoots her. She forgives him and, before dying, writes a mock suicide note. This piece of melodrama strikes a curiously inaccurate chord.

The play is saved from dullness by the workmen, by Father Boheroe, an interesting and complex character outside the pale of O'Casey's usual psychology, and by one very typical piece of comic invention. A statue of Saint Tremolo – somebody should compose a litany of O'Casey's saints – makes a trumpet-like noise whenever it disapproves of anything that happens or is said. This is an inspired piece of fantasy and a wickedly barbed comment on an element of Irish Catholicism. The rest of the play repeats points that O'Casey had already made with greater power and effectiveness in earlier work.

'The Drums of Father Ned' is a better play. It, too, is con-cerned with the preparations for an event, this time a festival; the villagers of Doonavale are about to celebrate 'An Tostal'. Thematically it bears a strong resemblance to the struggles in 'Cock-a-Doodle Dandy' and it utilises almost every theatrical manner which O'Casey had discovered in his writing career. Father Ned never appears but his influence is almost as strong as that of the Cock. The play opens with a 'Prerumble' in which a number of Black and Tans encounter two young potential gombeens called McGilligan and Binnington. They hate each other with such intensity that they refuse to shake hands even when ordered to do so at the point of a rifle. But the Black and Tan officer, a far-seeing man, decides to let them live. 'These two rats', he says, 'will do more harm to Ireland living than they'll ever do to Ireland dead.'

The subsequent acts justify his contention.

Thirty-four years pass. Binnington is now Mayor and McGilligan is his Deputy; though in constant contact they haven't spoken a friendly word to each other since the Troubles. Binnington's son, however, is in love with McGilligan's daughter; they are young and joyful and defy the dour protests of their parents and Father Fillifogue. Whenever they do so, the drums of Father Ned, who has given them this capacity for joy, can be heard beating in the distance.

Many of the play's scenes are extremely funny. A pageant depicting the Irish Rising of 1798 is being rehearsed and Mr Murray the choir-master, a high-farcical creation, reaches heights and depths of enthusiastic frenzy. And Alec Skerighan, an Ulsterman, has a memorable affair with a maid called Bernadette Shillayley. When she produces her 'ferocious chastity', Skerighan displays his Northern sense:

SKERIGHAN: Domn it, girrl, it was yoursel' led me int' it! Everything was innocent on' firm, tull ye pranc'd round swingin' your skirt, twirlin' your legs, on' sailin' ahead twutterin' your luddle bum!

BERNADETTE: (prostrate on the sofa – horrified) Twittherin' me luddle bum! Oh, blessed saints above, d'ye hear that! Oh, the villianous action! Twittherin' me little bum! Me that never heard th' word utthered before, an' guess only dimly at its meanin'!...'

At the end of the play, the two young people, who proudly confess that they have slept together, are determined to take over their fathers' jobs, banish the darkness that has loomed over Doonavale and live by the spirit and be guided by the drums of Father Ned. It is a more gentle play than 'The Bishop's Bonfire' and a good deal funnier; its satire, though sharp, is prompted by real affection and the invisible Father Ned is one of O'Casey's happiest creations.

O'Casey published three more plays before he died. They seem written to be read rather than staged and they leave one with the uneasy feeling that their author, having discovered how to state his themes with gusto and brilliance, was then preoccupied with restating them mildly. 'The Moon Shines on Kyleamoe' is an amusing little farce but like the other two plays 'Behind the

Green Curtains' and 'Figuro in the Night', it is minor work by a dramatist who, at the height of his career, achieved real greatness.

The Dreamer inspired Jannice to accept life. Two unfortunate British businessmen found that it is impossible to live in the past. Ayamonn inspired his fellow Dubliners to see a shining vision of a new Ireland. The Cock inspired some villagers to seek life and love. Father Ned inspired youth to reject past darkness and look to the glory of the future.

Sean O'Casey – whose own youth was bitter – believed that life was a joyful inspiration that should never be tarnished by anything that even remotely resembled a sense of sin. He believed in the dignity of freedom and the liberty of joy; nothing, one imagines, would have given him more pleasure than an opportunity of joining God in declaring that Nieztche was dead. He was a man of powerful vision and enormous energy, the most irrational yet likeable voice in twentieth-century theatre. An early and most vocal member of the Disestablishment, he was unable to resist sitting targets but he knocked them with brilliance and built alternatives with fierce integrity and considerable compassion. He added several new dimensions to the theatre, influenced many of the best contemporary dramatist of whom one can think, and wrote the most brilliant dialogue of our time.

Don't be misled by those who say that he was out of touch with Ireland. He wasn't. His plays have real relevance for they go back, in modern dress, to investigate the archaic, hypocritical and furtively puritanical thinking of the Irish past which still so strongly influences the mildly sophisticated thinking of the Irish present. Some day our society will change, broaden, solidify, and the old crawthumpers will be safely stored away and something approaching honesty will take the place of compromise in our politics, our religion and our thought. Then we will realise the extent of his genius. Or will we? There is a bitter, worrying sting in the tail of his *A Stance on the Silver Tassie*:

'What to such as they, anyhow, such a poet as I? Therefore leave my works,
And go lull yourself with what you can understand and with piano tunes,
For I lull nobody, and you will never understand me.'

NOTES

1. *My Works* by Ernst Toller, translated by Marketa Goetz. Tulane Drama Review. March 1959

2. *New York Times.* October 21, 1934

3. In *Collected Plays*, Vol. II (Macmillan and Co. Ltd, 1959) which also contains 'Within the Gates' and 'The Star turns Red'

4. *Under a Coloured Cap* by Sean O'Casey (Macmillan and Co. Ltd, 1963)

5. *Sean O'Casey, the Man I Knew* by Gabriel Fallon (Routledge and Kegan Paul, 1965)

THE AUTOBIOGRAPHIES OF SEAN O'CASEY

By Ulick O'Connor

THE famous dramatic critic, James Agate, called Sean O'Casey's three plays, 'The Shadow of a Gunman', 'The Plough and the Stars' and 'Juno and the Paycock', 'blazing masterpieces' when they were first produced – and added that not since the Elizabethans had there been a writer of tragi-comedy to compare with him. Today, thirty years later, all three have become classics.

But why, critics ask, after this brilliant start did O'Casey go on to write six volumes of quite unexceptional autobiography? More frequently, of course, it has been the other way round. Novelists and poets have failed when they have tried their hand at drama. Joyce could never understand the failure of his one play 'Exiles'. Tennyson, Byron, Browning, all wrote plays that flopped.

O'Casey's poverty as a young man, his struggle for recognition, the unique period in which he grew to manhood should have provided ideal material for a notable autobiography. Yet what he has given us is on the whole second-rate. The style frequently verges on the ludicrous. Sometimes it has the merit of accurate reportage. Very occasionally when he is moved by some event close to himself he becomes detached and unsentimental. Here O'Casey the artist is at work. His descriptions, for instance, of both his sister's and his mother's deaths are self-searching and clinical. 'Why did he promise Ella and his mother in a foolish moment that he'd give sixpence a week towards the rent. To help get rid of them – devil a haporth else and if he were honest he'd say so. But was he really concerned about his mother? Well yes, for it was bound to be a trouble to him if anything happened to her. Anyhow he had a right to think of himself. How could he read right, study things and write the way things were.'

But passages like this do not make up for the frequent glaring pastiche of Joyce's later style in the autobiographies, the barrage of bad puns, his over-use of adjectives, his immature attempts at fantasy! The conversational passages in the autobiographies are curiously unsuccessful. The marvellous dialogue of the plays, slightly orchestrated for dramatic effect and so effective when heard across the footlights, seems to lose credibility when it is read without being heard. Occasionally O'Casey brings off a descriptive passage. But when he describes nature he can become maudlin. On p. 381 of Volume 1 of the autobiographies (Macmillan) he uses the word 'golden' (a dubious adjective) four times in six sentences . . . 'golden hand' – 'golden glamour' – 'golden pool' – 'golden light'.

At times he blatantly romanticises himself. The boys whom he describes at school sound as if they were out of Stalky and Co. His descriptions of sexual encounters are as unlikely as situations in cheap novelettes. Sometimes an image passes before his eye and he gets it down before it is swallowed up in pretentious pastiche. 'A stout tall man built up by nature to resemble a lusty pig gradually assuming the shape of a man, all dressed in a Sunday suit . . . lightened by a gold watch-chain flowing across the wide bulging belly like a streak of summer lightning' is vivid and satisfying.

Re-reading the autobiographies one is struck by O'Casey's preoccupation, almost obsessional, with those whom he disliked. At times it becomes like the whining of a spoilt child. A whole chapter is devoted to blackguarding George Orwell simply because he wrote an article criticising O'Casey. Captain Jack White (son of the Defender of Ladysmiths) who drilled the Citizen Army, Countess Markievitch, Mrs Bernard Shaw, Denis Johnston, and F. J. McCormick, the Abbey actor, are others who are chastised in public simply because at one time or another they criticised O'Casey or his plays.

O'Casey seems to have had in financial affairs a keen sense of honesty and an admirable pride. It is hard to reconcile this aspect of his character with the dishonest methods which he uses to attack people whom he has had a disagreement with – this is particularly true when these happen to be people prominent in political life in Ireland, in the years when O'Casey himself was involved in politics up to 1915.

His treatment of Griffith for instance is indefensible. 'Griffith does not understand Ireland', O'Casey writes in *Drums under the Window*, 'a lighter of little gas lamps to show the Irish where to walk . . . the sword of light would turn him to ashes if he ever tried to hold it'. The leaders of the Rebellion, however, thought so much of Griffith's understanding of Ireland that they sent him home from the Post Office, because they thought he could keep alive through his paper the ideals they were fighting for. Griffith, in fact, understood his countrymen so well, that he provided them with the superstructure (abstention from Westminster and the setting up of a rival government in Dublin) upon which they were able to erect the subsequent physical force movement.

Stanley Baldwin (hardly a constructive statesman) on the other

Abercorn Road, where he lived in his early years

hand was according to O'Casey 'a most honest and kindly man'. The difference of course was that Baldwin met with O'Casey, gratified his excessive touchiness and asked his advice. Griffith had taken a stand on the 1913 strike based on the proposition that Irishmen should never accept help from England, even from English Labour; for this he was forever damned in O'Casey's eyes.

A.E. (George Russell) is dismissed with a cheap phrase 'Dublin's glittering guy'. O'Casey makes no reference to the years of devoted labour that A.E. gave to Ireland, cycling round the country villages organising the Co-operative Movement which was to free the small farmer from the tyranny of the gombeen man. In O'Casey's eyes A.E. was a man consumed by inordinate vanity immobilised by airy idealism. Yet if there is one thing that is remarkable about A.E. it is that with all his excursions into the world of fantasy, he was possessed of an acute and practical mind when it came to putting his ideas into action.

Douglas Hyde is also dismissed with a sneer. Yet the Gaelic League was his creation, one of the important forces in the building of modern Ireland.

A guilt complex may have been at work in O'Casey's criticism of these men. They had all done practical work for Ireland. O'Casey's National record is a dubious one. He had a history of constant personal quarrels until he pulled out altogether by resigning as secretary of the Citizen Army in 1913. In the Black and Tan War, as far as one can find out, he took no active part. As an artist he was entitled to be concerned with people more than politics. But he ought not to have developed what amounted to an obsessional hatred against those whose lives had been devoted to the political struggle in Ireland.

His early poverty and illness left its scar on O'Casey. Considering his background he can show himself at times fair-minded and generous. But the frustration of exile added to the tensions inherited from his early years and increased his pre-occupation with his wounded ego. 'The Silver Tassie' row kept him whining in London. Having gone into an exile, which his fierce Dublin pride prevented him from ending, he became increasingly obsessed with a sense of injustice. Of course, he did have detractors in Dublin. Not all of them were religious or political fanatics either. The intellectuals joined up. 'Sean O Faolain, Austin Clarke, Liam O'Flaherty, Frank O'Connor all weighed in with the opposition.' Of course this type of malice helped Yeats – 'the daily spite of this unmannerly town'; for him it was an astringent, like tartare sauce on sole, to irritate his intuition into action. But Yeats had a background of four generations of solid middle-class breeding behind him. So had Swift. Indignation erupted into imagery in their case. In O'Casey's it prevented him from taking the most practical steps he could have done for the renewal of his creative gift – to return to Ireland.

Outside Ireland, O'Casey doesn't seem to have been a complete person. He didn't possess the massive portmanteau of notes and freak, blotting-paper memory for dialogue that Joyce carried with him into exile, virtually bringing Dublin with him. Away from the music of Dublin, O'Casey was like an actor playing from memory rather than from the heart, relying on audience reaction to produce what is demanded. He became, to some extent, the victim of his own image. The world, as the world will, created him into a fiction, and in the end he was fool enough to believe in that fiction. Dublin would have pulled him down to size; he was manufactured there, and the citizenry would have spotted flaws in the product as it was submitted to wear and tear. The cut and thrust of Dublin life was necessary for him – the combustion of its dialogue. But pride kept him away, a refusal to admit that anybody but Sean O'Casey was right, where O'Casey's own works were concerned.

Perhaps this is a reason for the mediocre quality of the auto-biographies – mediocre that is by the standard of his dramatic work. He may have used them as a means of getting rid of what another man might have got off his chest on the psychoanalyst's couch.

Whatever the reason, it was a loss to literature. For had O'Casey not siphoned off his energy on autobiography, he might have exceeded the 'blazing masterpieces' by which the world remembers him today.

5

O'CASEY IN HIS LETTERS

By Catherine Rynne

THERE are different ways of expressing love. Gentle, tender and
mild, with total acceptance. Or harsh and scolding, always trying
to bring the loved object up to one's own strict standards. This
is the way O'Casey loved Ireland.

He scanned the Irish papers for items that might call for his
disapproval. And then got out his typewriter to express this in
no uncertain terms. About the only form of constant favouritism
he received from the land of his birth was the hospitality of
editorial columns. And he used this space to the full. The letters
section began to sprawl all over the newspaper once O'Casey
joined a discussion. With mock humility he would begin: 'Permit
me a few last defensive words . . .' or 'Please allow me one last
letter'. And then he would meander on for nine or ten enormous
paragraphs.

Writing letters was almost a vocation with him. Dr David
Krause, his American biographer, is making a collection of them
and has some 6,000 to consider; 'a bloody big cargo', as their
author described them disparagingly in a telephone interview.

However, it wasn't all militant. Sometimes his letters were
encouraging and wise, though wisdom is not a virtue many
would allow him. In September 1950 he told a Belfast Trade
Union Council: 'I regret very much that I will not be able to
attend the peace conference, but head and heart I am with you
for the cause of peace. This is surely a cause for which orange
and green can unite. If we don't prevent war, many an orange
sash and many a green one will be laid aside, for those who wore
them will be no more. In the next war, should it come, it will not
be a case of one being taken and the other left. Both will be
swept away.'

He assures the Council that he loves Belfast as much as
Dublin, Cork and Galway, and has no wish to see it a hill of
rubble: 'Let Churchill nurse the atom bomb to his bosom if he
wants to and make it his guardian angel – "the bomb before me,

the bomb behind me, the bomb on my right and the bomb on my left hand", but we, the people, won't let it come within striking distance of us. We are too busy with life to let ourselves be interrupted with death.' Enclosed in the letter is a subscription of a pound 'to help your fund for the fight'.

Another kindly message is sent to the Irish Workers' League in Dublin who invited him to attend a Larkin memorial lecture in January 1956: 'I wish I was young enough to be with you all when you commemorate what the Great Jim Larkin was, what he fought for, and what he did to give the workers courage, resolution and hope.

'Lots would like him to be but a stone with a name on it stuck in the ground in Glasnevin. But Larkin is not a stone, but a flame, a flame that set the Irish workers afire with discontent, and a resolution to make life better than it had been.' This flame lit the flame in Easter Week, and lit other fires which are still burning fiercely in China, the USSR, France, Italy and many other lands. 'It is an old flame, faint at times, but never to be put out till the whole world of man realises that an injury to one is the concern of all. All that Irish workers have today they owe to Big Jim Larkin. There can be no life without Labour. When Labour downs tools, life stays still.'

And he wrote in much the same tone to the Northern Ireland Committee of the Irish Congress of Trade Unions, who were planning a cultural conference in Belfast for February 1963: 'Culture begins with the mother teaching the child a nursery rhyme. She and the child must have the environment of a pleasant and colourful home so that culture may be natural all round the family. Then, and only then, can the family know what it is to enjoy music, art and reading. All these delightful things depend on what are called wages. They must be sufficient to provide the things we need.' He sends his blessings to the committee, telling them that he prays for 'success in every effort and fight Labour makes and everything that Labour does. For the Labour of man is the one thing that is eternal. All depends on what the workers do. God be with you. Yours, very sincerely.' There follows a touching postscript: 'Overlook any mistakes. I am 83 and nearly blind.'

A movement for the release of Irish political prisoners was bound to receive support from this ex-member and biographer of the Irish Citizen Army. Thus, in December 1947, he told one of the organisers of the appeal that the Irish Government had been as indifferent about the Lane pictures as they were now about their own imprisoned boys. Asking whether there was a single member of the Government who had not avowed the very principles for which the men were in prison, he adds: 'As far as I know, de Valera has never expressed regret for heading the Civil War, which did so much material harm to Ireland, a harm a million and more times more terrible than all that was done and all that was thought to be done by these I.R.A. lads.'

A second letter on the subject was addressed to Mr Eoin O'Mahony within the month. Here O'Casey makes a plea for the thirty Irishmen in Parkhurst Prison, Isle of Wight, whom he describes as 'squeezing out the ripe youth of life behind bars. Young men whose one fault was that they loved Ireland, not wisely, but too well'. He goes on to say that, if prison be a corrective, further imprisonment would be vindictive: 'A year longer, a month, a day, an hour, would be just cold and bitter vindictiveness. It's not democratic, not broadminded, not fair.' He closes the letter with a flourish by accusing the two Governments of Eire, past and present, of having done more damage and caused more suffering than those lads 'were they multiplied by a thousand and could or would carry on for the next ten hundred years.'

Anything about Russia or Communism was likely to draw an O'Caseyism from Devon. He advises a reader of the *Irish Times* in 1957 to 'cease bothering about the Red Star in O'Casey's coat and bend to the better job of getting his Government to give up their silly boycott of the Soviet Union', suggesting that they invite the Red Army Assembly to the Theatre Royal in Dublin for the next 'Tostal'; or send two of Ireland's first-class hurling teams to Moscow, adding that there is trade in that city too.

Again, he answers another attack on Communism in 1958: 'It is time we said farewell to the stupid hatred of Communism and Communists everywhere, and began to realise that this force is here to say and to grow and conquer unless Christianity can evolve a force grander and greater than this ideal, forged in historical realism, now moving hearts, minds and bodies of so many millions of men and women in every land.'

Improved political relations between Northern and Southern Ireland was a subject which interested O'Casey greatly and his ideas on it were *avant-garde*. The Government has now given a lead in this matter. It is fashionable at least to pretend to cordial feelings towards our fellow-countrymen north of the Border.

There was no such atmosphere of goodwill in 1957, when O'Casey wrote to *Irish Times* columnist, Quidnunc: 'What a heaven-sent thing it would be if all the North were as of the South – all Catholics; or if all the South were as of the North – all Protestants! Then one damned problem would be solved anyhow. But it isn't so, and so we are where we are. How then bring them together, if not in a bond of faith, then in a little closer companionship?'

Pointing out that Catholics should be the most charitable, loving, and kindest hearted people in the Christian world, he says that they are all these fine things individually but not collectively. As they have the privilege of being in the true Church with its added responsibility of showing a light to the world, he begs them to 'start by showing this gracious light of goodwill and charity to the Irish folk in the North.'

Next, he asks the Irish Government to 'invite the Orange Order to hold its celebrations of the Twelfth of July, not in Belfast, but in Dublin; they should ask the Orangemen to come to the capital as guests of the Republic, march through the chief streets of Dublin, and hold their meetings in the green glades of the Phoenix Park . . . Certainly, there will be no union till an Orange sash can walk the streets of Dublin without protest, and a Green sash can walk the ways of Belfast, with many a look, maybe, but without a murmur. So let Dublin start on the fight for fraternity between the North and the South.'

The year he died, O'Casey brought up the subject again in his last letter to Ernest Blythe, managing director of the Abbey Theatre. Blythe had written to ask permission for the Abbey Players to perform 'Juno and the Paycock' in Derry. He replied enthusiastically in the affirmative, adding the suggestion that a green and orange flag should be erected in the hall during the three nights' run.

Nothing was too trivial for O'Casey. Here, in the *Irish Times* of May 1957, he replies to a priest who had said at a Christus Rex congress that Irish writers might have been forced to forsake the real Ireland in writing for a world market: 'What is the "real Ireland"? Ireland, like all other lands, is a land not of one, but of many realities.

'If he looks at our Irish Christmas cards, he'll find them covered with designs ostensibly taken from the Book of Kells – a bad habit just as amusing and as irritating as one covered over with shamrocks.' The cards he himself has received from Irish people living in America show him 'houses made of shamrocks, lads and lassies swathed in them, round towers growing out of them; and, let me add, those who sent them me were far from being fools. . . . I'm afraid that the shamrock, round towers and shilellagh Ireland is, in its own way, as real as any other aspect of our country.'

O'Casey could be melodramatic in his letters too, as when he wrote to the *New York Times* editor about a revival of 'The Plough and the Stars' in that city's Phoenix Theatre: 'The Dublin première produced a great roar, a roar that shook the homes of Dublin and the corn waving in Ireland's four beautiful fields! Scholars, saints, hurlers and bards shouted "Down O'Casey" and in spite of the indomitable poet, Yeats, I felt as Ruth felt among the alien corn. I was an alien in my own land. The next day, angry and abusive letters against the play shone darkly from the Dublin papers, and O'Casey was told by many symbols in speech and letter that the shamrock wasn't for him to pluck. It was time to . . . go.' This contrasts with the opinion of his biographers, who maintain that his going to England then was neither premeditated nor intended to be final.

He loved young people. Over the years, he wrote numerous letters giving them advice, or merely information. A group of students at Abraham Lincoln High School, Brooklyn, sent him some questions after a visit they paid to a Broadway production of his 'Red Roses for Me' in June 1962.

The eighty-two-year old writer, by now nearly blind, might have been excused had he failed to reply. Instead, he patiently sat down to compose yet another letter, addressing them fondly as his 'golden lads and lassies'. He wished he could answer each one of them separately, he told them, 'but I have too many things to do and this is not by any means concerned only with writing plays. There is homework to do', instancing washing up, emptying rubbish, making his own bed, peeling potatoes.

Wealthy? asked a student: 'In one sense, I am not indeed; but in a lot of other ways I am immensely wealthy. I know a good deal about painting; I delight in the music of Mozart, Beethoven, Verdi and many others; I know a good deal about flowers. I take a keen interest in all branches of science; and a Gaelic writer (Gaelic is our Irish language) with whom I lived for a while has recorded that O'Casey was forever chanting songs as if he were a Robin Redbreast. And, best of all, I have a gallant wife. So you see, I'm quite a wealthy fellow.' He confides to another young

244

writer that he had never been able to compose bedtime stories for his children when they were small: 'My poor mind became a dark blank; a clean black-out.'

Even when he was in his early twenties, O'Casey was known in his family for a scurrilous tongue, although he was otherwise described as gentle and manly. Censorship was a subject liable

The new Liberty Hall, Dublin's first skyscraper, home of the Irish Transport & General Workers' Union

to bring his scurrility to the fore. In fairness, it must be admitted that he suffered from both public and private censors. Although he declared in one letter, 'I am in the fortunate position of not caring a tráithnín whether a single book of mine is delivered to Ireland or not', this was not altogether true. The regulation banning of his works by the Censorship Board was bad enough; in addition, customs officers impounded them for indefinite periods and, apparently, they also fell foul of the Post Office. Priests wrote angrily to the newspapers and spoke in the same vein at public meetings. The C.Y.M.S. in Galway condemned him out of hand. All this embittered him, albeit with some justification.

May and June of 1957 saw a lengthy debate about censorship in the *Irish Times*, with O'Casey in the thick of it. 'A word or action is obscene only when the mind thinks it to be so; and, odd enough, this obscenity in Ireland seems to be exclusively connected with sex. But sex laughs at cleric and censor. When it comes, a physiological upsurge, the robin sports a redder breast, the lapwing gets himself another crest, a livelier iris changes on the dove, and dodging into secret places go the lover and his lass.'

A little later, he is saying: 'This insignificant bunch of censors, I suppose, have been designed by God to make no mistake in banning any book written by any man or woman with mind or imagination. If they miss any, then there are others waiting in ambush, hordes of them. If not the Board, then a cardinal, a politician'. If all these miss out, then the librarians act as censors. One girl burnt a hundred books off her own bat. Next, he says, come the confraternities and the Legion of Mary, followed by the readers themselves. He quotes a newspaper report of a librarians' congress at which it was said that often books allowed by the Appeal Board were denounced by local readers, and so removed from the shelves.

His next paragraph starts humourously and ends on a more serious note: 'The banners are like the fleas – a big flea has a little flea on his back, and the little flea a lesser one, set there just to remind him to seize a writer's naughty word and knock it down, and bind him. It is near time these banning boobies realised that God made the bottom as well as the top of the body, and not to go running about roaring about human things. . . . We should be up against, not what brings life, but against all things that take it away till old age sends us into a gentle sleep; for a start, up against the hydrogen bomb and all nuclear weapons, till, grown stronger, we strike against war everywhere. The banning of bombs is more to the point than the banning of books, and Christians should know this better than anyone else, instead of going into hysterics over the natural merrymaking of a Jack and Jill.'

In the course of the same correspondence, O'Casey describes Ireland as 'an island full of tremolos, full of sour noises; the body

246

trembling with tension in its resolution to defend God's Kingdom from any nosey parker; and the Irish writers trembling in fear of writing anything that might start the bookineeno blaring.'

Next, he crosses swords with a doctor who had quoted the late Dr R. D. Gillesby, consulting psychiatrist to Guy's Hospital, London, in his support against O'Casey: 'He thinks to stun us with his "indecent books were the greatest extra-familial collateral cause for sexual corruption". Does he think that an Irish writer has the time or the thought, when he is writing anything, to rush over to have a chat with Dr Gillesby in order to ask him whether or not what he was writing might possibly be an "extra-familial collateral cause for sexual corruption"?'

Writers are not supposed to answer back. They are expected to take in decent silence any abuse that is heaped on their work, no matter how ill-informed the origin. This was not the O'Casey method. From his earliest youth, he was a staunch believer in the maxim that attack is the best method of defence. As a child he is reported to have whacked over the head a teacher who blamed him in the wrong. As a young man he walked out of a job rather than touch his cap when collecting his wages. As a dramatist, he defended his plays.

Taking it on its purely human level, the constant harping back to the famed trilogy, with the almost continual dismissal of later plays, would have annoyed any playwright. O'Casey wrote to an actor friend rather sadly: 'If an angel did the production of an O'Casey play, and another had leaned over me shoulder when writing it, it would still be a wretched work to the Irish professional critics'. He wanted them to love all his work. They didn't. So he abused them roundly and got rid of some of his disappointment that way.

He was defiant. Concluding a long letter to the *Irish Press* in 1935, he writes: 'I am in no way whatsoever ashamed of one, single, solitary word or phrase appearing in "The Silver Tassie", and the storm of abuse that the play has received only convinces me that "The Silver Tassie" is a greater play than I thought it to be. Thank you.'

He was heavily sarcastic. In April 1944 he wrote a letter to the *Irish Times* in answer to remarks by Roddy the Rover, *Irish Press* columnist, about the flag being dishonoured by being brought into a pub in 'The Plough and the Stars'. He describes Roddy as 'that tealogian, antiqueerian, playwrong, jennologist, litterary and dhrimin dhu dreama critic, hystorian and heaven knows what else.'

He went into tremendous detail, as in December 1949, when he wrote seven lengthy paragraphs to the *Irish Times* drama critic who had suggested that 'Cock-a-Doodle Dandy' couldn't happen in Ireland. In instancing several unsavoury happenings reported in the Irish papers, he states: 'These are but a few of the things I have written down in a record covering thirty pages of tight-packed typescript which shall appear one day.'

He was childish, as when he wrote an open letter to the *Irish Press* drama critic, Niall Carroll, in March 1958: 'Your pre-dumbinent "drama critic" in Monday's issue of your valuable journal, in the course of other remarks, says "I think it is fair enough to record the statements (record the statements – what pompous phrases!) of responsible people who have read the O'Casey manuscript . . . Well, I regret to say (he regrets to say!) that competent theatre personages (personages!) who have read the script carefully (carefully!) have made no secret of their disappointment (disappointment!) In brief, and without mincing words, they have informed me (not told him; informed him) that it is a 'very mediocre stuff".'' '

In March 1955, in a letter to the *Irish Times* about 'The Bishop's Bonfire', he describes Irish drama critics as 'fluttering drama-angels of the denunciations', threatens a book against them, adding: 'I am so used to them now that anything nice from them would get me down. Their reviews are a bewildering mass of dismissals, denials, denunciations, declensions, and deviations from their party line'. He quotes critic George Jean Nathan in defence of the play (he often brought Nathan in for his own self-defence), adding that this 'may provoke them to stick their necks again out of their thick, enveloping hoods, and give them something more to think of and talk about'.

The O'Casey of the public battle-field wrote quite a different letter when he was O'Casey, the private correspondent. Here he was mild, very human, and the style is not at all literary or posed, but almost bald. He corresponded quite often with his bachelor brother, Mick, who was living on a British Army pension and was generous with what he had. At Christmas 1938 he said: 'We've come to Devon, finding London too expensive to live in; and here there's a school we like for the boys. Hope you are well.' The letters were signed Jack, as he was known to his family. There was usually a Russian stamp on the back of the envelope and nearly always a pound inside, with the pious wish that it would be spent on something other than drink.

In April 1946 he tells his brother: 'I haven't got much out of the play yet – it is performing in small theatres. If it continues to go, I'll send you some more. All the best.' The following July, he writes: 'The photograph was fine. You look very venerable in it – like G.B.S. I hope you have quite recovered from the weakness in the legs; or recovered enough to let you go around the world easily. All well now, bar the youngest, who still has an attack of tonsillitis.'

He also wrote to his niece, Mrs Bella Murphy, with whom Mick lived, calling her by her family petname, Babsie, and signing himself Uncle Jack. In January 1947, both Mick and Bella's daughter Mary, aged twenty-six, died within a few days of each other: 'I am very sorry to hear about your daughter Mary. I don't remember ever seeing her but she must have been a young woman. What happened to her? It doesn't matter about Mick; he was an old man, had had his day. But Mary's death is quite different.' He goes on to speak of insurance policies belonging to both the deceased, promising to either send her on the policy money, or tell her how to get it, as soon as he settles with the agent. Some weeks later he asks for Mick's death certificate: 'This is done in haste as I am down with influenza', and he sends on the money in March, 'which I hope may be of some use to you. The delay was caused by influenza and pneumonia in the family.'

But there was one member of his family circle in Dublin to whom O'Casey wrote letters of a rather more literary nature. This was Lorraine Beaver, a grand-niece, who started writing to him in 1962, when she was eighteen. In her first letter she told him briskly that he should lift the Abbey ban before he died as she had never seen any of his plays. This started a correspondence: 'What a bold and impudent letter to send to a world-famous writer! It is almost past endurance (though it shows fine courage). What shall I do about it? What am I to say? You teenagers take one's breath away at times.

'There is no Abbey Theatre, young lady. That theatre died when the poet Yeats and the poet Fred Higgins died, and, shortly afterwards, the building they left behind them went up in flames. If the Abbey Theatre were there, my plays would be seen and heard there.'

He told her in early November that his eyes were so bad that he couldn't read, was almost unable to write and found it difficult even to type. She had sent him some drawings: 'I liked your portraits very much. Very graceful lines indeed. You should try to make sketches of places you visit, of flowers, houses, etc., if these give you pleasure. Many years ago I used to do myself the few Christmas cards I sent.'

The next month he reminisces: 'When I worked in Easons, I had to be in at 4.15 every morning, ending at six; and in the building trade the hours were from 6 to 5.30. It is fine to remember that I had a hand in changing all that and bringing a fairer disposal of time to the worker instead of it being wholly according to the will or whim of the boss.'

Then he talks to Lorraine about writing: 'It is a hard task and I should never venture to advise anyone to embrace it, for often it gets abuse rather than reward and a regular job is more secure and often far happier too. Not unless the urge to write be irresistible should writing be attempted.'

There is something of the unsuccessful lover condemning his would-be mistress in the next bit: 'No, my dear Lorraine, I am never homesick and I do not miss Ireland. I was glad to get away from Ireland's ignorance and humbug, religious and political. . . . She will have to make herself more attractive if she wishes to keep her people attached to her. If she is content to remain slovenly and shy, her people will continue to flee from her.'

When he wrote to his grand-niece in May 1963, he complained of his deteriorating eyesight and of all the letters he had to answer: 'There are upwards of 30 piled up waiting for me, American and Continental, but God knows when I shall be able to attend to them. . . . Eileen has to read letters for me now; I try to remember all that is said in them but usually fail, when they number so many, with others sailing in every morning.'

Letters from O'Casey to all and sundry gained a new significance in September 1964, when the dramatist, essayist, writer and most prolific sender of lengthy missives, died. Many hitherto unpublished ones saw the light of day in the national press. But a reader of Dublin's *Evening Herald* wrote sharply: 'I am disgusted at the spate of eulogiums poured out on the death of Sean O'Casey. The torrid spate of fulsome praise goes on.' He calls him a double deserter for giving up the Irish Citizen Army and his faith, dubs the Irish morons for praising him like this now that he is dead.

Silence. And there was something sad about it. He always answered back. Often happily joined in the fray uninvitedly.

What does O'Casey say about this, that or the other? What next will he react to in anger, scorn, disgust or, just possibly, approval? Nobody is scanning the papers now. No aged prophet in Devon is bothering about us any more. Loving us more than hating us through a lifetime of neglect and derision. There's no one to look out for us now. Forgive us, O'Casey. May you march in Elysian fields.

BOOKS ON SEAN O'CASEY

The Experiments of Sean O'Casey by Robert Hogan (St Martin's Press, New York, 1960)

Sean O'Casey, the Man and his Work by David Krause (Macgibbon and Kee, 1960)

Sean O'Casey, the Man Behind the Plays by Saros Cowasjee (Oliver and Boyd, 1963)

Sean O'Casey, the Man I Knew by Gabriel Fallon (Routledge and Kegan Paul, 1965)

The World of Brendan Behan

edited by Sean McCann

Here is the authentic Brendan Behan—as he was known to his friends and associates. In this unique book they reveal him as he really was. Among the contributors are:

Eamonn Andrews, who reviews Behan's relations with the BBC, and his controversial scripts.

Anthony Butler, who recalls the Dublin of the thirties, and Behan's interest in the I.R.A. He talks to the men who knew him in the movement, and who went to jail with him.

Kevin Casey, Ireland's most promising playright and author, who looks at Behan's works and evaluates their place in contemporary literature.

Tim Pat Coogan, who writes about Behan the Legend.

Marion Fitzgerald, who contributes an account of the women in Behan's life.

Benedict Kelly, who began his career in the Irish Press with Behan, describes the days spent with him travelling between The White Horse and the newsroom.

Michael MacLiammoir, who discusses the events that lead up to Behan's death, and the feeling in Ireland and abroad when he died. He concludes with The Ballad of Brendan Behan, by Irish ballad-writer Jimmy Hiney.

Catherine Rynne and Anthony Butler, who have gathered 'Behanisms' from many sources never before touched. They include literary editors, reporters, bookies, trade unionists—and barmen.

FOUR 4 SQUARE EDITION   3s. 6d.

The Great Hunger

by Cecil Woodham-Smith

In the short space of five years more than a million Irish died of starvation and of the diseases which accompany malnutrition. 800,000 Irish emigrants sailed for the United States and Canada. They took with them few possessions. But they took disease, particularly typhus, and a deep hatred of Britain. For they were convinced that it was Britain that was responsible for the appalling conditions from which they were fleeing.

Cecil Woodham-Smith, who has won a unique reputation with two best-sellers as an author of accurate history made exciting and readable to thousands, describes the Irish disaster which affected the history of Ireland, North America and England.

Among the characters, she draws fascinating portraits of Sir Charles Trevelyan, Lord John Russell, O'Connell the Liberator and William Smith O'Brien. But most vividly brought to life are the starving peasants, their women and children scattered 'like a flock of famished crows over the fields devouring raw turnips'.

FOUR SQUARE EDITION 7s. 6d.

The Informer

by Liam O'Flaherty

This is one of the most moving and memorable stories ever recorded about the Irish Rebellion. Set against a background of blazing patriotism, overwhelming hatred of the enemy and the implacable determination of an oppressed people, it is a work of incredible realism and understanding.

'*The Informer* by Liam O'Flaherty must be accounted a little masterpiece of its kind ... his portrait of the brutish informer is so marvellously vivid, and his whole narrative, with its slowly increasing atmosphere of terror, so perfectly unfolded that the book must be ranked very high indeed ... easily its author's best work. It is a quite unforgettable story.' *Sunday Times*.

FOUR SQUARE EDITION 3s. 6d.